SEED TECHNOLOGY AND PATHOLOGY

SEED TECHNOLOGY AND PATHOLOGY

By

Dr. Ashok Kumar

Deptt. of Zoology
Bundelkhand University
Campus Department
Jhansi (India)

DPH

DISCOVERY PUBLISHING HOUSE PVT. LTD.
NEW DELHI-110 002

Published by:
Tilak Wasan
DISCOVERY PUBLISHING HOUSE PVT. LTD.
4383/4B, Ansari Road, Darya Ganj
New Delhi-110 002 (India)
Phone : +91-11-23279245, 43596064-65
Fax : +91-11-23253475
E-mail : discoverypublishinghouse@gmail.com
sales@discoverypublishinggroup.com
parul.wasan@gmail.com
web : www.discoverypublishinggroup.com

First Edition: **2014**

ISBN: 978-93-5056-391-5

Seed Technology and Pathology

Printed at:
Dynamic Printers
Delhi

Preface

In recent years, with the advances taking place in the field of agriculture, seed technology and seed pathology, which seek to understand the conditions to which seeds are subjected, their improvement in quality through biotechnology and the diseases to which they are prone. As such, seed technology and seed pathology have proved to be highly crucial in comprehending what defines plant growth and development. Progress of agriculture depends on production and distribution of good quality seeds, of best yielding varieties with favourable characteristics. At the same time quality of agriculture depends on good quality seed.

—Author

Contents

1

Seed Germination

INTRODUCTION

Deciding appropriate germination test regimes for accessions so that germination tests reflect true viability with minimum interference from dormancy (and other factors which limit germination, such as hardseededness) can be one of the more difficult decisions which gene bank staff need to make. In the following chapters we have summarised useful information on the germination response of seeds of various genera to very many test regimes and dormancy-breaking treatments together with advice on suggested test procedures. In many cases, however, the information available is far from complete and accordingly much of the advice is very tentative. In such cases it is hoped that gene bank staff will be able to improve on the suggestions made. In order to help in this endeavour, in this chapter we discuss four different types of approach to determining appropriate germination environments.

ECOLOGICAL GUIDELINES TO DEVELOPING APPROPRIATE GERMINATION ENVIRONMENTS

A consideration of the ecology of a species may sometimes help to provide some guidance as to appropriate germination test conditions. At the simplest level tropical species generally require higher temperatures for germination than temperate species. However, there are other more subtle responses which relate to the strategy of the plant in relation to its natural environment and a consideration of these may help in the development of germination test conditions which minimise dormancy.

DORMANCY MAY PREVENT SEEDS FROM GERMINATING IN THE WRONG PLACE AT THE WRONG TIME

As mentioned the majority of mature seeds show innate (or inherent or primary) dormancy-a condition necessary to prevent germination on the mother plant before the seed is shed. Innate seed dormancy in most species tends to be gradually lost with time (except in some tree species), often at a rate depending on temperature and moisture content. But induced (or secondary) dormancy, in many respects similar to innate dormancy, may subsequently be induced by conditions which signal that the current environment is inappropriate for germination-*e.g.* high temperatures or an aerobic conditions. Furthermore enforced dormancy may be temporarily imposed by conditions which again appear to play a role in ensuring that the seed only germinates when there is a reasonable probability of the seedling growing to maturity. Dormancy in all its forms therefore tends to prevent seeds from germinating in the wrong place at the wrong time.

FIELD ENVIRONMENT

For example, many annual or ephemeral species produce large numbers of small seeds. At any one time it is common for there to be more dormant seeds in the soil waiting for appropriate conditions than there are growing plants. Since small seeds only contain small food reserves, only a small amount of seedling growth can occur before the seedling needs to start photosynthesising. Thus germination more than a few centimetres below the soil surface or beneath dense vegetation could lead to seedling destruction. It would seem that many species have evolved dormancy mechanisms which avoid these problems.

The seed needs to be able to respond to environmental factors that signal when it is at or near the soil surface. There seem to be two major environmental factors which many species use as indicators-light and alternating temperatures; and in most cases the seeds respond to both.

Light is obviously only present at or near the soil surface; and diurnal temperature alternations have a maximum amplitude (or diurnal range) at the soil surface: the range rapidly diminishes with depth in the soil profile. Furthermore even at the soil surface the amplitude is diminished by the presence of vegetation. Since vegetation contains chlorophyll which absorbs strongly in the red region of the spectrum, the quality of light beneath vegetation may be inhibiting since far-red light penetrates much more and thus the light quality tends to affect the balance of phytochrome in the seeds in favour of the inactive Pre form.

Accordingly it is very common for small seeds of annuals and ephemerals to be light-sensitive and to germinate in response to white (or red) light and alternating temperatures. In many cases neither of these factors on their own has a major effect and both are necessary for a maximum response. Both these factors also often interact with nitrate ions.

MATERNAL ENVIRONMENT

It may be worth considering the maternal environment in which the seeds develop as a further guide to distinguishing those species likely to require light treatments in order to promote seed germination. The light-filtering properties of the maternal tissues which surround the developing seeds, whilst they remain moist, can affect the sensitivity of seed germination to light in subsequent environments. Where the maternal tissues have a high chlorophyll content (that is are green) the seeds tend to require a light stimulus for germination (in subsequent tests).

In contrast those seeds which have developed within maternal tissues where the chlorophyll content declined whilst the seeds remained moist tend to be able to germinate subsequently in light or darkness (that is are light insensitive). This is because the seeds developing within green maternal tissues would have received light filtered by the chlorophyll. This light would have a low red/far red ratio and most of the phytochrome would be in the inactive Prform. In the latter case, however, the light would not have been filtered to such an extent; the red/far red ratio of the light received by the seeds would have been greater and thus more of the phytochrome would be in the active Pfr form which promotes germination. This Pfr would remain after desiccation and subsequent imbibition and accounts for the insensitivity of these seeds to light.

LARGE-SEEDED SPECIES OF ARID ENVIRONMENTS

As mentioned, sustained and/or high-intensity light can also inhibit the germination of some seeds. This response is more common amongst somewhat larger seeds of species of arid environments, where it is more important for seeds to germinate below the soil surface where short-term severe water shortage is less likely, and the probability of the shoot not reaching the soil surface before food reserves are reduced is lessened by the larger food reserves of the seed.

In desert regions where rains are infrequent and of limited duration, ephemeral plants have short life cycles and it is important for them to germinate only after a substantial fall of rain (and not after a minor shower which would not provide sufficient water for survival). In such cases seeds of some species appear to have their own 'rain gauge' which depends on the fact that it takes a certain minimal amount of rain to leach germination inhibitors. Thus in such cases germination may be stimulated by washing the seeds in running water.

PROBABILITY OF PLANT ESTABLISHMENT AND SURVIVAL

Dormancy mechanisms often also tend to ensure that the seeds do not germinate at times when the probability of the survival of the plant to maturity is poor. For example, many seeds in temperate latitudes tend to germinate after the winter, *i.e.* at the beginning of the main growing season. These seasonal considerations are often independent of seed size and thus many temperate species germinate best after a period of stratification (*i.e.* cool temperatures applied to moist seeds). Such a response ensures that seeds do not germinate at the beginning of winter.

In contrast, seeds of species from Mediterranean climates tend to avoid germination at the beginning of the hot, dry summer and germination at the beginning of the cool moist winter is more common. In such cases it would be less likely to find marked responses to stratification. This would also be generally true of tropical plants, but see the note below.

In tropical rain forests the temperature and water supply is always adequate for growth and so seeds of such species often show little dormancy. Seeds of many of the woody perennial species are also recalcitrant. Such seeds do not have to survive long periods in the dry conditions, and fresh supplies of short-lived seeds are produced regularly by the mature plants.

Many seeds of this type show little dormancy, and many are killed by cool temperatures (*e.g.* less than 10° to 15°C) which they would never normally experience. However, even in tropical forests some species are not recalcitrant, and some may show light responses to ensure that they only germinate when a gap arises in the forest canopy and/or the soil is disturbed after clearance, thus ensuring that early growth is not inhibited by low light intensity.

There are, of course, exceptions to these general principles. In particular it should be noted that laboratory treatments which emulate environments which the seeds would never experience in their natural habitat may sometimes promote germination. For example, low temperatures applied to moist seeds of some species of tropical and sub-tropical ecotypes can promote germination. Nevertheless the few examples above may be sufficient to indicate that a consideration of the ecology of the species may give useful clues as to the type of laboratory germination techniques which may be most appropriate.

ANATOMICAL APPROACH TO DEVELOPING APPROPRIATE GERMINATION ENVIRONMENTS

This approach has been developed largely by B.R. Atwater from long experience of attempting to germinate seeds of flower and ornamental species. Atwater's observations suggest that dormancy and germination requirements in these species are closely related to the maturity of the embryo and the structure and permeability of the seed coat coverings in the mature seed.

		A. Basal Rudimentary Embryo	B. Axillary Linear Embryo	C. Axillary Miniature Embryo	D. Peripheral Linear Embryo
SEED ANATOMY	embryo	small, show little differentiation,	linear in a central axillary	linear-spatulate in a central	curved in a peripheral position
		basal location	Position	axillary position	surrounding the perisperm or endosperm
	cotyledons	obscure and limited to a few cells	minimal: thin, narrow and shorter than the stalk	not expanded and equal to the stalk	thin, narrow and equal to the stalk
	endosperm	occupies most of seed and surrounds embryo	occupies half or more of seed and surrounds the central embryo	occupies half or less of the seed and surrounds the central embryo	centrally placed within the curved envelope
	seed coat	permeable and fibrous or reticulated	thin, reticulous or fibrous: may be semi-permeable	thin and fragile	thin testa, leathery outer coat and often parts of the calyx

	seed size	medium, 2-4 mm long	medium-large, 3-10 mm long	small, 1 mm long or less	medium-large, 2-6 mm diameter
	example	Anemone coranar ia	Cyclamen persicum	Nemesia strumosa	Portulaca grandiflora
	embryo	must develop before germination, hence delay	must develop before germination, hence delay		
BLOCKS TO GERMINATION	endosperm	inhibitors to germination may be present			
	seed coat	permeable, no block to germination	may be semi-permeable	permeable if light provided	may be impermeable and contain inhibitors
	temperature	temperate species 15°C; others 20°C, 20°/30°C	15° to 20°C; 10°/30°C or 20°/30°C	10°, 15° or 20°C; 20°/30°C, 10°/20°C or 5°/30°C	10°, 15° or 20°C (rarely 3°-6°C); 20°/30°C
	test duration	14-28d; in extreme cases 100-155d	14-28d; in extreme cases 40-60d	10-28d; in extreme cases 40-60d	5-28d; in extreme cases 65-75d
	KNO_3	*0.2%	*0.2%	*0.2%	0.2%
SUCCESSFUL GERMINATION TEST	GA_3	*100-400 ppm	*400-800 ppm	120-400 ppm	
	pre-chill	2w at 3°-5°C, or (rarely) test throughout at 5°-8°C	8w at 5°C	2-4w at 5°C	

REGIMES (*most widely applied treatments)	light	probably insensitive	*insensitive or sensitive (promotory, may aid imbibition)	*sensitive (promotory); supply red light for up to 70h either continuously or 12h per day	*may be insensitive or sensitive (promotory)
	seed coats	partial removal of pericarp	may be necessary to remove endosperm over radicle		*remove (calyx and) outer coats; pierce, chip (clip)
	pre-soak	hot water; 0.5h in 1N KOH or other alkaline solutions			pre-wash in water
Plant Families With Species Exhibiting These Characteristics		Araliaceae, fumariaceae, papaveraceae, ranunculaceae	Ericaceae, Gentianaceae, Primulaceae, Resedaceae, Solanaceae, Tropaeolaceae, Umbelliferae	Begoniaceae, Campanulaceae, Crassulaceae, Hypericaceae, Lobeliaceae, Saxifragaceae, Scrophulariaceae, Solanaceae	Aizoaceae, amaranthaceae, cactaceae, capparidaceae, caryophyllaceae, chenopodiaceae, mesembryanthaceae, nyctaginaceae, polygonaceae, portulacaceae

Atwater has described eight basic forms of seed structure. These categories have been described. Within each of these categories it is suggested that the seeds have similar dormancy and germination patterns, but it should be emphasised that the mechanisms suggested are hypotheses rather than established facts.

SEEDS WITH DOMINANT ENDOSPERM (ENDOSPERMIC SEEDS) AND IMMATURE DEPENDENT EMBRYOS (THAT IS EMBRYOS NOT READY TO GERMINATE)

Basal Rudimentary Embryos

The rudimentary embryos are the principal cause of delayed germination in this group. Inhibitors found in the endosperm may also contribute to the delay. Treatment consists of neutrali-zation of the inhibitors with leaching, or with extra oxygen at low temperature followed by higher temperatures favourable to rapid embryo growth. Gibberellic acid increases the rate of embryo development if added to the substrate.

Axillary Linear Emxillary Linear Embrtis

Linear embryos are similar to the above. An additional block is added by the seed coats which may limit oxygen entry, but seed coat permeability may be increased when the seeds are exposed to light. Gibberellic acid added to the substrate increases the rate of embryo development.

Axillary Miniature Embryos

Miniature seeds having minimal embryos are protected by thin seed coats showing a light requirement for oxygen permeability. Germination is prompt. Gibberellic acid is an aid, but not a substitute for light.

Peripher Linear Embryos

Peripheral embryos which surround the food storage organ rather than being contained within it have multiple seed coverings which contain inhibitors, and which form barriers to both oxygen and water. Treatment is primarily leaching of the inhibitor but cold or light treatments may be required to increase permeability.

Removal of the seed covering structures is also effective. Summaries of seed anatomy, blocks to germination, successful germination test regimes and families exhibiting these characteristics are provided in Table for endospermic seeds.

Table 1.1 Endospermic Seeds Anatomy and Germination

		A. Axile Foliar Embryos with Hard Seed Coats	B. Axile Foliar Embryos with thin, Mucilaginous, Seed Coats	C. Axile Foliar Embryos with Woody Seed Coats and Inner Semi-permeable Layer	D. Axile Foliar Embryos with Fibrous Seed Coat and Separate Inner Eemi-permeable Membranous Layer
Seed Anatomy	embryo	spatulate, bent or folded and fills seed cavity	spatulate or bent and fills most of seed cavity	fills most of seed cavity	spatulate and fills most of seed cavity
	cotyledons	large, thickened and dominant over the stalk	large, thickened and dominant over the stalk	expanded and dominant	large and dominant embryo
	endosperm	reduced to a thin layer or lacking	thin layer around embryo or lacking	surrounds axillary embryo forming a lining of the seedcoat or none	thin layer(s) lining the membranous testa

(Contd...)

	seed coat	hard	thin, may exude mucilage when wet, or contain a mucilaginous layer within	woody, usually achenes with fused or separate membranous testa	
	seed size	medium-large; 2-15 mm long	small-medium; 1-6 mm long	medium-large; 2-10 mm long	wedge-shaped achenes; 1-10 mm long
	example	Ipomoea purpurea	Iberis amara	Verbena x hybrida	Dimorphothecasinuata
	embryo				inhibitors present in cotyledons
Blocks To Germination	endosperm	possibility of inhibitors in residual endosperm			impermeable to oxygen, gibberellins and inhibitors
	seed coat	impermeable when desiccated; imbibition through specialized valves or after scarification	becomes impermeable to oxygen and other gases as it absorbs water	permeable to moisture, but impermeable to some gases and inhibitors may be present within the seed coat	inhibitors may be present
	temperature	20°C; 20°/30°C	15°C, 20°C; 15°/25°C or 10°/30°C	15°, 20°, 25°C; 20°/30°C, 25°/35°C,	15°,20°C; 15°/25°C or 20°/30°C

(Contd...)

				15°/25°C or 15°/30°C	
	test duration	14-28d; in extreme cases 40-50d	10-28d; in extreme cases 56-90d	9-28d; in extreme cases 40-60d (but excised embryos 2-4d only)	5-14d; in extreme cases 21-40d
	KNO_3		*0.2%	*0.2%	0.2%
	GA_3		*100-400 ppm	5 ppm	5-10 ppm
	pre-chill				60d at 2°-5°C with high oxygen conc.
Successful Germination Test	light	insensitive	*insensitive or sensitive (promotory)	*insensitive or sensitive (promotory)	insensitive or sensitive (promotory)
REGIMES (*most widely applied treatments)	seed coat	*file; chip (clip); excise embryo	excise embryo	*excise embryo; pierce, remove over radicle	*excise embryo from endosperm and seed coat; chip (clip) radicle end
	scarification	*mechanical; conc H_2SO_4 for 15 min to 4 h; absolute ethyl alcohol for 20-72 h; percussion (shake)			

(Contd...)

	pre-soak	water at 50°-90°C for 30 sec-24h		400 ppm GA_3 or warm water for 24h	*in water or 5% chlorox or leach (even with excised embryos) away inhibitors with water
	after-ripen	dry at 95°C for 6 mins; dry over $CaCl_2$		2-3m dry storage	
Plant Families with Species Exhibiting these Characteristics		Anacardiaceae, convolvulaceae, geraniaceae, leguminosae, malvaceae, rhamnaceae, sapindaceae	Balsaminaceae, cruciferae, labiatae, linaceae, plantaginaceae, violaceae	Acanthaceae, apocynaceae, balsaminaceae, boraginaceae, cistaceae, dipsaceae, euphorbiaceae, hydrophyllaceae, labiatae, limnanthaceae, loasaceae, onagraceae, passifloraceae, plumbaginaceae, polemoniaceae, rosaceae, valerianaceae, verbenaceae, zygophyllaceae	Compositae (Only)

SEEDS WITH ONLY RESIDUAL OR NO ENDOSPERM (NON-ENDOSPERMIC SEEDS) AND MATURE INDEPENDENT EMBRYOS (THAT IS EMBRYOS READY TO GERMINATE)

Hard Seed Coat

Hard (impermeable) seed coats are present which limit the entry of water for imbibition. Treatment for allowing water entry is necessary and may be mechanical scarification, acid treatment, percussion, high temperature treatment or soaking. for more information on treatments to overcome hardseededness.)

Thin Seed Coat with Mucilaginous Layer

Mucilaginous seed coats limit oxygen availability to the embryo after imbibition. Gibberellic acid is the most effective additive but light and potassium nitrate are also helpful, particularly when treatment with the two agents is combined.

Woody Seed Coat With Inner Semi-permeable Layer

Woody-textured and membranous multi-layered seed coverings cause blocks to germination which are most difficult to overcome. They readily admit water for imbibition but contain strong inhibitors which do not leach readily. Some of these are probably located in the thin residual endosperm surrounding the embryo or within the cotyledons of the embryo and are blocked from leaching by the semi-permeable membranous testa incorporated in the coverings. Excised embryos germinate promptly.

Fibrous Seed Coat with Separate Semi-permeable Membranous Coat

The Compositae family forms a specialised group which is similar to the preceding section. Embryos contain inhibitors in their cotyledons. Testa and thin endosperm form a separate membranous semi-permeable coat. An outer fibrous coat offers various dispersal forms. Extracted embryos grow promptly if leaching is complete.

Summaries of seed anatomy, blocks to germination, successful germination test regimes and families exhibiting these characteristics are provided in Table for non-endospermic seeds.

Atwater has developed her ideas and experience almost to the stage of providing species prescriptions. Much of this information is summarised in subsequent chapters, but the problems inherent in species prescriptions are discussed below. Note also that certain plant families have species in more than one category of seed anatomy (*e.g.* Solanaceae, If Tables are used to develop germination test environments and dormancy-breaking treatments, it should be remembered that combinations of different dormancy-breaking agents are more likely to be successful than treatment with a single agent alone.

PRESCRIPTIONS FOR GERMINATING ALL ACCESSIONS OF A GIVEN SPECIES

This approach to determining germination test environments is exemplified by the Rules of the International Seed Testing Association (ISTA) and the Association of Seed Analysts of North America (AOSA). Commercial seed testing has evolved over the past 130 years to provide a certain degree of assurance to farmers, growers and foresters that any seeds of agricultural, horticultural or arboreal crops that they may purchase are capable of germinating under normal field conditions, emerging above the soil surface and developing into plants which yield an adequate crop. Thus, by assessing the quality of seed lots before they are sown, commercial seed testing minimises the risk to the farmer, grower or forester of sowing seed lots which do not have the ability to produce an abundant crop. Since this assessment will be done by only one of many laboratories and since there is also considerable international trade in seed of many species, assessments by different seed testing laboratories must give similar results.

COMPATIBILITY BETWEEN SEED TESTING STATIONS

To achieve compatibility of germination test results between different laboratories ISTA and AOSA co-ordinate and produce agreements between seed testing laboratories on the procedures to be applied for each species. We have discussed in Chapters how the proportion of seeds which will germinate in a germination test can be affected by the test environment.

Thus if seed testing laboratories used very different germination test conditions the results obtained in different laboratories could differ substantially. To aid compatibility ISTA and AOSA seek agreement between laboratories as to the most appropriate environment for testing the germination of a given species. In theory this implies agreement upon a single germination test environment. In practice alternative environments are often specified for a given species. This is either because of disagreement between laboratories as to the single most appropriate environment, or because of the need to provide alternative procedures for certain seed lots, or because of practical difficulties in providing certain environments (for example, alternating temperatures) in some laboratories.

The rules of the ISTA and AOSA list the prescribed germination test conditions for each species. These prescriptions specify the substrata, temperatures and test duration which seed testing laboratories must adhere to, Additional directions are provided for special treatments which may be required for certain species together with recommendations for breaking dormancy. These prescriptions and directions are summarised in the chapters which follow.

Now, these rules and directions are intended to give the most regular, rapid and complete germination for the majority of samples of seed of a particular species. To that end we presume the rules are successful, but how closely does the above aim coincide with the problems facing those testing seeds within gene banks?

PRESCRIPTIONS ARE NOT AVAILABLE FOR ALL SPECIES

First, ISTA and AOSA tend to only provide rules for those species in which certian individual seed testing stations have knowledge of the germination behaviour of a large number of seed samples. Thus the species listed in the ISTA and AOSA rules are those in which there is considerable trade in the sees; the seed-propagated crops. In contrast gene banks will often need to germinate seeds of species which are not yet in substantial trade in the developed world (*e.g.* the tropical pasture species), true seeds of vegetatively propagated crops (*e.g.* potato, Solanum tuberosum), and seeds of species which do not have crop status such as wild and weedy relatives of modern crop species (*e.g.*

teosinte, Euchlaena mexicana). Thus the first drawback for gene banks of the ISTA/AOSA rules is that for many species on which gene banks require advice on germination test conditions no information is provided.

PRESCRIPTIONS DEVELOPED FOR MODERN CULTIVARS

Secondly, within those species for which ISTA and AOSA prescribe test conditions the range of seed lots which seed testing stations test for germination, and upon the results of which ISTA precriptions are based, are generally limited to relatively non-dormant, high quality, modern, genetically homogeneous cultivars. That is in most cases the cultivars with which the rules have been developed are likely to have been subjected to considerable selection pressures. In contrast gene banks will be testing seeds of primitive cultivars and genetically heterogeneous landraces which may also show considerable dormancy and/or be of poor quality. Thus the second drawback for gene banks of the ISTA/AOSA rules is that the prescribed conditions for a particula species will not necessarily be suitable for those acessions within gene banks which are dissimilar to modern cultivars-or of poor quality.

RELATIVE PRIORITIES OF THE AIMS OF SEED TESTING

Thirdly, for some crops seed testing stations may operate under considerable pressure at harvest time. For example, in temperate countries autumn sown cereal seeds are sown only five or six weeks after harvest. Thus seed testers may need to complete germination tests in as short a time as possible. Hence seed testing stations' aim of providing conditions which give rapid germination. Now in at lest one group of species—the temperate cereals—although the conditions prescribed by the rules may give rapid germination this is only achieved in our experience by using supra-optimal temperatures at the cost of the parallel aims of achieving regular and complete germination which are better achieved at much lower temperatures.

In contrast to seed testing stations, gene banks are not under any pressure to give priority to rapid germination over achieving regular and complete germination. Thus the third drawback for gene banks of the ISTA/AOSA rules is that the aims of rapid and complete germination may not always be compatible. Note that this criticism does not apply to the rules for all crops. In the case of tree species, for example, considerable periods are allowed for dormancy-breaking and germination test treatments by ISTA and AOSA rules, and the requirement for complete germination takes precedence over the requirement for rapid germination.

FIELD PLANTING VALUE

The purpose of commercial testing is to provide information on the comparative field planting value of different seed lots. In general the ISTA and AOSA prescriptions make no attempt to enable those viable seeds which will not germinate under field conditions to germinate in the laboratory test. If, for example, dormancy is a problem in laboratory tests, but not in field sowings (for example, due to differences in temperature between the two regimes) then directions to break dormancy must be provided in the rules—otherwise the field planting value may be underestimated. However, where dormancy is a problem in both laboratory tests and field sowings then to obtain an indication of field planting value the rules may not necessarily provide dormancy-breaking directions—since the removal of dormancy in laboratory tests may result in an overestimate of field planting value.

Again whether or not this objective of ISTA or AOSA prescriptions and recommendations makes them unsuitable for viability testing in gene banks depends on the species. For example, in tree species directions for dormancy removal are suggested to enable viability to be estimated in laboratory tests and these directions must also be followed in field sowings if laboratory results are to provide a reasonable estimate of field planting value. In contrast in some species where hardseededness prevents germination no recommendation is made to render the seed coat permeable.

Instead the proportion of hard seeds is reported. Thus the fourth drawback of ISTA/AOSA rules is that no attempt may be made to overcome a wide range of physiological phenomena which may prevent the germination of viable seeds under both laboratory and field conditions. Of these phenomena the most important are hardseededness and strong dormancy. In contrast to seed testing stations, gene banks aim to provide conditions which will enable all viable seeds to germinate both in laboratory tests and in subsequent field or glasshouse sowings.

OTHER SOURCES OF PRESCRIPTIONS

Numerous groups of workers have attempted to provide prescriptions for germination tests of species for which no ISTA/ AOSA rules are available or which overcome certain of the deficiencies of the ISTA and AOSA prescriptions for species where rules are available. Particular emphasis has been placed on overcoming dormancy since this can be an important problem for plant breeders, and also for seed testers if considerable dormancy is experienced when the seeds are tested but which is likely to be lost during storage before sowing.

However, much of this information is also of limited use in gene banks. This is because the majority of such information relates to the application of single dormancy breaking agents alone. It was explained that if this approach is used then the treatment concentration (if a chemical agent) or duration (if another form of treatment) required to break dormancy in the most dormant seeds would be likely to damage less dormant seeds, particularly if these are also of poor quality.

THE AIM OF DEVELOPING A SPECIES PRESCRIPTION FOR USE IN GENE BANKS

We believe that the ultimate desirable aim of a prescriptive test for a given species is to be able to provide within one test environment or procedure those conditions which enable all viable seeds of that species—whether strongly dormant, moderately dormant, weakly dormant or non-dormant, and of high or low quality—to be able to germinate. This means that any stimulus or combination of stimuli used to promote the germination of dormant seeds must not be damaging to other non-dormant seeds in the sample or to intolerant genotypes.

DEVELOPING A PRESCRIPTION FOR A SPECIES

Whether this aim can in fact always be achieved is a matter for debate, but two considerations are important in attempting to achieve it. The first is to ensure that the germination test temperature is suitable for poor quality seeds; within this range attempts can then be made to determine the most suitable temperature regime which will minimise the expression of dormancy. In certain species this first step may result in an adequate single germination test environment without any need for further treatment. In temperate cereals this appears to be the case, where a single low constant temperature is appropriate for both purposes.

However, in other species simple solutions of this type may not be available and so it is necessary to take a second step and provide further stimuli to break dormancy which do not impair the germination of less dormant seeds. In our opinion this is often best attempted by combining more than one additional stimulus with all stimuli being applied at relatively low dose-levels. This is an attempt to utilise the positive interactions observed between many dormancy-breaking agents. The treatments developed for Oryza spp. and Vitis spp. provide examples of this type of procedure (these and other prescriptions are described in the appropriate chapters of this volume).

Gene banks considering developing their own germina-tion test prescriptions may be discouraged by the wide range of different treatments—and the even wider range of different treatment combinations—which may be of potential benefit in promoting the germination of viable seeds. Consequently it is worthwhile considering which factors should receive priority in any investigation. We believe that the three most important factors to consider first are to ensure that the seeds have imbibed moisture without damage and then to attempt to determine the most suitable temperature (probably alternating temperature, and light regimes for germination.

Provided a prescription is already available for a species which is suitable for application in a gene bank then this would be the simplest approach for gene banks to use. However, even where a prescription is well-tried, gene banks will still need to be alert to the possibility that some accessions may be discovered for which the prescription does not appear to work. Furthermore, for many years to come, there will continue to be a large number of species for which there are no adequate prescriptions. Accordingly alternative approaches to providing suitable germination test environments are also considered in this handbook.

USE OF TETRAZOLIUM TEST TO DETERMINE EFFICACY OF A PRESCRIPTION

Although a gene bank can never be absolutely certain about the efficacy of any approach to germinating seeds, do not forget that the efficacy of a species prescription on a particular accession can be tested by comparing the results of the germination test with that of the topographical tetrazolium test on a sub-sample of the seed lot and by also applying a tetrazolium test to the seeds remaining ungerminated at the end of the test. In this way one can determine the proportion (if any) of viable seeds which are either killed by the germination test procedure or remain dormant at the end of the germination test procedure.

In the above we have detailed objections to the wholesale and unquestioning adoption of either ISTA or AOSA prescribed germination test procedures as gene bank germination tests. However, this certainly does not mean that such prescriptions should be ignored by gene banks. The ISTA and AOSA rules summarise a wealth and depth of expertise and experience which is unmatched. Thus where available, the prescribed conditions represent a control against which any proposed alternative should be tested; and, despite our earlier comments, certain of these prescriptions will be suitable for gene bank use.

TAXONOMIC ALGORITHMS TO DETERMINE APPROPRIATE GERMINATION TEST ENVIRONMENTS

As mentioned above, germination test prescriptions are available for only a small proportion of seed-producing species. What environment should be chosen to test the germination of seed accessions of species for which no prescription or no acceptable prescription is available? This is exactly the problem which faced staff at the Royal Botanic Gardens Kew, Wakehurst Place Gene Bank, for almost all their accessions, because this gene bank deals entirely with seed collections of species which do not have great commercial significance. The method that they developed to answer the question posed above provides another approach to developing appropriate germination test regimes for seed accessions maintained in gene banks.

ALGORITHM THE SHORTEST SERIES OF TESTS TO DEFINE A SUITABLE TEST ENVIRONMENT

This approach acknowledges that the most suitable environment for testing each accession is unknown. Thus, instead of a single prescription, an attempt has been made to develop the shortest series of tests which is likely to give a solution to the problem of defining a suitable test environment. The decision as to which test to try next depends on the results obtained in the previous test(s), and so we call this series of tests an algorithm. For gene banks a truly universal algorithm would be one appropriate to all seed-producing species, irrespective of taxonomy. However, such an approach would be rather unwieldy and require a large number of tests. Certain similarities in the response of seed germination to environment for species within a family can be recognised. Consequently this approach provides a separate algorithm for each family where sufficient knowledge has been accumulated.

Where available, the algorithms developed by the staff at the Wakehurst Place Gene Bank are presented according to family. However, it is necessary here to provide some explanation of how the algorithms were developed, their possible faults, and how they should be applied.

THE DEVELOPMENT OF THE RBG KEW WAKEHURST PLACE ALGORITHMS

Storage at the Wakehurst Place Gene Bank began in 1974. Since then all accessions entered into storage have been tested for germination as soon as possible thereafter. In many cases accessions were tested in more than one germination test environment, the reason for this being an inadequate proportion (less than 85 per cent) of seeds germinating in the first test. Thus for many accessions it was possible to compare germination test results over a number of different environments with and without the imposition of various additional dormancy-breaking treatments. For each accession the best germination test regime was noted, and this regime was then used for all subsequent germination tests of that accession. In addition the results of all the different germination tests carried out on each accession were filed according to species to provide a growing information bank on the response of seed germination to different test conditions. The below table provides an example of the information generated and filed from such tests for a single accession of Veronica verna.

Table Example of germination test results recorded by staff at the Wakehurst Place Gene Bank used in subsequent analyses to determine algorithms for determining suitable test regimes: germination (per cent) and classification of non-germinating seeds after testing seeds of a 1977 collection of Veronica verna under four different regimes (100 seeds per test).

Test Date	Germination Test Regime	Total Test Duration (Days)	Cumulative Germination (%) at End of Test	Non-germinated Seeds at End of Test[1]		
				Fresh	Mouldy	Empty
16/12/77	21°C	42	0	100	0	0
16/12/77	21°/11°C (12h/12h)	157	48	52	0	0
18/4/78	26°C for 28 days (imbibed) then 11°C	48	100	0	0	0
18/4/78	2°C	73	88	12	0	0

Note: [1]expressed as the percentage of the original number of seeds tested

The two original tests on seeds from this accession, begun on 16/12/77, demonstrated a high proportion of dormant seeds (those designated as fresh at the end of the test. At 21°C all seeds exhibited dormancy (Table). The alternating temperature 'regime of 21°/11°C was only partly successful in breaking this dormancy (Table). Therefore towards the end of the latter test, a decision was made to sample more seeds from the accession and begin two additional germination tests in different conditions (which are known to promote germina-tion in several species). One of these additional regimes-consisting of a preliminary period during which the imbibed seeds were exposed to 26°C (sometimes described as a warm stratification treatment) followed by subsequent exposure to 11°C-was entirely successful at breaking dormancy, enabling all the seeds tested to germinate. Consequently this regime will be used for any subsequent germination tests to monitor the viability of this accession.

Over the past ten years or so a considerable amount of information on the response of seed germination to various test regimes (similar to that described above for Veronica verna) has been generated by staff at Wakehurst Place. This raw information has subsequently been analysed, principally by Mr. S. Linington, in the following manner. For a particular family all the routine test data for all accessions (each similar in form to that provided in the above Table) were examined. It was (arbitrarily) decided that test regimes in which 85 per cent, or more, of the full seeds germinated would be classified as successful. For each accession all the successful regime(s) (if there were any) were listed. For example, two regimes would be listed as successful for the accession shown in Table: 2°C constant; and 28 days at 26°C followed by 11°C constant.

When this first stage of analysis was completed a pattern of successful regimes within each family was sought. Emphasis was placed on determining those simpler regimes (that is those employing few dormancy-breaking agents) which were successful for the greatest number of accessions. These regimes are those which are now used as the first step in the algorithms which have been developed. More complicated regimes (involving the use of many dormancy-breaking treatments) which are successful for fewer accessions are then provided as subsequent alternatives (later steps) in the algorithm if the first step does not provide a suitable environment for germination testing.

POSSIBLE LIMITATIONS OF THE ALGORITHMS

There are a number of possible faults inherent in this method of analysis. First, by excluding from the analysis all accessions which failed to reach 85 per cent germination under any test regime, the response of accessions which are either very dormant, or very poor quality and vulnerable in certain germination test environments may have been ignored. Secondly, it is based on tests of accessions within the Wakehurst bank which, at least in the past, were biased towards collecting in temperate regions. Not only may this result in an algorithm more suited to temperate collections, but it may also result in algorithms more suited to certain tribes within each family. For example, the algorithm for the Leguminosae was based largely on accessions of the Papilio-noideae tribe and little data was available for accessions from either the Caesalpinoideae or Mimosoideae tribes. Finally it should be noted that the analysis was based on data obtained over only a limited range of treatments. Other, untested, treatments may be superior and there is as yet no way of knowing whether this will be the case.

SUCCESS OF THE ALGORITHMS MAY VARY BETWEEN FAMILIES

Despite these reservations, the algorithm approach to determining germination test environment works well at Wakehurst and is likely to be useful in other gene banks. Tests at Wakehurst on previously untested accessions using the algorithms for the Amaranthaceae, Gramineae, Leguminosae and Solanaceae families have shown that 100 per cent, 50 per cent, 90 per cent and 75 per cent of accessions within each family reached 85 per cent germination or greater.

In view of the importance of the Gramineae in food production the limited success of the algorithm for this family is disappointing. One group of species within the Gramineae whose seed is particularly difficult to germinate is the tropical pasture species. Unfortunately tests on five seed lots of tropical pasture species at Reading confirm that the present algorithm for the Gramineae is not particularly helpful for determining germination test environment in these species.

DEMONSTRATION OF THE USE OF AN ALGORITHM

Nevertheless, Table can be used to explain the method of applying the algorithm. Table should be studied together with the

Gramineae algorithm provided in Chapter. In Table every feasible combination of dormancy-breaking agents within the algorithm was applied to the seeds, amounting to some 24 separate test environments. Note, however, that only a few of these tests would have been applied if the algorithm had been followed. The pathway through the tests which would have been followed if the Gramineae algorithm had been applied is shown by the boxed values in Table (*see on next page*), the sequence being from the top of the table to the bottom. Table Normal germination (expressed as percentage of full seeds tested) after 28 days in germination test [lower figures in square brackets after 56 days] for five tropical grass seed lots. If the Gramineae algorithm had been followed in the manner intended only the tests in square boxes would have been investigated.

Three details of the work reported in Table differ from the Gramineae algorithm provided by the Wakehurst Place Gene Bank. First the germination test temperatures are not identical, but are within 1°C-except for the upper limit of the alternating temperature regime where the difference is 2°C. These minor differences are unimportant and result from differences in the standard temperatures available at Reading and Wakehurst. Secondly the comment in the algorithm to test at constant temperatures either below 20°C or above 25°C depending upon which gave the higher test result was not followed, since previous experience with dormant seed lots of these species indicated that alternating temperatures were essential to promote germination. Thirdly, following on from the last point, seeds were also tested for germination at the two additional alternating temperature regimes of 15°/30°C and 10°/30°C.

To enable the reader to understand fully the use of the algorithm, an explanation is provided below of the sequence of tests and decisions that would have been applied for tests on the accession of Brachiaria decumbens. The first stage in the algorithm was to test the seeds at constant temperatures of 20°C and 25°C. These test results were inadequate (less than 85 per cent germination).

Treatment	SPECIES																			
	Brachiaria Decumbens				Brachiaria Humidicola				(Gatton Panic) Panicum Maximum				(Green Panic) Panicum Maximum				(Riversdale Guinea) Panicum Maximum			
	Temperature, °C				Temperature, °C				Temperature, °C				Temperature, °C				Temperature, °C			
	20	25	35/20	(15/30,10/30)	20	25	35/20	(15/30,10/30)	20	25	35/20	(15/30,10/30)	20	25	35/20	(15/30,10/30)	20	25	35/20	(15/30,10/30)
Control (constant temperature)	[4]	[1]			[0]	[4]			[39]	[25]			[18]	[18]			[2]	[0]		
	[5]	[3]			[0]	[4]			[39]	[26]			[18]	[18]			[3]	[0]		
Alternating temperature			[19]	(10,10)			[21]	(74,73)			[46]	(90,92)			[18]	(13,7)			[31]	(57,69)
			[22]	([10],[15])			[57]	([75],[77])			[49]	([92],[93])			[18]	([15],[8])			[44]	([58],[70])
10^{-3} M KNO_3	3	3	[28]	(13,17)	0	1	[18]	(66,-)	61	31	[59]	(93,82)	14	14	[13]	(14,14)	3	0	[40]	(64,79)
	[4]	[3]	[30]	([13],[19])	[1]	[2]	[64]	([67],-)	[61]	[31]	[64]	([97],[90])	[16]	[14]	[13]	([17],[14])	[6]	[0]	[51]	([64],[80])
Dehusk	15	14	65		0	2	[14]		11	8	7		14	15	[18]		1	2	35	
	[17]	[15]	[66]		[0]	[2]	[45]		[12]	[10]	[12]		[14]	[15]	[19]		[10]	[2]	[41]	
Dehusk + KNO_3	14	15	[63]		4	3	12		17	11	[9]		14	21	13		18	3	[61]	
	[15]	[16]	[63]		[4]	[4]	[40]		[19]	[13]	[26]		[14]	[22]	[14]		[19]	[3]	[69]	
8 week pre-chill	0	0	0		0	0	[3]		33	21	16		0	0	[2]		35	54	59	
	[0]	[0]	[0]		[0]	[0]	[4]		[34]	[21]	[18]		[0]	[0]	[2]		[35]	[54]	[62]	
Dehusk + pre-chill	1	7	38		0	0	5		11	27	25		0	2	2		35	31	46	
	[2]	[7]	[38]		[1]	[0]	[12]		[11]	[27]	[26]		[0]	[3]	[4]		[38]	[31]	[49]	
KNO_3 + pre-chill	1	1	1		1	0	4		8	20	[25]		2	2	2		49	62	59	
	[1]	[1]	[1]		[1]	[0]	[5]		[8]	[20]	[25]		[2]	[2]	[2]		[49]	[62]	[62]	
Dehusk + KNO_3 + pre-chill	0	9	[35]		0	0	6		24	18	30		4	2	7		31	45	[62]	
	[0]	[10]	[35]		[2]	[0]	[9]		[24]	[18]	[30]		[5]	[3]	[9]		[33]	[45]	[62]	
Viability (tetrazolium test)		[94]				[75]				[97]				[25]				[76]		

Now, according to the algorithm the next step would have been to look for trends in the results of these two tests (*i.e.* was germination greater at the higher or lower tempera-ture?) and test for germination at either a more extreme higher or a more extreme lower constant temperature accordingly. This, however, was not done for the reasons given above and we proceeded to the second step of the algorithm which was to test a fresh sample of the seeds in an alternating temperature regime of 35°/20°C (the nearest regime available to the standard 33°/19°C Wakehurst regime). The germination obtained in this test was substantially greater than at either of the two constant temperatures, but again inadequate as a germination test regime. Consequently further tests were required.

The third step according to the algorithm was to test a fresh sample of the seeds in a medium containing 10^{-3} M KNO_3 at, in view of the difference observed between the results at steps 1 and 2, an alternating temperature of 35°/20°C. Again the result of this test at step 3 was an improvement on the result at step 2 but inadequate as a germination test regime since 85 per cent germination was not achieved.

Thus the fourth step was to remove the seed covering structures from a fresh sample of the seeds and test in a medium containing 10^{-3} M KNO_3 (since the result at step 3 was greater than the result at step 2) at an alternating temperature of 35°/20°C. Once again the result of the test at this step was an improvement on the previous test result (suggesting that dehusking was a worthwhile treatment), but the percentage of seeds germinating was still unsatisfactory.

Consequently the final step in the algorithm was applied. Namely dehusked imbibed seeds were pre-chilled at 3°-5°C for 8 weeks and then transferred to an alternating temperature regime of 35°/20°C in a medium containing 10^{-3} M KNO_3. Unfortunately this test resulted in substantially fewer seeds germinating than the previous test. Thus the conclusion reached by using the algorithm is that dehusked seeds of this accession of Brachiaria decumbens should be tested on a substrate containing 10^{-3} M KNO_3 in an alternating temperature regime of 35°/20°C.

Note that the decision making procedure at each step in the algorithm did not result in the algorithm missing more favourable treatment combinations. For example, if the algorithm had been followed dehusked seeds would not have been tested at 35°/20°C without 10^{-3} M KNO_3 in the germination medium. In fact this treatment gave a very similar result (that is there was no significant difference) to the treatment with dehusked seeds which did include 10^{-3} M KNO_3 in the germination medium. Thus it appears that the use of 10^{-3} M KNO_3 in the medium is in fact not necessary, but its use (apparently necessary if the algorithm had been followed) does not result in a significantly lower proportion of seeds germinating.

In that sense we can regard the decision-making procedure within the algorithm as being successful, but unfortunately the algorithm itself was not successful since the level of viability indicated by the tetrazolium test was not achieved in these germination tests.

SENSITIVITY OF GERMINATION TO THE TEMPERATURE REGIME

In addition to all the possible germination test regimes according to the Gramineae algorithm, Table also presents results of tests carried out in two additional alternating temperature environments (15°/30°C and 10°/30°C) and also in combination with 10^{-3} M KNO_3 (where sufficient seeds were available). These results suggest that, for some seed lots at least, those gene banks testing tropical grass species would be well advised to include additional alternating temperature regimes as the second step of the algorithm. For three of the seed lots tested here small differences in the alternating temperature regime greatly influenced the proportion of seeds which germinated (*see table 1.2 on page 27*). Not only did this result in almost full germination of viable seeds, but it would have avoided the need for several stages of the algorithm in the case of Gatton Panic.

In passing note that the results shown in Tables emphasise that seed germination can be particularly sensitive to the temperature regime in which the seeds are tested. It cannot be overemphasised that gene bank staff must make strenuous efforts to get this right first before embarking on investigations as to the efficacy of other dormancy-breaking agents.

POSSIBLE USE OF UNGERMINATED SEEDS FROM PRIOR STEP IN ALGORITHM FOR THE CURRENT TEST

In the algorithms provided here additional tests are carried out by drawing a fresh sample of seeds from the accession bulk in storage. In some cases, for example if the supply of seeds is severely limited, it is possible to test the response to additional treatments by applying these to those ungerminated seeds which remain fresh and firm at the end of a previous test.

This is particularly suitable for scarification, dehusking or puncturing treatments since it may avoid the need to apply these time-consuming procedures to all seeds tested. For example, if 70 per cent of seeds tested of a legume accession germinate without scarification it is easier to scarify the remaining proportion of seeds and to return these to the germination environment than to draw a fresh sample of seeds from storage and scarify all of the seeds to be tested.

DURATION OF GERMINATION TESTS

During each step of the algorithm it is necessary to decide when to terminate the germination test and whether to pursue the next step in the algorithm. Since both aged and dormant seeds may only begin to germinate in a test after a substantial delay it is not possible to provide categorical advice. In Chapter 10, Volume I, an example is provided of how to decide when to terminate a germination test by constructing a germination progress curve.

This technique can be used for each step in the algorithm, but each test should not be continued for an excessive period because the next step in the algorithm might result in a more suitable and more rapid procedure. That is if the progress of germination is very slow it might be better to pursue the next step in the algorithm.

A minimum germination test period of 28 days is suggested. A comparison of results after 28 and 56 days in test, for example, shows substantial germination after 28 days in test for only the Brachiaria humidicola accession tested at 35°/20°C. Consequently it is suggested that the decision to test a further sample of seeds in the next step of the algorithm can generally be made once the 28-day test result is known, but that the current test be continued for a further period dependent upon the shape of the germination progress curve. In tests at a very low temperature (*e.g.* 6°C), however, it may be better to delay a decision as to whether to continue through the algorithm until the 56-day test result is known.

USE OF ALGORITHMS AT ACCESSION RECEIPT

It is suggested that the algorithms could be applied soon after an accession is received if the standard advice on germination test procedures and dormancy-breaking treatments is unsatisfactory or if no advice is available. The number of seeds tested in each of the regimes required by the algorithm need not exceed 100 (and 50 seeds may well be sufficient), but the seeds should be sampled from the accession at random and replication in each test is advisable Once a suitable test procedure has been developed a further sample of 200 seeds can be withdrawn from the accession and tested by this procedure in order to 'estimate initial accession viability. Subsequent monitoring tests of accession viability will also apply the same germination test procedure, but may be either fixed sample size tests or sequential tests. Note that it is envisaged that the algorithms would only be applied once, *i.e.* when the accession is first received: the subsequent monitoring tests would employ the most appropriate regime already determined.

SEED DORMANCY

The fruits are usually surrounded by a persistent perianth. B.R. Atwater classifies seed morphology as endospermic seeds with peripheral linear embryos. Light, alternating temperatures, pre-washing and removal of the seed covering structures can promote germination, but some care may be required in defining promotory treatments in detail. Detailed information on seed germination is provided for the genera Amaranthus and Celosia in this chapter. A limited number of other recommended germination test procedures is provided in Table and the algorithm below may be helpful in developing suitable germination test procedures.

RBG KEW WAKEHURST PLACE ALGORITHM

The first step of the algorithm is to test three samples of the seeds at constant temperatures of 26°C, 31°C, and 36°C with light applied for 12h/d. If full germination has not been promoted and there is a trend in germination response to constant temperatures, then test further samples of seeds at more extreme constant temperatures.

That is: if germination was greatest at 26°C then test at constant temperatures of 16°C and 21°C with light applied for 12h/d; but if germination was greatest at 36°C then test at a constant temperature of 41°C with light applied for 12h/d. If, however, germination was greatest at 31°C then go to the next step of the algorithm.

If full germination has not been promoted, the second step of the algorithm is to test a further sample of seeds in an alternating temperature regime of 33°/19°C (12h/12h) with light applied for 12h/d during the period spent at the upper temperature. If full germination has not been promoted, the third step of the algorithm is to estimate viability using a tetrazolium test.

If the result of the tetrazolium test indicates that the failure to achieve full germination is due to the presence of dead seeds and that one of the above regimes promoted the germination of all, or almost all, the viable seeds, then this regime is used for all subsequent germination tests. If, however, the result of the tetrazolium test indicates that dormancy has not been broken by the regimes applied so far in the algorithm, then experiment with modifications to the above regimes. Clues to possible satisfactory dormancy-breaking treatments and promotory germination test environments can be obtained from the information provided in this chapter for the genera Amaranthus and Celosia and from Table.

Table 1.2 Summary of Germination Test Recommendations for Species Within the Amaranthaceae

Species and Authority	Substrate	Temperature	Duration	Additional Directions	Source
Gomphrena globosa L.	TP; BP	20°/30°C; 20°C	14d	Potassium nitrate	ISTA
	TP	20°/30°C	14d	light, potassium nitrate	AOSA
		20°/30°C'	10d	Light	Atwater

AMARANTHUS

A. Albus L.	Tumble Pigweed
A. Blitoides Wats.	Prostrate pigweed
A. caudatus L. [A. paniculatus L.; A. cruentis L.]	Grain amaranth, pigweed, love-lies-bleeding, tassel flower
A. Graecizans L.	Tumbleweed, prostrate pigweed
A. Hybridus L.	Edible amaranth, smooth pigweed
A. Hypochondriacus L.	
A. Lividus L.	
A. Palmeri Wats.	Palmer amaranth
A. Powellii Wats.	Powell's pigweed
A. Retroflexus L.	Green amaranth, redroot pigweed
A. spinosus L.	Spiny amaranth
A. tricolour L.	

Evidence of Dormancy

Almost without exception seeds of Amaranthus spp. show considerable dormancy. This is possibly because the majority of references cited here concern seeds from weedy plants of Amaranthus spp. Only in a minority of papers has the dormancy of seeds from cultivated plants within the genus Amaranthus been investigated. Nevertheless it is clear that dormancy can also be considerable in seeds from cultivated plants-*e.g.*

After-ripening treatment periods required to remove dormancy from the majority of seeds can be considerable: 180 days (4,22), 300 days or as many as 4 years for seeds of A.

retroflexus; and 6 months for seeds of A. blitoides and A. graecizans.

Comment

Comparatively few treatments have been reported which are able to break the dormancy of all seeds within accessions ofAmaranthus spp. Light is a factor of critical importance. At first sight the literature may appear confusing, since the effect of light on germination has been reported as both stimulatory and inhibitory. Inhibitory action occurs when the light is of the wrong wavelength-for example, far red-or the dosage is too high. To obtain the maximum promotion from light additional parameters are important: these include tempera-ture, the timing of the light application, and-more occasio-nally-the presence of other dormancy-breaking agents.

At constant temperatures, high temperatures are required for the germination of dormant seeds: above 30°C, 30°–37°C, 35°C, 35°–40°C, or 40°C. Alternating temperatures can promote germination: 20°/35°C (16h/8h) is reported to be superior to 20°/30°C (16h/8h)-the AOSA prescribed regime-whilst both are better than high constant temperatures; 30°/25°C (day/night) is superior to 25°/20°C, 20°/15°C, or 15°/30°C (day/night); 25°/8°C (18h/6h) is reported to be better than constant temperatures between 25° and 28°C; and 23°/35°C (12h/12h) is superior to constant temperatures of 30°C or 35°C, but to obtain maximum promotion the initial imbibition temperature should be 23°C, not 35°C-that is 23°/35°C, not 35°/23°C.

However, neither constant nor alternating temperatures alone can be regarded as satisfactory. For example, testing dormant seeds from five Amaranthus spp. at constant temperatures between 29°C and 38°C, or alternating temperatures of 19°/23°C, 20°/32°C or 22°/43°C in the dark resulted in no more than 10 per cent germination in any one environment, with no significant difference in germination between the various germination test regimes.

At high constant temperatures the germination of dormant seeds is promoted by only a very short duration light treatment, for example in A. blitoides and A. retroflexus. As little as 45–60 seconds can be sufficient to promote the germination of the majority of dormant seeds-for example, promoting germination from 25 per cent to 92 per cent.

However, the timing of the light treatment in relation to the start of imbibition is critical: in A. hybridus the maximum promotion is reported after 80-150 hours; in A. blitoides after 48 hours; and in A. retroflexus after 96 hours. Moreover, the response to light can be considerably increased in the presence of other dormancy-breaking agents-particularly potassium nitrate. Although the above times appear to vary—probably due to differences of irradiance reaching the seeds-once the maximum sensitivity to light has been achieved during imbibition, delaying the light treatment does not reduce the germination of seeds of Amaranthus spp.

Given the wide differences in the level of seed dormancy between accessions within the genus Amaranthus it is difficult to make precise recommendations. Nevertheless, the following regime is tentatively suggested: imbibe seeds in the dark at 35°C for four days with 0.2 per cent potassium nitrate co-applied; expose briefly to red light-1×10^{-9} mol cm^{-2} is probably sufficient. Although one exposure is probably satisfactory, it might be worthwhile to provide this daily in case some individual seeds require a longer period of imbibition before they reach maximum sensitivity to light.

It is likely that an alternating temperature regime would be preferable to a constant temperature of 35°C; 20°–25°/35°C (12h/12h) is suggested, again with potassium nitrate and red light as described above, but this must be regarded as untested as yet. Finally, if it is difficult to provide a suitable light environment it is worth noting that pre-chill treatments can reduce the need for light in subsequent germination tests; try 14 days at 3°–5°C and then transfer to 35°C in the dark for the germination test.

2

Seed Testing

OVERVIEW

This chapter provides a brief overview of the process from sampling to detection. Further details of sampling and detection are then discussed in subsequent chapters. The International Seed Testing Association (ISTA) and the International Organization for Standardization (ISO) have developed standards for sampling lots of seed and grain, respectively. ISO terminology refers to primary samples as increments, the composite sample as the bulk sample and the submitted sample as the laboratory sample (Figure). In this report, sampling terminology and sampling protocols are based on ISTA standards for discussion on seed-for-sowing and on ISO standards for discussion on grain.

Based on ISTA terminology, the sampling process (*Fig. 2.1*) involves taking a number of primary samples from the original seed lot. The number of primary samples required depends on the size of the seed lot and how well it is mixed. If adventitious GM material is unevenly distributed throughout the lot then more primary samples are required to accurately represent what is in the lot. The primary samples are combined and mixed to form a composite sample which is representative of the whole seed lot. As the concentration of GM material in the lot decreases, larger composite samples are required to ensure that the composition of the lot is accurately reflected. If the composite sample is too large to be sent to the laboratory, it is reduced in size (with very thorough mixing) into a submitted sample. In the laboratory, the submitted sample is mixed and further subdivided into one or more working samples which are then analysed using the chosen test method.

Where GM and non-GM crops are being developed and grown in the same country, AP could theoretically be introduced at any point in the supply chain, from initial pre-breeding, through breeding, seed-increase, on-farm production, transport and storage through to use (delivered for export, food or feed processing). For example, AP would occur at storage sites if GM grain was inadvertently mislabelled or mixed with non-GM grain. Monitoring for such inadvertent errors could be undertaken using an on-site test with a relatively low sensitivity since such mislabelled or misdirected truckloads are likely to contain a very high level of GM grain. Commercially available tests would need to be assessed to ensure that they have adequate sensitivity.

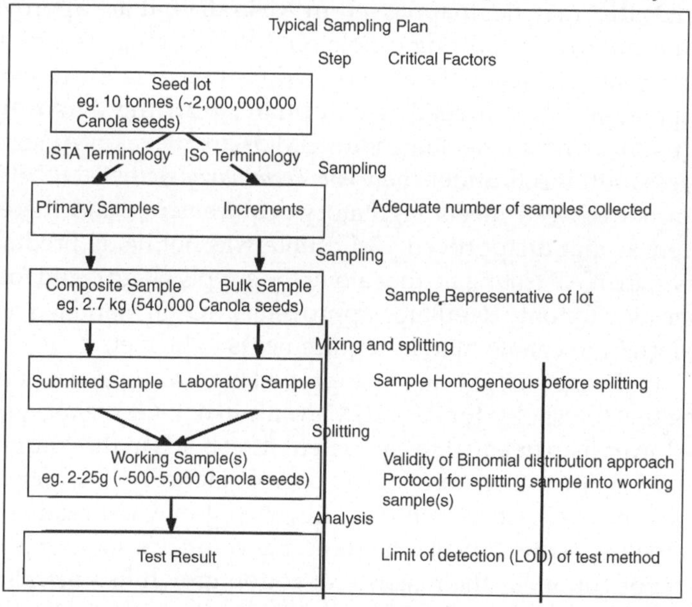

Fig. 2.1 Steps Involved in a Typical Sampling Plan for Detection of GM Seed in a Seed lot. An Accurate Test Method has Limited Value If the Working Sample Does Not Accurately Represent the Seed Lot from Which it Originated

To minimise errors with sampling and possible heterogeneity at storage sites, grain arising from entirely different sources would preferably not be combined prior to sampling and testing. The appropriate test method can be protein-or DNA-based, and would be selected depending on the limit of detection and the level of specificity for GM events that are required. A method can screen for a range of GM events, or it can be specific to one particular event.

SAMPLING

WHEN SHOULD SAMPLING BE DONE

Australia imports seed and also grain for food and feed from countries that commercially produce GM varieties. Using the example of imported labelled non-GM canola seed for breeding purposes; it could be tested for the presence of both GMOs that are approved in Australia for commercial release, and those GMOs that may be unapproved in Australia but are approved in the countries exporting canola seed to Australia. Testing for unapproved GMOs in imported seed for breeding in Australia helps ensure sown seed is compliant with the Australian regulatory system; dealings with GMOs are illegal in Australia unless authorised under the *Gene Technology Act 2000* (Cwlth). If imported seed meets regulatory requirements, and there is sureness that unapproved GM canola was not being bred and sown, then AP testing further along the supply chain could focus on testing for only Regulator-approved GMOs in marketed non-GM grain to enable market requirements to be met.

In the case of GM canola approved for sowing in Australia, labelling thresholds for AP of GM events in non-GM canola grain are lower than or equal to equivalent thresholds in the countries to which Australian canola is exported. Hence, if the non-GM canola meets Australian thresholds, then it may not require re-testing to ensure it meets the receiving country's standards.

For cotton, as the majority of cotton grown in Australia is GM, testing for the AP of GM events in cottonseed is required only in the case of certified non-GM cottonseed that is being exported to niche markets. For soybean and maize, no GM events have been approved by the Regulator for commercial release.

HOW SHOULD SAMPLING BE DONE

The strategies and techniques used in taking, mixing and reducing the samples are designed to ensure that the composition of the working sample analysed in the laboratory corresponds as closely as possible to the composition of the original lot (*Fig 2.2*). In reality this process does not work perfectly, and the errors associated with each of the sampling steps need to be considered when estimating the total uncertainty of the sampling process.

Two linked factors are involved in developing strategies for sampling and testing. The first is the level of confidence required. This is a measure of how confident one can be that a calculated result is correct. A confidence level of 100 per cent means that 100 out of 100 times, the result given is correct. A confidence level of 95 per cent means that 95 out of 100 times, the result is correct. Also to be taken into account is the relative uncertainty of the measurement (often expressed as the error). Uncertainty is given as a projection of how far away the actual value could be from the calculated result due to the cumulative errors of the processes leading to that result. It is expressed as a range around a value (*i.e.* 1 per cent GM ± 0.05, or 1 per cent GM with 5 per cent relative uncertainty).

The application of confidence levels and uncertainty to AP testing plays a very large role in deciding the sample size required for testing. Statistics can identify the minimum bulk sample size required to provide a specified level of confidence that the GM content of the sample lies within a specified error range of the actual composition of the lot (*Fig 2.2 on page 36*). As shown in Figure for an 'ideal' homogenous seed lot, larger numbers of seeds are required as the proportion of GM content in the lot decreases. In the case of a perfectly homogenous lot, only a single increment of the requisite size would be needed. However, as it cannot be assumed that real lots are homogenous, most sampling protocols specify the collection of multiple increments from different parts of the lot with the aim of obtaining a bulk sample representative of the average composition of the lot.

At a specified threshold level (per cent GM), to decrease the relative uncertainty, the size of the sample collected should be increased. In addition, the sample size also needs to increase as the threshold level decreases. This is because the lower the relevant concentration (*i.e.* the allowable threshold) of GM material in a seed lot, the more seeds are required in the collected sample to accurately detect and measure it.

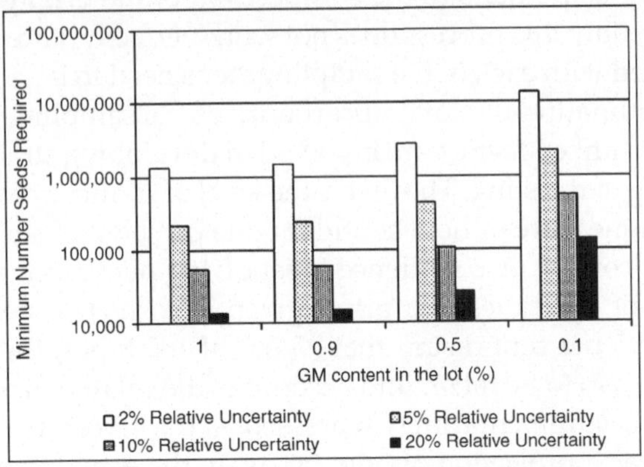

Fig. 2.2 The Number of Seeds Required in a Composite Sample to be 98 per cent Certain that the Sample is Representative of the Composition of the Original Lot (to within 2, 5, 10, or 20 per Cent of the True Value, Assuming that all of the Seeds have an Identical Size and are Completely Mixed)

aaWhere there is AP of a GM event, it would be very difficult to know how well dispersed any GM presence may be within any given seed lot. Therefore, most grain and seed sampling and testing protocols require that a large number of primary samples are taken (see Figure 2.3 (c) for an example of sampling GM grain), and that the maximum lot size to be tested is limited, to minimise the uncertainty inherent in the sampling.

ISTA has developed rules for sampling seed lots that are designed to provide confidence that the submitted or laboratory sample is representative of the lot in most cases. The maximum seed lot size for maize should be 40 tonnes (± 5 per cent), and for canola 10 tonnes (± 5 per cent). There should be documentary evidence that the lot being tested is all from the same source and batch. ISTA rules define the minimum number of primary samples to be collected, in containers ranging from less than 15 kg up to the maximum permitted (and also for a seed stream), and state that the primary samples should be approximately the same size as each other. In the case of a 10 tonne seed lot for any seed, the ISTA rules specify the collection of twenty 500 g primary samples. The maximum lot size recommended for grain is much larger. For instance, ISO guidelines specify a maximum lot size of 500 tonne when sampling grain.

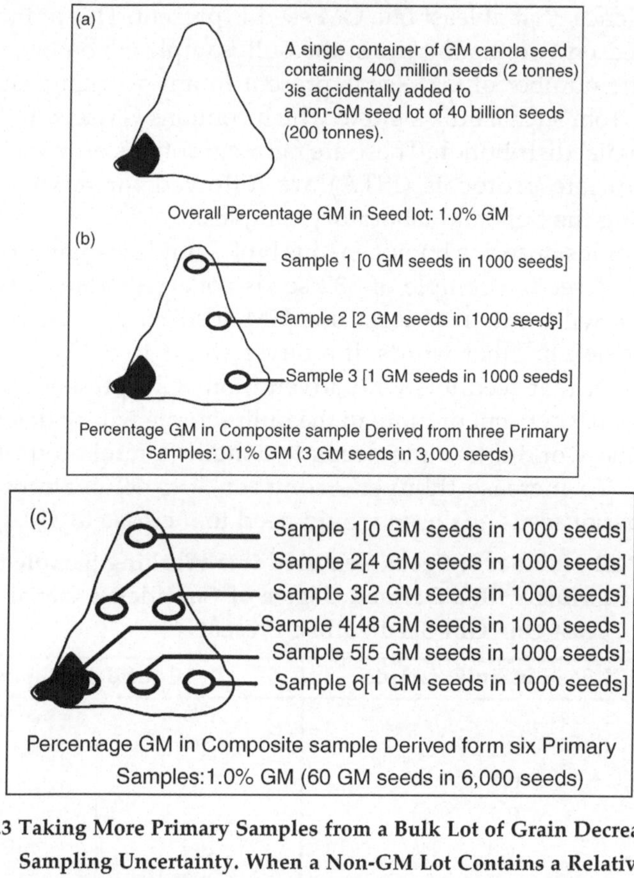

Fig. 2.3 Taking More Primary Samples from a Bulk Lot of Grain Decreases Sampling Uncertainty. When a Non-GM Lot Contains a Relatively Small Amount of GM Grain (as Shown in *(a)*), Unless the GM Seed is Evenly Distributed, a Small Number of Primary Samples (Such as the Three Samples Shown in *(b)*) May not Accurately Represent the Composition of the Entire Lot. Taking More Primary Samples (as Shown in *(c)*) Increases the Confidence Level that the Composite (or bulk) Sample Accurately Represents the Original Lot

The minimum number of seeds that needs to be collected from the bulk sample for analysis depends on the relevant threshold level for AP of GM seed and the level of confidence required in the result. Based on these two factors, a statistical approach can be used to determine the minimum number of seeds required in a sample to ensure, with a defined of confidence, that at least one GM seed is present. This approach is based on two assumptions: the bulk sample is homogenous, and the number of GM seeds present in any working sample taken from such a bulk sample which contains GMseed follows a binomial distribution. These are fairassumptions provided that appropriate protocols (ISTA) are followed for mixing and dividing the bulk and laboratory samples.

For instance, if a homogeneous bulk sample contains 0.9 per cent GM seed, a sample of 332 seeds collected from the bulk sample will contain at least one GM seed 95 per cent of the tim(Table). In other words, if a buyer wants to be 95 per cent confident that seed lots with adventitious GM presence at the level of 0.9 per cent or more in the bulk sample will be detected, then the working sample needs to contain a minimum of 332 seeds. To increase thbuyer's confidence to 99 per cent, the number of seeds analysed would need to increase to 510.

Table 2.1 Number of Seeds Required in a Working Sample to Ensure with a Defined Degree of Confidence that at Least Onc GM Seed will be Present

%GM Seed in Bulk Sample	Confidence Level	
	95%	99%
0.1	2995	4603
0.5	598	919
0.9	332	510
1.0	299	459
3.0	99	152
5.0	59	90

These estimates for the minimum number of seeds to be analysed are valid for use with a *qualitative* analytical method only if the method has no false positives or false negatives. Under these circumstances, a positive result from a qualitative test would indicate, with thdefined level of confidence, that presence of GM material in the bulk sample exceeded the threshold level (in this example presence of GM material greater than or equal to 0.9 per cent).

The measurement uncertainty associated with DNA-based*quantitative* assays is relatively large due to the intrinsic nature of the amplification process of the polymerase chain reactioassay that is used to detect the DNA. Sampling error is not likely to be a significant contributoto the total uncertainty provided that good sampling practice is used—small sample sizes should not be chosen and the sampling error should be below 20-30 per cent. The total measurement uncertainty of a quantitative result should be taken into accounif such an assay is to be used to screen for the presence of GM material in grain and seed.

In practice the level of confidence for results from a qualitative assay is also affected by the uncertainty introduced by the sampling process. If a sampling protocol introduces a 10 per cent relative uncertainty, this can be allowed for by targeting the testing at the lower limit of the uncertainty range (Table 2.2) (*i.e.* test for 0.9 per cent GM instead of 1.0 per cent GM by taking a sample of 510 seeds instead of 459 seeds). The sampled seeds are combined to form a working sample before testing—they are not tested individually.

Table 2.2 Suggested Number of Working Samples Required to Meet Target Confidence Levels when Operating at an Assay Limit of Detection of one GM Seed in 1000 Seeds and Taking into Consideration of a Relative Uncertainty in Sampling of 10 per cent

Acceptable Threshold Level (% GM Seed)	Lower Limit of Sampling Uncertainty (% GM Seed)	Number of Working Samples		95% Confidence Level	99% Confidence Level
0.1	0.09			4	6
0.5	0.45	2	2		
0.9	0.81	1	2		

As outlined above, statistics can be used to determine the minimum number of seeds to beanalysed to ensure with a defined degree of confidence that at least one GM seed will be present in the sample if the bulk sample contains GM seed above a defined threshold (Table 2.2). Assay methods used to test for the AP of GM events in non-GM grain should be validated under the conditions of use to verify their limit of detection.

If the analytical method is capable of detecting a single seed in this minimum number of seeds, it can be used directly on a representative working sample of the appropriate size. However, in some cases the chosen analytical assay may not be sensitive enough to detect a single GM seed in the sample. If this is the case, then the sample should be split evenly into several working samples and the number of seeds in the working samples should be selected to ensure that the analysis is conducted within the detection limit of the assay. Each of these working samples should be analysed using the same method.

ZERO PRESENCE LEVELS

Analytical testing to a zero presence level is not possible. It is possible to test only as low as the limit of detection of the analytical method will allow. For example if a test is capable of detecting down to a concentration of only 0.1 per cent GM (that is one GM seed in 1 000 non-GM seeds), then a negative result (no GM material detected) does not mean that there is no GM material present. There could still be GM material present at a concentration lower than 0.1 per cent. Therefore, detection will always be limited by the sensitivity of the analytical testmethod and the number of seeds analysed in the working sample(s).

DETECTING GMOS

All GMOs contain at least one transgenic construct inserted into their genome (*Fig 2.4*). The two main approaches for detecting constructs in GM seed are DNA-based assays to detect novel DNA sequences and protein-based assays to detect novel proteins. For identification of specific GM events, DNA tests are required.

The most cost-effective approach for a monitoring programme that covers a large number of GM events is to test the sample initially using one or more screening methods that can detect several GMOs. Screening methods may be either DNA-or protein-based. If required, subsequent analysis can then be undertaken to identify and, if needed, quantify the specific GM event(s) detected in a sample.

The detection limit of the assay will play a significant factor in choosing which method to use. In particular, some protein-based methods are not sensitive enough for practical purposes when analysing GM seed at the thresholds for AP. Even DNA-based methods should be carefully validated to ensure that they are sensitive enough to meet the requirements of the working sample size.

PROTEIN-BASED DETECTION METHODS

Several immunoassays have been developed to detect the novel proteins that are expressed by different GM plants. The sensitivity of these immunoassays depends on the level of expression of the novel protein in the plant tissue being analysed. For example, some GMOs have been specifically designed so that the novel protein is expressed in leaf tissue with relatively weak expression in seeds. Use of a protein assay on seeds under these circumstances may not be feasible due to lack of assay sensitivity. Since the same novel protein may be expressed by plants containing different GM events, protein assays are not event-specific but may be usefulfor screening and for qualitative analysis.

The most sensitive protein-based detection technique is the enzyme-linked immunosorbent assay (ELISA). ELISA works by detecting the presence of either antibody or antigen in a sample. The tag indicating the antibody-antigen affinity can either be an enzyme or a fluorescent dye (Pita *et al.* 2008). For the basic ELISA, molecules of an antibody specific tothe target protein are bound to the walls in each well of a microtitre plate and used to bind to the target protein, if present in the sample. A second antibody, that is also specific to the targeprotein, is then added. This antibody is labelled with an enzyme that catalyses a colour reaction. After removing unbound labelled antibody from the wells through washing steps, the amount of colour is proportional to the amount of target protein present. A number of ELISA assays are on the market for detection of different herbicide-tolerant or insect-resistant traits.

In general, these assays require some level of sample preparation and laboratory instrumentation for analysis. One disadvantage with ELISA relates to the large number of incubation and wash steps that are required when using enzymatic activity as the detection system as it makes the procedure difficult to automate when screening large numbers of samples, and prolongs the time taken to obtain results. Using fluorescent dyes as opposed to enzymatic activity for detection can help overcome some of these difficulties. Velappan *et al* comment that by avoiding the extensive washing steps required when using enzyme tags, the use of fluorescent dyes can significantly reduce the time required to carry out assays. A concurrent reduction in the number of incubation steps will also facilitate automation of the technology.

The most rapid detection method that requires minimal sample preparation and equipment is the lateral flow strip device. This is a test strip containing immobolised antibodies in specific zones on the strip. Sample preparation simply involves crushing the sample and mixing it withthe protein extraction solution provided in the kit. The lateral flow test strip is dipped into the prepared sample extract which migrates up the strip by capillary action. As it moves up the strip, the sample passes through a zone of reagent that contains antibodies, usually labelled with colloidal gold. This labelled antibody binds to the GM protein, if present in the sample. The antibody-protein complex then continues to move up the strip until it reaches a second zone of antibodies, which in this case are immobilised onto the test strip.

The complex concentrates into this immobilised antibody zone where the gold becomes visible as a red band. The test strip also contains an immobilised control zone that binds a control complex that is present in the extraction solution and also produces a visible line. If there is no target GM protein present only a single line will form at the control zone. A result is called positive when both the control line and the line indicating presence of target GM protein change colour. Theoretically, lateral flow strips are suitable for analysis in the field. However, their robustness under field conditions may require further research.

It is most likely that expression levels of the novel protein being tested will vary between seeds. Consequently, if the assay system is protein-based, the detection limit when testing working samples containing a single GM seed in the working sample will not be as good as the detection limit when testing working samples derived from a larger, uniform, homogenise-dsample containing the equivalent percentage of GM seeds since the level of expressed protein in a large, homogenised sample will reflect the average expression level over a number of GM seeds. On the other hand, a working sample that contains an individual GM seed with an expression level of the novel protein that is less than the average expression level for the GM seeds may not be detected by the assay.

DNA-BASED DETECTION METHODS

DNA-based detection methods include end-point and real-time polymerase chain reactions (PCR), microarrays, and DNA fingerprinting techniques. DNA-based detection methods are designed to be specific for a short sequence of DNA, generally much smaller than a gene. Todetect GM events, these techniques target the transgenic DNA of a construct (*Fig 2.4*).

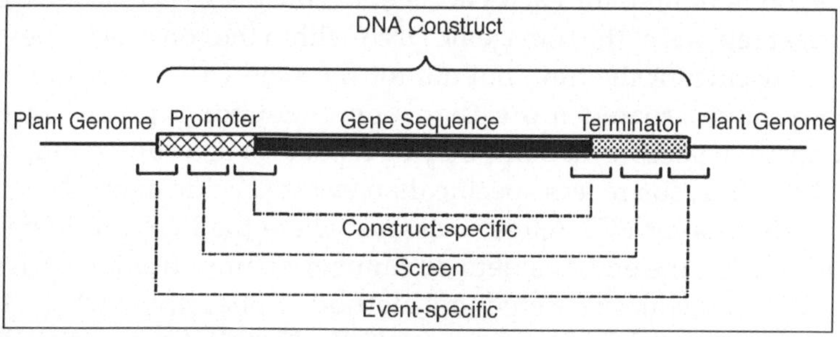

Fig. 2.4 Simplified Diagram of a DNA Construct and the Range of DNA Tests Available

END-POINT PCR

PCR works by making multiple copies of the targeted DNA sequence through a process known as DNA amplification. PCR detection can provide both *qualitative* results (whether or not the target sequence was present) and *quantitative* results (the amount of DNA that is amplified in the reaction can be used to calculate the percentage of transgenic DNA that was in the original sample). PCR assays can be designed to detect a specific region of the transgenic DNA. The region used will determine how selective the test is. For instance, a method that detects a promoter or a terminator sequence (*Fig 2.4*) is useful as a screen since these regulatory sequences are common to a number of GM constructs.

These sequences are most commonly derived from viruses or bacteria so their detection in a sample does not absolutely confirm the presence of a GM event. An additional, more selective test would need to be conducted to be more certain that the sample contained GM material. A false positive result could be obtained if the virus or bacterium from which the promoter or terminator were derived, is itself present. For a number of reasons, PCR assays can also produce false negative results; this is another reason why the laboratory testing methods used need to be both verified and standardised.

PCR assays which are event-rather than construct-specific (*Fig 2.4*) are designed to detect the DNA at the junction between the plant genomic DNA and the inserted construct. This junction region is unique for each GM event. Construct-specific assays target regions of the transgenic DNA within the construct. These are specific for the trait, but not for the event; as the developer may have created more than one event for a given trait. Construct-specific methods may be capable of detecting multiple GM events, so are less specific than event-specific methods.

End-point PCR refers to assays where the PCR product is detected at the end of a defined number of amplification cycles and is a *qualitative* detection method. Generally, each PCR product is amplified in a separate tube. Hence, if one sample is to be screened for the presence of several different genetic elements, a series of individual PCR assays is needed.

Real-time PCR

Real-time PCR refers to assays where the PCR product is detected during the amplification process by monitoring an increase in fluorescence throughout the PCR and can be used as a *quantitative* detection method. The fluorescence detection system is either based on a fluorescent dye or probes. In each case, the intensity of the fluorescence is directly related to the amount of amplified product. Whether assays are *qualitative* or *quantitative,* controls are still required to verify that the assay is working correctly and to convert results to a 'per cent threshold' level.

Microarray Techniques

Microarray technologies simultaneous detection of a number of DNA sequences and, theoretically, are highly suited for use as a screening tool for GMO analysis. In late 2007, the first commercially available microarray system for GMO screening was validated in the EU through a collaborative study which was coordinated by the Joint Research Centre of the European Commission. The performance of the DualChip® GMO assay (DualChip is a registered trademark of Eppendorf Array Technologies) was assessed as a qualitative method for screening for authorised GMOs in the European Union. In the collaborative study, different genetic elements were detected at a concentration of 0.1 per cent GM with an accuracy rate of 95 per cent using blind DNA reference samples.

DNA FINGERPRINTING TECHNIQUES

The Canadian Food Inspection Agency (CFIA) has developed a DNA fingerprinting technique for qualitative detection of approved and unapproved GM crops. The technique targets common genetic elements such as promoters and terminators, and provides a characteristic 'fingerprint' pattern based on the gene sequence adjacent to the promoter or terminator (the coding region of the introduced gene). The CFIA have obtained specific and reproducible DNA fingerprint patterns to identify GM presence down to a LOD of 0.5 per cent GM seed or grain in a non-GM lot.

This technique is not a quantitative method, it cannot be used to verifyAP above or below threshold levels, but it does have the potential to be used as a screening method to simultaneously monitor for the presence of a large number of GMOs. NMI, in Australia, currently has a collaborative agreement with CFIA to validate the methods within a second laboratory and develop additional fingerprint patterns relevant to Australia.

METHODS AND PROTOCOLS

Throughout this section, references are made to the approval processes for GMOs in Australia's main trading partners for the four crops of interest. The approval process for GMOs and the language used to describe the process differs from country to country. Most countries, including Australia, approve GMOs for a specified use. In Australia, the Regulatorlicenses dealings involving intentional release of GMOs, which includes approval of GMOs for commercial release. FSANZ approves foods derived from GM crop lines.

The EU authorises GM events for marketing, where authorised for marketing means that the product is reviewed and approved for sale for a specified use including import, cultivation, processing, food, feed and/or industrial. In the USA, GM plants are not approved for cultivation but rather they are 'regulated articles' until they have been favourably reviewed by the relevant agencies. A GM plant that has been 'reviewed for cultivation' and has received a positive assessment is grant 'non-regulated' status and is no longer subject to oversight by USA regulatory agencies. GM plants are similarly 'reviewd for human consumption (or food)' and 'for animal consumption (or feed)'.

REGULATORY REQUIREMENTS FOR CANOLA

In Australia, eight GM canola lines have been approved for commercial release by the Regulator, as well as some hybrids of these lines. Food derived from these approved GMOs has also been approved by FSANZ. To date, only one GM canola line has been commercially grown in Australia. The technology provider will not commercialise all Regulator-approved lines; Bayer

CropScience has indicated that it does not intent to commercialise the lines T45, Topas 19/2, MS1, RF1 and RF2 (or hybrids containing these) in Australia (OGTR 2006a). Approvals for these GM lines were nevertheless sought to obtain consistency with overseas regulatory approvals.

Consumers and some markets require the integrity of non-GM seeds and grain to be maintained. This may require labelling. Maintaining 100 per cent product purity is not practical and/or cost-effective, and governments around the world have therefore introduced thresholds for GM presence (for approved events) in non-GM seed and grain, below which the seed and grain can still be labelled as non-GM.

In Australia, as discussed previously, industry has adopted a threshold level for labelling of non-GM canola grain and seed which may contain some GM seed and grain approved by the Regulator. Adventitious presence (AP) thresholds are 0.9 per cent GM canola in non-GM canola grain and 0.5 per cent GM canola in non-GM canola seed-for-sowing.

EXPORTS

The Australian canola industry is strongly export oriented. Approximately 60–75 per cent of the crop is exported in any given year, the majority to markets in which Australia competes predominantly with Canada. The major customers (in terms of the share of total Australian canola exports in the five years to 2006/07) were: Japan (67.5 per cent); Pakistan (25 per cent); Bangladesh (9 per cent); China (3 per cent); UK (2 per cent); Nepal (1 per cent) and other EU countries (0.5 per cent).

For export of non-GM canola to these countries, the regulatory requirements and approval status for GM canola within each country, which are summarised below, must be considered in relation to the allowable threshold levels and approval status of GMOs within Australia. Appendix A contains more detailed information for each of these countries.

Japan

Under the Japanese Food Sanitation Law, if the GM content of the top three ingredients in foods exceeds 5 per cent of the total weight of the foods, they must be identified with either the phrase 'Biotech Ingredients Used' or 'Biotech Ingredient Not Segregated' if the rawmaterial is not accompanied by certificates of identity preservation handling. Under the Japan Agricultural Standards law, Japan has set an informal tolerance level of 5 per cent for GM ingredients in products that are identified 'Non-Biotech' provided that the event(s) have been approved in Japan. The 5 per cent tolerance level applying to GM canola is above the threshold for non-GM canola set within Australia. Therefore, canola meeting Australia's domestic threshold requirements, would also meet Japan's non-GM importing requirements.

Five of the eight GM canola lines that have been approved in Australia for commercial release by the Regulator, as well as the GM hybrid intended for commercial production, have also been approved in Japan for food and feed and so can be exported to Japan. Three canola lines (MS1, RF1 and RF2) that have been approved in Australia have not been approved in Japan. However, the resulting hybrids from these parent lines (MS1×RF1, MS1×RF2) have been approved for food and feed in Japan. GM canola with any of these three GM events are not intended to be grown commercially in Australia.

China

China has placed its listed agricultural GMOs (soybean, maize, canola, cotton and tomato) under a mandatory labelling system. China requires that all products derived from listed GM crops be labelled and prohibits the importation and sale of any unlabelled or mislabelled GM products. China has not approved any of the GM canola varieties licensed in Australia for commercial growing in China; however, since GM canola is a 'listed GMO' in China's regulatory scheme, it may still be imported and used for oil and meal provided its products are labelled appropriately as being derived from a GMO.

EU

The EU has set a threshold level of 0.9 per cent for AP of GM events authorised in the EU fofood and feed use, with labelling required for products above this level. For GM events that have not been authorised but have received a positive EU risk assessment, the adventitious presence level is set at 0.5 per cent, while products containing GM events above this level are not allowed into the EU market. GM events without a positive safety assessment are not permitted at any level in the EU.

All of the GM canola lines and hybrids approved for commercial release in Australia have also been authorised in the EU for use in food. Authorisation for the cultivation and placing on the market of GM events MS1, RF1, RF2 and Topas 19/2 was withdrawn in the EU from 18 April 2007, as varieties containing these events were no longer offered for sale on a global basis and Bayer CropScience indicated to the European Commission that it had no intention to submit an application for renewal of the authorisation(European Union 2007c; b; a). AP of this event will still be tolerated in the EU at a level of up to 0.9 per cent until 25 April 2012 (European Union 2007c) and, after this date, at a level up to 0.5 per cent. Again, GM canola varieties with these events are not intended to be commercially grown in Australia.

Other Countries

Bangladesh, India, Nepal and Pakistan do not set a tolerance for AP of GM events in non-Gcommodities. These countries have not formally approved any of the GM canola varieties approved for commercial release in Australia. However, these countries import GM canola fromCanada.

IMPORTS

Imports of non-GM canola seed from overseas, such as New Zealand, Japan, Canada and theUSA, are permitted. New Zealand does not grow GM canola. While all of the GM canola events currently approved for commercial release in Australia have been approved for cultivation in Canada and reviewed for cultivation in the USA, there are four events either approved in Canada and/or reviewed for planting in the USA, that have not been approved by the Regulator under the *Gene Technology Act 2000* (Cwlth) for commercial release in Australia.

These are GM canola events 18, 23, GT200, and Westar-oxy-235; not considered for approval in Australia because applications have never been made to the Regulator. Two (event 18 and GT200) of these four events, however, even though approved in Canada and the USA have not been commercialised there (Biotechnology Industry Organization 2008) and the other two events have not been sold in North America for a number of years.

CANOLA TESTING OPTIONS AND CAPABILITIES

Test protocols for GM events will differ depending on the sampling point along the supply chain and the commodity being sampled. Protocols may not involve monitoring for all events at each sampling point. In the majority of cases where testing is required, one approach is for an initial screen to be conducted. If any GMO was detected in the screen, the level of GM presence may need to be determined to ensure that it is below the specified threshold. Identification of the specific GM event could be required, for example to confirm if it is approved in Australia or not.

There are twelve GM canola events relevant to Australia's domestic and international tra(eight of the events are approved in Australia and four of the events are approved overseas but unapproved in Australia). There is no single genetic element that is present in all twelve GM canola events relevant to Australia. to detect all twelve GM events, a combination of at least three screens would be required. A similar number of screens would be required to only detect the GMOs approved in Australia.

In the first instance, a combination of screening tests is most suitable for detecting unapproved GM canola varieties (*example in Figure 2.5*). If these results indicate GM material is present, possible GMOs present in the sample can be deduced from the pattern of results. In the case of GT73 and GT200, further testing may be required if an initial screen suggests that one of these two GM events is present; one (GT73) is Regulator-approved and the other (GT200) is not, so confirmation would be needed about which one is present. AP of unapproved GT200 GMOs would require this additional testing, preferably using a validated event-specific method for conclusive evidence.

For detection of approved GMOs, a combination of screening tests (*Figure 2.6*) would be most suitable in the first instance. If the correct number of working samples with the required number of seeds is analysed at the screening stage, these results could be used to estimate whether or not any AP of GM seed in the seed lot is above the threshold level. Samples falling above the threshold would most probably require further testing to confirm and identify the GM event present in the sample.

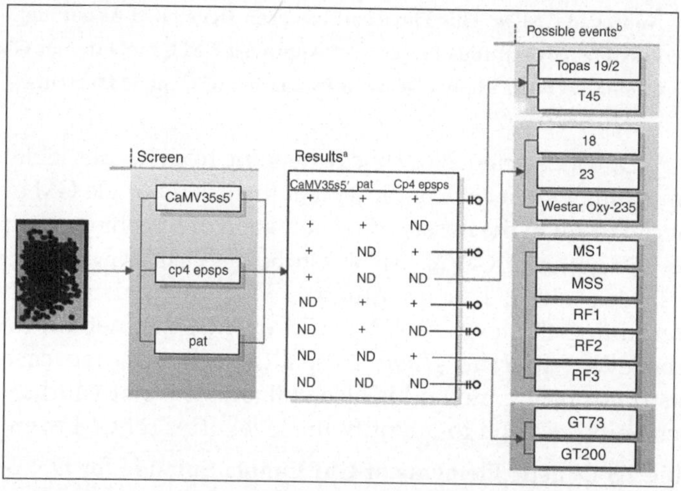

Fig. 2.5 Flow Chart Representing the Process to Screen Canola Seed Imported from the USA and Canada for Unapproved GMOs. This Flowchart has been Developed Assuming Possible Adventitious Presence of a Single Unapproved GMO in non-GM Plant Seed Based on a Desktop Evaluation of Genetic Elements within Events. Unapproved GMOs are Shaded

ND, not detected. Flow lines extending from Results table and terminating with a circle indicate that there is no single GM event that can result in the observed combination of screening results.

Note: [a] A positive result for the CaMV35s 52 may indicate the presence of the Cauliflower Mosaic Virus itself and not a GM event.

[b] The approved GMOs, MS1, MS8, RF1, RF2 and RF3 are not detected using this screenincombination.

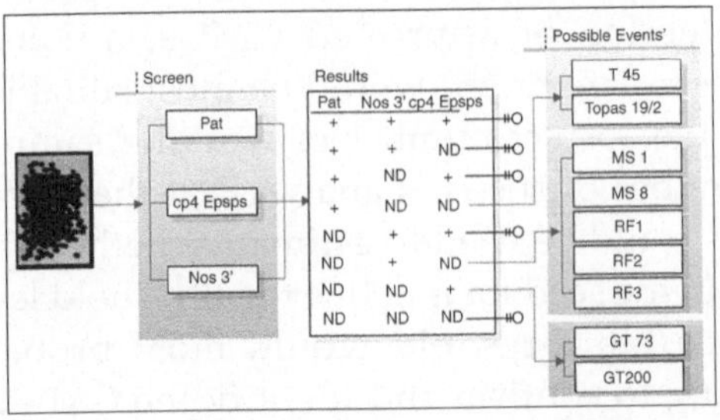

Fig. 2.6 Flow Chart Representing the Process to Screen Canola Seed for Approved GMOs. This Flowchart has been Developed Assuming Possible Adventitious Presence of Approved GM Canola in non-GM Canola Seed Based on a Desktop Evaluation of Genetic Elements within Events

ND, not detected. Flow lines extending from Results table and terminating with a circle indicate that there is no single GM event that can result in the observed combination of screening results.

Note: [a]Unapproved GMOs that would be detected using this screen are shaded in red. If a quantitative PCR method is used for determining the level of AP of GM events, the method needs to be event-specific (*Table 2.3*), although in some cases a construct-specific method is also suitable. It is not valid to use a screening method to quantify the level of AP of GM events.

Table 2.3 Genetic Elements of GM Canola Suitable for DNA-based Screening Methods

	Target DNA for Screening						
Event(S)	CaMV35s5'	nos 3'	nptII	CMoVb35s 5'	Pat	Bar	CP4 epsps
18 23	✓	-	✓	-	-	-	-
GT73 GT200	-	-	-	✓	-	-	✓
MS1 RF1 RF2	-	✓	✓	-	-	✓	-
MS8 RF3 MS8xRF3	-	✓	-	-	-	✓	-
T45 Topas 19/2	✓	-	-	-	✓	-	-
Westar-Oxy-235	✓	✓	-	-	-	-	-

REGULATORY REQUIREMENTS FOR COTTON

The major customers for Australia's exported cottonseed (note this is traded as a distinct commodity to cotton fibre) as a share of total exports in the five years to 2006/07 were Japan (79.9 per cent), the Republic of Korea (19.7 per cent) and Taiwan (0.4 per cent). For export of cotton to the small niche markets that require non-GM, the regulatory requirements and approval status for GM cotton within the relevant country should be considered. In Australia, five GM cotton varieties (three with stacked events) have been approved for commercial release by the Regulator.

All GM cotton crops approved for commercial release in Australia have been approved in Japan and they have also been approved in Korea for food and feed. The tolerance levels for approved GM ingredients in non-GM consignments in Japan (5 per cent w/w) also apply to GM cottonseed.

The Republic of Korea applies a 3 per cent tolerance level for the AP of GM material in non-GM raw agricultural products (*i.e.* grain) used to produce processed foods and for products used for animal feed. However, the tolerance level does not apply to the processed product itself (*e.g.* cottonseed oil) and applies only to the 20 raw agricultural products approved by Korea, including canola, maize, soybean and cottonseed. A 0.5 per cent tolerance level is currently applied to all other, non-approved, raw agricultural products.

Recently proposed changes to the Republic of Korea's KFDA GM labelling regime, which are yet to come into force, include:

- Processed foods that contain any GM agricultural ingredients must be labelled;
- Previously exempt products (*i.e.* highly processed food such as soy sauce or cottonseed oil) must be labelled (a three year grace period for this requirement is proposed);
- GM-free labelling will be available but there will be zero tolerance for unintentional GM presence;
- GM-free labelling cannot be applied to products that can't be tested for GMOs (*i.e.* highly processed foods such as soy sauce or cottonseed oil);
- GM labelling will also be alcoholic beverages.

COTTON TESTING OPTIONS AND CAPABILITIES

There is no single assay which will detect all GM cotton events relevant to Australia's domestic and international trade. However, all five GM cotton varieties approved by the Regulator for commercial release in Australia contain the *CAMV35s* 5' DNA sequence and four of the five events contain the *nos* 3' sequence (*see table 2.4 on next page*). Therefore, a single DNA screen is sufficient to detect all GMOs approved by the Regulator and our major trading partners for cottonseed. A combination of two or more assays will provide additional information regarding the specific events taht may possibly be present in a sample.

In some cases, available screening tests will not distinguish approved from non-approved GMOs. For instance, the approved GMO MON1445 event and the unapproved GMO MON1698 event both contain the same DNA targets for screening, so a PCR screen will not distinguish between these two events. An event-specific test (PCR or other) would be required.

Dealings with GMOs are illegal in Australia unless authorised under the *Gene Technology Act 2000* (Cwlth). Hence, if unauthorised GMOs are detected in seed lots there is no need to determine the level of GM presence, because any level is illegal.

Currently, the only cotton varieties that have been commercialised in another country but are not approved in Australia are varieties with the 281 or 3006 events, and varieties (with stacked events) containing at least one of these events. Since both of these events contain the pat gene which is not present in any of the Regulator-approved GMOs, a simple *pat* screen could be used to monitor for AP of these events in approved GM cottonseed. Confirmation of presence of the specific unapproved GMO would require additional testing, preferably using a validated event-specific method for conclusive evidence.

Lateral flow strip assays would be suitable screens for monitoring the AP of approved GM cottonseeds in non-GM cotton provided that the detection limit of the assay is taken into account. Alternatively, a single PCR screen to detect the CaMV35s 5' DNA sequence would be suitable (Table 2.4).

Table 2.4 Genetic Elements of GM Cotton Suitable for DNA-based Screening Methods and Laboratory Capabilities

Events	Target DNA for Screening					
Event(s)	CaMV35s5'	nos3'	nptII	CMoVb35s5'	Pat	Bar
MON1445 MON1698	✓	✓	✓	✓	-	-
MON531	✓	✓	✓	-	-	-
LLCotton25	✓	✓	-	-	-	✓
MON15985	✓	✓	-	-	-	-
10211 10222 31807 31808 BXN MON757	✓	-	✓	-	-	-
MON88913	✓	-	-	✓	-	-
COT102	-	✓	-	-	-	-
MON1076	-	-	✓	-	-	-
281 3006 MXB-13	-	-	-	-	✓	-
19-51a COT67B	-	-	-	-	-	-

REGULATORY REQUIREMENTS FOR SOYBEAN

Australia imports soybean grain from the USA for processing and some seed. Ten GM soybean events have currently been reviewed and approved for cultivation in the USA. There have been no applications for commercial release of GM soybean in Australia.

The Regulator has approved import and processing of GM soybean grain under Dealings Not Involving Intentional Release (DNIR) licences. These licences have included conditions to prevent the accidental or deliberate release of the imported grain into the environment, including transportation in sealed vehicles and processing so the grain is devitalised (*i.e.* made non-viable). DNIR licences are time-limited and do not confer general ongoing approval for import. Currently, four of the GM soybean lines that have been reviewed in the USA for cultivation have been approved by FSANZ for use in food. According to the relevant agricultural biotechnology companies, GTS 40-3-2 is the only GM soybean event that has been commercialised, although the commercialisation status of MON89788 was not supplied in the database.

SOYBEAN TESTING OPTIONS AND CAPABILITIES

In Australia, the Regulator has not licensed any GM soybean lines for release into the environment (*i.e.* field trials or commercial release). Importation of viable soybean seeds for breeding or for seed-for-sowing could therefore be the primary sampling point along the supply chain for GM AP testing; if a GMO was detected, there would be no need to determine the level of GM seed or grain because any level of presence in such seed would be illegal. Where GM soybean lines have been approved for import and processing under DNIR licences, they are permitted in grain for processing. For the GM soybean events that have been reviewed for cultivation in the USA, there is no single assay which will detect them all.

Nine GM soybean events have been approved by the USA for planting. Eight GM soybean varieties (including the three GM lines derived from event 206.05) contain the *CAMV35s* 5' DNA sequence, and the remaining variety contains the *cp4 epsps*gene (Table). So the minimum screening approach to detect all the relevant GM events and lines is a combination of two PCR assays that target the *CAMV35s* 5' and *cp4 epsps* genes (Figure). Not all soybean events reviewed in the USA have been approved by FSANZ (Table), and there is no screening combination that will differentiate all FSANZ-approved GM lines from those not approved by FSANZ (Table).

There are no PCR screening options that will distinguish the FSANZ-approved GM lines, A2704-12 and A5547-127, from the unapproved lines, A2704-21, A5547-35 and GU262. If this is required, further testing would need to be undertaken if the initial screen suggested that a sample may contain one of these five GM events (Table 2.5), although methods to distinguish between these events are limited. The suggested screening option (Figure 9.3) does not distinguish between FSANZ-approved and unapproved GM events. Further testing, such as for the *bar* and *pat* genes, would be required to determine if the AP, in this case, was due to a GM line that was approved by FSANZ.

Table 2.5 Genetic Elements of GM Soybean Suitable for DNA-based Screening Methods and Laboratory Capabilities

Event(s)	Target DNA for Screening: CaMV35s5'	nos 3'	bar	Pat	Cp4 epsps
W62 W98	✓	✓	✓	-	-
GTS 40-3-2	✓	✓	-	-	✓
[a] 260-05 G94168 G94-1 G94-19	✓	✓	-	-	-
[b] A2704-12 A2704-21 A5547-35 A5547-127 GU262	✓	-	-	✓	-
MON89788	-	-	-	-	✓

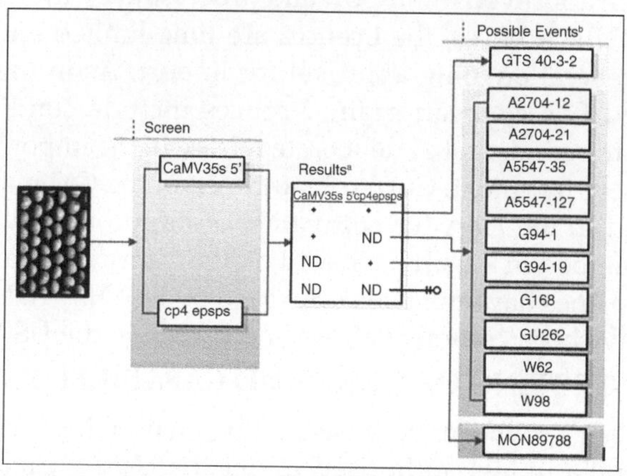

Fig. 2.7 Flow Chart Representing the Process to Screen Soybean Seed and Grain Imported from USA for GM Events. This Flow chart has been Developed Based on Possible Presence of a Single GM Event in non-GM Plant Seed Based on a Desktop Evaluation of Genetic Elements Within Events. None of these GMOs are Approved for Commercial Release by Regulator

ND, not detected. The flow line extending from Results table and terminating with a circle indicates that there is no single GM event that can result in the observed combination of screening results.

[a] A positive result for the CaMV35s 5' may indicate the presence of the Cauliflower Mosaic Virus itself, and not a GM event.

[b] GM lines that have not been approved by FSANZ are shaded in red.

REGULATORY REQUIREMENTS FOR MAIZE

Australia imports small amounts of maize seed (mainly from New Zealand, which does not grow GM crops) and grain for processing (from the USA, where twenty-five GM maize events and one stacked event (MON88017/MON88010) have been reviewed for use in food and feed and seventeen events have been reviewed for cultivation). In Australia, no GM maize varieties have been approved for commercial release by the Regulator, therefore the presence of any GM maize events in imported maize seed-for-sowing is illegal. Where GM maize lines have been approved for import and processing by the Regulator under DNIR licences, the licences are time-limited and do not confer general ongoing approval for import. As in the case of imported GM soybean grain, licences include conditions to prevent the accidental or deliberate release of the imported grain into the environment. Currently, thirteen of the GM maize lines reviewed in the USA for cultivation are approved by FSANZ for use in food in Australia. Based on the information available, only two lines have not been approved by FSANZ—DLL25 and T14—have been commercialised and grown in the USA.

MAIZE TESTING OPTIONS AND CAPABILITIES

As with soybean, because dealings with GMOs are illegal in Australia unless authorised under the *Gene Technology Act 2000*(Cwlth), imported maize seed-for-sowing could be one of the primary sampling points along the supply chain for GM testing. If unauthorised GMOs were detected in imported seed, there would be no need to determine the specific level of AP of the GM event; any level of presence is illegal.

Testing of maize for the presence of GM material could commence with an initial screen. If any GMO is detected, identification of the specific GMO may be required to determine if it is an unapproved event.

Twenty-one of the twenty-four GM maize events reviewed for use in the USA contain the *CAMV35s* 5' DNA sequence or a modification of this sequence (Table). Based on a desktop evaluation, a combination of two screens, for the *CaMV35s* 5' and *nos* 3' DNA sequences, should detect twenty-three of the twenty-four GM maize events. However, there is no single screen available to detect the Ly038 event. Event-specific methods are available to identify and quantify the majority of GM maize events.

Table 2.6 Genetic Elements of GM Maize Suitable for DNA-based Screening Methods and Laboratory Capabilities

	Target DNA for Screening					
Event(s)	CaMV35s5'	nos 3'	bar	cryIAb	Pat	cp4 epsps
MS3 MS6	✓	✓	✓	.	.	.
Bt-11	✓	✓	.	✓	✓	.
[a]MON802 MON809 MON80100(MON801) MON88017/MON810	✓	✓	.	✓	.	✓
MON810	✓	✓	.	✓	.	.
MON88017 NK603	✓	✓	.	.	.	✓
MON863	✓	✓	.	.	.	.
Bt-176	✓	.	✓	✓	.	.
[a]6275 DBT418 DLL25(B16)	✓	.	✓	.	.	.
[a]676 678 680 T14 59122 1507 T25	✓	.	.	.	✓	.
GA21 MIR604	.	✓	.	.	.	.
LY038	.	.	.	.	.	.

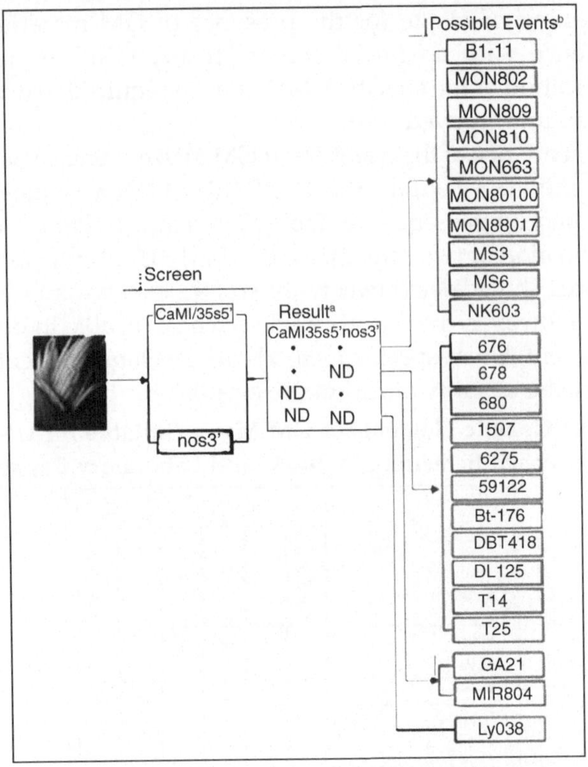

Fig. 2.8 Flow Chart Representing the Process to Screen Maize Seed and Grain Imported from the USA for GM events. This Flow-chart has Been Developed Based on Possible Presence of a Single Unapproved GM Line in Non-GM Maize Seed Based on a Desktop Evaluation of Genetice Elements Within Events. None of these GMOs are Approved for Commercial Release by the Regulator

Note: [a] A positive result for the CaMV35s 5' may indicate the presence of the Cauliflower Mosaic Virus itself, and not a GM event;

[b] GMOs that have not been approved by the FSANZ are shaded in red; c Event Ly038 cannot be detected using common screens.

HARMONISATION AND STANDARDISATION OF METHODS USED IN GMO TESTING LABORATORIES

A major issue in testing for the presence of GMOs is taht crops are tested using a variety of methods and instruments and in many different laboratories, in diverse countries. Results need to be accurate and comparable.

The choice of method can add variability to analytical results. Many different methods may be available to test for the same thing. Not only are there published methods, but custom methods are also commonly developed within a given laboratory. Bodies such as ISO, Codex, CRL-GMO and the JRC have the express aim of standardising testing methodology. They develop, validate and/or publish 'standard methods'. These methods have been shown to work and be fit-for-purpose, and are made available with the intention that they be used as common methodology among laboratories.

Certified reference materials are used to verify that both standard methods and laboratory developed methods are able to produce results that are accurate and comparable. A reference material is a substance whose value (*i.e.* per cent GMO content) is known, and is used to ensure that the detection method is capable of giving the correct results. There are commercially available reference materials for genetically modified crops that can be purchased as intact seed, ground seed, and extracted DNA, provided with a Certificate of Analysis specifying the GM content.

However, reference materials are not available for all approved GM crops, let alone for unapproved crops. Also, there are only very limited sources of GM reference materials that are certified appropriately to ISO Guide 34:200030 (International Organization for Standardization 2000) so that the supplied value can be trusted (Accreditation in GMO Testing Laboratories). Certified reference materials are available from AOCS in the USA or the Institute for Reference Materials and Measurements in the EU. Import and use of these reference materials in Australia is costly and as the materials are designed as quarantine materials, strictly controlled. Australia does not currently produce or supply reference materials.

The absence of reference materials in Australia is a major limitation to the development of standard protocols for seed testing. This is because a lack of reference materials may negate the ability to use quantitative PCR methods (*i.e.* real-time PCR) and is a major issue in regard to being able to evaluate the reliability of tests against false positives and negatives.

Any method used, whether it is a standard method or a method designed witihin the laboratory, should be shown to be capable of repeatedly producing accurate results and to be appropriate for the intended use. This is done through the process of validation. Standard methods have already been validated, but it should be verified that the results achieved are as expected when applied within the laboratory. This is generally done by assay of reference materials. The validation process in laboratory-designed methods is more in-depth, and guidelines have been published by the JRC that define the minimum performancerequirements of a GMO analytical method. Before a GM food or feed can be authorised in the EU, there needs to be analytical method for its detection validated to these requirements. The CRL-GMO maintains an online register of these validated methods for use as standard methods. GIPSA's Rapid Tests Performance Evaluation Programme performs a similar validation function for commercially available lateral flow strip test kits.

Inter-laboratory collrative studies are where multiple laboratories perform the same analytical method on 'identical' sample materials. These are an integral part of the validation of a method, proving that the method is robust enough to be applied between laboratories and still achieve accurate and reproducible results. Inter-laboratory proficiency testing schemes are where multiple laboratories perform their own method of analysis on 'identical' sample materials. This has the purpose of demonstrating the competency of the participating laboratories to accurately perform the analysis. Participation in proficiency studies is paid for by the participating laboratory. ISTA and the Food Analysis Performance Assessment Scheme are the main suppliers of this service for GMO analysis, conducting proficiency testing schemes multiple times per year.

Accreditation in GMO Testing Laboratories

The techniques described in the above section are used within a GMO testing laboratory to achieve harmonisation and standardisation of analytical techniques. The use and effectiveness of these techniques are demonstrated in industry by accredited compliance with the appropriate International Standard. 'ISO/IEC 17025:2005(E). General requirements for the competence of testing and calibration laboratories' (International Organization for Standardization 2005) was initially issued by ISO in 1999 and updated in 2005, and is the main standard used by testing and calibration laboratories.

ISO/IEC 17025:2005(E) is a tool for a testing laboratory to demonstrate their competence on an international scale in both laboratory management and technical capability. Accreditation to ISO/IEC 17025:2005(E) is not a blanket endorsement. Accreditation is only given for specific methods that have been audited and shown to conform to the standard. Accredited methods are reassessed periodically to ensure their continued compliance, and accreditation can be rescinded if the requirements of the standard are not met. If a laboratory is not accredited, it does not mean that it is incapable of doing the testing, but it means that it has not demonstrated its capability to the accrediting body. To maintain accreditation, laboratories are required to participate in relevant proficiency testing programmes.

Testing laboratories demonstrate their compliance with ISO/IEC 17025:2005(E) by gaining accreditation from the relevant National Accreditation Body (Figure 2.9). In Australia, the National Association of Testing Authorities (NATA) is the only National Accreditation Body, and it is also a member of the International Laboratory Accreditation Cooperation (ILAC). ILAC is an international organisation with the aim of facilitating trade by promotion of acceptance of accredited test and calibration results.

The ILAC Mutual Recognition Arrangement provides a peer-reviewed evaluation that accreditation bodies maintain conformance with their own relevant ISO standard (ISO/IEC 17011), and in so doing ensure that laboratories accredited by them are truly compliant with ISO/IEC 17025:2005(E). A similar function is performed by the Asia Pacific Laboratory

Accreditation Cooperation (APLAC), but APLAC membership is restricted to National Accreditation Bodies within the Asia Pacific Region. In the USA there are multiple national accreditation bodies capable of accrediting to ISO/IEC 17025:2005 (E), including the American Association for Lab Accreditation (A2LA), Assured Calibration and Laboratory Accreditation Select Services (ACLASS), the International Accreditation Service, Inc (IAS), the National Voluntary Laboratory Accreditation Programme (NVLAP) and the Laboratory Accreditation Bureau (L-A-B). Canada has the Standards Council of Canada (SCC).

There are many national accreditation bodies in the European Union providing accreditation to ISO/IEC 17025:2005(E) including the United Kingdom Accreditation Service (UKAS) in the United Kingdom, in Germany the Deutches Akkreditierungssystem Prufwesen (DAP), and in Belgium BELAC, the Belgian Accreditation Structure.

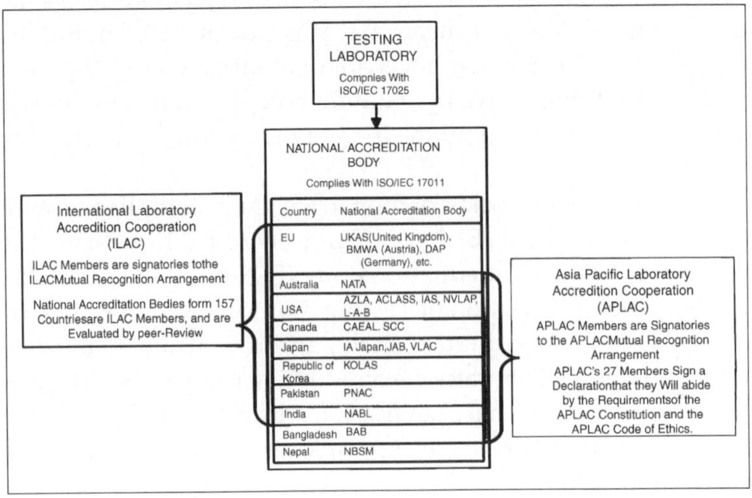

Fig. 2.9 Laboratory Accreditation Process

Limitations to Use of Sampling and Testing Methods

There are intellectual property restrictions on the use of analytical methods designed within individual laboratories for the detection and/or quantification of GM adventitious presence.

Unpublished methods are the property of the laboratory that developed them, whereas standard methods or published methods have no restrictions on their use.

GMO LABORATORY TESTING CAPABILITIES

Three laboratories in each of Australia, North America (USA/Canada) and the EU (nine in total) were surveyed by NMI for this study to give an indication of GM testing capabilities in these countries. The information included in this section indicates only whether any of the laboratories surveyed within these regions has indicated a capability to conduct GM testing methodologies.

Laboratory Testing Capabilities for Screening Methods

Screening techniques are conducted to narrow down the possibilities of which adventitious GM events could be present by identifying groups of events with common elements. The capabilities of the surveyed laboratories to conduct screening techniques are not consistent between Australia, North America and the EU (*see table 2.7*). Not all of the screens recommended in the best practice screening packages described in Chapter 11 are currently able to be conducted within the Australian laboratories surveyed.

The 'screening packages' described in the following chapter are for sampling and testing for AP of GM events at several points along the supply chain. They outline details such as the stage in the supply chain, seed lot details, sampling protocol, analysis details and assay protocol. Depending on the situation and also on market demand, the packages could be used to screen for GMOs approved in Australia and for unapproved GMOs in imported commodities.

Once screening methods have been used to narrow down the possibilities of what adventitious GM events may be present in a lot, either trait-specific (protein) or event-specific (DNA) testing methods can be used to identify which event(s) are present within the seed sample submitted to the testing laboratory.

Table 2.7 Canola, Cotton, Soybean and Maize—Laboratory Testing Capabilities Using Screening Methods

Target Genetic Element	Screening Package (Chapter 11)	Screening Method Available ?		
		Australia	USA/Canada	EU
Canola				
CaMV35s 5'	Table 11.1	–	✔	✔
nos 3'	Table 11.1.11.3	✔	✔	✔
CMoVb35s 5'		✔	–	✔
nptII		✔	✔	✔
cp4 epsps	Table 11.1,11.2, 11.3	–	✔	✔
bar		✔	–	✔
Pat	Table 11.1,11.2, 11.3	✔	✔	✔
Other		✔	✔	✔
Cotton				
CaMV35s 5'	Table 11.4	✔	✔	✔
nos 3'		✔	✔	✔
CMoVb35s 5'		✔	–	✔
nptII		✔	✔	✔
cp4 epsps		✔	–	✔
bar		✔	–	✔
pat		✔	–	✔
Other		✔	–	✔
Soybean				
CaMV35s 5'	Table 11.5	✔	✔	✔
nos 3'		✔	✔	✔
cp4 epsps	Table 11.5	–	✔	✔
bar		✔	–	✔
Pat		✔	✔	✔
Other		✔	–	✔
Maize				
CaMV35s 5'	Table 11.6	✔	✔	✔
nos 3'	Table 11.6	✔	✔	✔
nptII		✔	✔	✔
cp4 epsps		–	✔	–
bar		✔	✔	✔
pat		✔	✔	✔
cry1Ab		✔	✔	✔
Other		✔	–	✔

For the laboratories surveyed, trait-specific or event-specific testing methods are not available for every canola, cotton and soybean event of interest to Australia's national framework. However, there is at least one trait-specific or event-specific testing method available for all maize events of interest in the laboratories surveyed.

Laboratory Testing Capabilities for Trait-specific and Event-specific Methods

The laboratory capabilities identified by NMI do not appear to allow for comprehensive GM AP testing solely within Austalia, but this does not mean that these capabilities are not present in other Australian laboratories not surveyed for this study.

Canola

From the 2008-09 season, Australia will be growing both GM and non-GM canola. If required, it may be necessary to test—for the purpose of meeting customer requirements in both domestic and export markets—declaring non-GM canola grain for the AP of Regulator-approved GMPs. Australia also imports canola seed for breeding, and potentially grain from time to time, from countries where GM canolas are commercially grown. As discussed previously in this report, Australian seed breeding companies already carry out comprehensive AP testing in generating commercial seed-for-sowing so additional testing may be required only to confirm the integrity of imported non-GM canola grain.

Based on the laboratories surveyed, it appears that ten of the fifteen canola events of interest cannot be identified within the USA, Canada and the EU (Table). However, it is important to not that in the laboratories surveyed, there is a qualitative and quantitative event-specific test available in Australia for the GM canola lines intended for commercial release in Australia and approved by the Regulator (GT73, MS8 and RF3). Five other GM canola events have been approved for commercial release by the Regulator (T45, Topas 19/2, MS1, RF1 and RF2); and, as mentioned above, there are no intentions to commercialise these lines in Australia at this time. Of the remaining lines in Table, some (GT200 and 18) were never commercialised, and others have not been sold in North America for a number of years (T45, last seed sales in 2005; Topas 19/2, MS1, RF1 and RF2, last seed sales in 2003; Westar-Oxy-235, last seed sales 2001; and, last seed sales 1998).

Table 2.8 Canola-testing Capabilities in the Surveyed Laboratories for Trait and Event-specific Methods

Approval for Cultivation in Australia[a]	Canola Event	Trait-Specific Method Available			Event-Specific Method Available					
					Qualitative			Quantitative		
		Australia	USA/Can	EU	Australia	USA/Can	EU	Australia	USA/Can	EU
Approved	GT73	–	✓	–	✓	✓	✓	✓	✓	✓
	MS1	–	✓	–	–	–	–	–	–	–
	RF1	–	✓	–	–	–	–	–	–	–
	RF2	–	✓	–	–	–	–	–	–	–
	MS8	–	✓	–	✓	✓	✓	✓	✓	✓
	RF3	–	✓	–	✓	✓	✓	✓	✓	✓
	MS1xRF1[c,]	–	✓	–	–	–	–	–	–	–
	MS1xRF2[c,]	–	✓	–	–	–	–	–	–	–
	MS8xRF3	–	✓	–	✓	✓	✓	✓	✓	✓
	T45[b]	–	✓	–	✓	✓	✓	✓	✓	✓
	Topas 19/2[c]	–	✓	–	–	✓	–	–	–	–
Unapproved	18[e]	–	–	–	–	–	–	–	–	–
	23[f]	–	–	–	–	–	–	–	–	–
	GT200[e]	–	✓	–	–	✓	–	–	–	–
	Westar-Oxy-235[d]	–	–	–	–	✓	–	–	✓	–

Lateral flow test strips (trait-specific) may be commercially available for some GM canolas of interest; however, the Australian laboratories surveyed for this report did not report that they had such tests available. This does not mean that such tests are not used by other Australian laboratories not surveyed for this study.

Cottonseed

Australia imports cottonseed for use as germplasm in domestic cotton breeding programmes. However, as discussed earlier, such germplasm would be extensively tested by the seed breeding companies to ensure that it is either non-GM, or if it is intended to be GM, that only the intended GM events are present and that there is no AP or unintended GM events. Traditionally, Australia has not imported bulk shipments of cottonseed for processing into food and feed. As the majority of domestically produced cottonseed comes from GM cotton, if required by the market it may be necessary to test any identified non-GM cottonseed intended for export markets for the AP of Regulator-approved GMOs. There does not appear to be a demand for non-GM cottonseed in the domestic market. Of the laboratories surveyed by NMI, it appears that fourteen of the nineteen cotton events of interest cannot be identified by trait or event-specific methods within Australia, two of which also cannot be identified within the USA, Canada and the EU (*Table 2.9*). However, from Table, it is important to note that in the Australian laboratories surveyed, there are event-specific methods available to test for all the GM cottons except for MON88913 approved by the Regulator for commercial release in Australia. Some other GM cottons may have been used in field trials but have never been commercialised.

Soybean

Australia may import soybean for use as germplasm in breeding programmes and grain for processing (crushing). Soybean seed imported for use as germplasm undergoes extensive testing by seed companies for the AP of GM events. As stated earlier, no GM soybean is approved by the Regulator for commercial release in Australia. Of the laboratories surveyed by NMI, it appears that of the twelve soybean events of interest, ten cannot be identified by trait or event-specific methods in Australia and eight of these events also cannot be identified within the USA, Canada and the EU (*see table 2.10*). This does not mean that the remaining events cannot be tested by other laboratories not surveyed. Further, it is important to note that a number of these events, whilst they may have been reviewed for planting in the USA, have never been commercialised.

Table 2.9 Cotton-testing Capabilities in the Surveyed Laboratories for Trait and Event-specific Methods

Approval for food or Cultivation in Australia	Cotton Event	Trait-Specific Method Available			Event-Specific Method Available					
					Qualitative			Quantitative		
		Australia	USA/Can	EU	Australia	USA/Can	EU	Australia	USA/Can	EU
Approved for food and Cultivation	LLCotton25	–	✓	–	✓	✓	✓	✓	✓	✓
	MON531[b]	–	✓	–	✓	✓	✓	✓	✓	✓
	MON1445	–	✓	–	✓	✓	✓	✓	✓	✓
	MON15985	–	✓	–	✓	✓	✓	✓	✓	✓
	MON88913	–	✓	–	–	✓	–	–	✓	–
Approved for food only	10211	–	–	–	–	–	–	–	–	–
	10222	–	–	–	–	–	–	–	–	–
	COT102	–	–	–	–	–	–	–	–	–
	MON757	–	✓	–	–	✓	–	–	–	–
	MON1076[a]	–	✓	–	–	–	–	–	–	–
	MXB-13	–	✓	–	✓	–	✓	✓	–	✓
Unapproved for Either Cultivation or food	19-51a[a]	–	–	–	–	–	–	–	–	–
	281	–	✓	–	–	✓	✓	–	✓	✓
	3006	–	✓	–	–	✓	✓	–	✓	✓
	31807	–	✓	–	–	–	–	–	–	–
	31808	–	✓	–	–	–	–	–	–	–
	BXN	–	–	–	–	✓	–	–	–	–
	COT67B	–	✓	–	–	–	–	–	–	–
	MON1698[a]	–	✓	–	–	✓	–	–	–	–

Table 2.10 Soybean-testing Capabilities in the Surveyed Laboratories for Trait and Event-specific Methods

Approval for food in Australia	Soybean Event	Trait-Specific Method Available			Event-Specific Method Available					
					Qualitative			Quantitative		
		Australia	USA/Can	EU	Australia	USA/Can	EU	Australia	USA/Can	EU
Approved	A2704-12[a]	–	✓	✓	✓	✓	✓	✓	✓	✓
	A5547-127[a]	–	✓	–	–	–	–	–	–	–
	G94-1[a]	–	–	–	–	–	–	–	–	–
	G94-19[a]	–	–	–	–	–	–	–	–	–
	G168[a]	–	–	–	–	–	–	–	–	–
	GTS 40-3-2	–	✓	–	✓	✓	✓	–	✓	✓
	MON89788	–	✓	–	–	✓	–	–	–	–
Unapproved	A2704-21[a]	–	✓	✓	–	–	–	–	–	–
	A5547-35[a]	–	✓	✓	–	–	–	–	–	–
	GU262[a]	–	✓	–	–	–	–	–	–	–
	W62[a]	–	–	–	–	–	–	–	–	–
	W98[a]	–	–	–	–	–	–	–	–	–

Maize

Australia may import maize seed for use as germplasm in breeding programmes or as grain for processing (crushing). Maize seed imported for use as germplasm undergoes extensive testing by seed companies for the AP of GM events. As stated earlier, no GM maize is approved by the Regulator for commercial release in Australia.

Table 2.11 Maize-testing Capabilities in the Surveyed Laboratories for Trait and Event-specific Methods

Approval for food in Australia	Maize Event	Trait-Specific Method Available			Event-Specific Method Available					
					Qualitative			Quantitative		
		Australia	USA/Can	EU	Australia	USA/Can	EU	Australia	USA/Can	EU
Approved	1507	–	✓	✓	✓	✓	✓	✓	✓	✓
	59122	–	✓	–	✓	✓	✓	✓	✓	✓
	Bt-11	–	✓	✓	✓	✓	✓	✓	✓	✓
	Bt-176	–	✓	✓	–	✓	✓	–	✓	✓
	DBT418[a]	–	✓	✓	–	✓	–	–	✓	–
	GA21	–	–	✓	✓	✓	✓	✓	✓	✓
	LY038	–	–	–	–	✓	–	–	–	–
	MIR604	–	✓	✓	✓	✓	✓	✓	✓	✓
	MON810	–	✓	✓	✓	✓	✓	✓	✓	✓
	MON863	–	✓	–	✓	✓	✓	✓	✓	✓
	MON88017	–	✓	–	–	✓	–	–	✓	–
	MON88017/ MON810	–	✓	✓	–	✓	–	–	–	–
	NK603	–	✓	–	✓	✓	✓	✓	✓	✓
	T25	–	✓	✓	✓	✓	✓	✓	✓	✓
Unapproved	676[b]	–	✓	–	–	–	–	–	–	–
	678[b]	–	✓	–	–	–	–	–	–	–
	680[b]	–	✓	–	–	–	–	–	–	–
	6275[b]	–	✓	–	–	–	–	–	–	–
	DLL25 (B16)[a]	–	✓	✓	–	✓	–	–	✓	–
	MON802	–	✓	–	–	–	–	–	–	–
	MON809[b]	–	✓	✓	–	–	–	–	–	–
	MON80100 (MON801)[b]	–	✓	✓	–	–	–	–	–	–
	MS3	–	✓	–	–	–	–	–	–	–
	MS6	–	✓	–	–	–	–	–	–	–
	T14[a]	–	✓	✓	✓	✓	✓	–	✓	–

Of the laboratories surveyed by NMI, it appears that fifteen of the twenty-five maize events of interest cannot be identified by trait or event-specific methods within Australia. Considering also the capabilities of the laboratories in the USA, Canada and the EU, all of the maize events of interest can be identified (*see table 2.11*). It is important to note that although the GM maize events below may have been approved for commercial production overseas, many of them were never for commercial seed production, so a capacity for testing all the listed events would probably not be needed.

In addition to using trait-specific and event-specific methods to identify GM events, there are other techniques currently available and in the process of development. These include micorarrays, dynamic arrays and DNA fingerprinting techniques, but laboratory capabilities for these techniques were not evaluated in the laboratory capabilities survey for this report.

RECAP ON CO-EXISTENCE, SEGREGATION AND THRESHOLDS

The National Framework to Develop Co-existence Strategies for GM and Non-GM Crops summarises the factors which determine the thresholds established and maintained by industry as including:

- Thresholds established in export markets by customers and if premiums will be paid for achieving those levels
- The technical and practical ability of the supply chain management system to process and deliver product consistently to levels below the threshold
- Availability of appropriate testing technology.

For canola in Australia, the thresholds which have been adopted by the peak industry bodies, the Australian Oilseed Federation and the Australian Seed Federation, are 0.9 per cent GM canola grain in non-GM canola grain and 0.5 per cent GM canola seed in non-GM seed-for-sowing. Thresholds established by current and potential international trading partners in export markets are equal to or above the Australian industry thresholds. Therefore, providing Australian industry thresholds are met, other countries' thresholds should not present any barriers to trade, and growing GM canola in Australia would not be expected to impede access to markets.

This report has emphasised that managing segregation and working with thresholds is not new to the Australian seed and grain supply chain. For example, growers already manage for a threshold level of 0.4 per cent for barley in wheat, significantly lower than the 0.9 per cent threshold set for GM and non-GM canola. Growers also manage the segregation of products that cannot be differentiated by visual inspection, such as malting barley and barley used for animal feed which attract a significant price differential. The malting barley supply chain delivers a varietyal purity standard of 98 per cent to maltsters.

The technical and practical ability of supply chain management systems to process and deliver product consistently to levels below thresholds has therfore been demonstrated in Australian agriculture. Thresholds are met and product integrity is maintained through effective segregation practices. In the case of the canola industry and GM/non-GM coexistence, segregation practices have been identified for canola seed breeders, growers, and grain handlers to ensure that the AP of GM canola in non-GM seed and grain is below the 0.9 per cent threshold for GM canola in non-GM. Provided these canola coexistence practices are upheld, AP thresholds would be met, with human error being perhaps the most likely potential risk (for example, a truck with GM seed being accidentally directed to unload into a non-GM silo at a grain receival site).

The National Framework also refers to specific coexistence strategies to incorporate 'access to sampling and testing regimes, with the aim of confirming, or providing evidence, that market and regulatory requirements are being met'. Sampling and testing confirms that segregation is being managed adequately and that the product's integrity has been maintained.

CURRENT SAMPLING AND TESTING FOR GM IN THE SUPPLY CHAIN

Australia currently imports canola seed for breeding purposes, use by seed companies for seed increase, and also as grain for processing for food or feed or for oil extraction. Grain and seed of soybean and maize are also imported, mainly for crushing for processing for food or feed but also small quantities for breeding or for seed increase. Most imported canola and maize is from New Zealand. Cotton germplasm is imported for breeding from time to time. Imported seed of maize, soybean and cotton (but not canola) require quarantine becuase they are 'quarantine restricted species'; restrictions relate to disease and pest risks, not to any risks arising from potential AP of GM events.

Some of the countries from which the seed and grain is imported have either commercialised or are in the process of reviewing for commercial release GM events for these four commodities. No sampling and testing for AP of GM events in imported bulk commodities is required at the border; and no quarantine risk associated with a specific GM event has been identified with any type of import of these commodities. The *Quarantine Act 1908*(Cwlth) requires prior approval via an import permit to import declared GM seeds and grain. AQIS relies on the declaration by the importer as to a shipment's GM status.

In the case of canola seed currently imported for plant breeding (germplasm enhancement), testing for the presence of both Australian-approved and unapproved GMOs is undertaken by industry.

Only GM events approved by the Regulator are allowed to be bred into canola, maize, cotton and cotton breeding lines. Any imports of seed which are GM would require a licence from the Regulator, unless already approved for commercial release in Australia. Conventional non-GM seed imported into Australia by seed companies would be certified seed.

At the time of writing, the only GM broadacre crop in Australia to have been grown commercially and processed through the complete supply chain is GM cotton. GM and non-GM cottonseed was segregated by the Australian cotton industry when GM cotton was first introduced, but following the lack of significant market demand for non-GM cotton, the latter is now delivered in a single supply chain. As a result, there is no requirement for the cotton industry as a whole to segregate or to carry out sampling and testing for AP of GM events past the seed breeding stage. There are few examples of non-GM cotton being segregated.

The Australian Bureau of Agricultural and Resource Economics (ABARE) reported that in 2005 around 20 000 t of Australian cottonseed was certified as derived from non-GM cotton and virtually all of this was exported. For this reason, the cotton industry does not serve as an example or model for GMO sampling and testing needs and capabilities in a coexistence framework, or for managing segregation, for the Australian grain supply chain generally or for the canola supply chain specifically.

An AP threshold does not apply to cotton production in Australia. Furthermore, no GM soybean or maize is grown in Australia. Therefore, the only crop for which there is an AP threshold for GMOs in a non-GM crop is canola. Australian seed companies carry out appropriate sampling and testing of imported non-GM seed for breeding to ensure that it is free from the AP of any GMOs not approved by the Regulator. Sampling and testing is performed according to the ISTA guidelines and their own internal protocols. Such sampling and testing maintains the integrity with respect to the non-GM status of the commercial non-GM seed supplied to growers.

In summary, the only part of supply chains where sampling and testing of conventional non-GM seed and grain for AP of GM material is currently conducted is in breeding and supply of certified seed by breeders and seed companies, as this is a critical stage where unapproved GMOs could enter supply chains.

Importing seed-for-sowing without testing would be a potential source for the introduction of unapproved GMOs into farm production systems, if the seed was imported from a country which grew GM crops and was intended for direct use by farmers in farm production. However, we are unaware of any canola, soybean, maize or cotton seed that is imported into Australia for such direct use by farmers; but if it was, it would need to be certified seed. Seedis imported in small quantities either for breeding or for seed increase by seed companies; or, in the case of soybeans and sometimes maize, in larger quantities for processing for food or feed. All imports of GMOs require authorisation under the *Gene Technology Act 2000* (Cwlth) and any release of a GMO to the environment requires a licence from the Regulator.

POTENTIAL FUTURE

Canola

For the 2008 season, about 10 000 ha of GM canola have been sown in NSW and Victoria. The crop is expected to yield 10 000–15 000 t of grain depending on the seasonal conditions. All harvested grain will be sold to appointed marketers and delivered to pre-determined receival points. For this season, GM canola grain will be stored separately from non-GM canola, and will be marketed by only specified companies. Other segregation arrangements of GM/non-GM canola would be expected to be made as larger amounts of GM canola are cultivated in coming seasons.

Extensive adoption by farmers of GM canola could see the need for sampling and testing for AP of Regulator-approved GM events introduced to points in the supply chain other than seed breeding. This would be dependent on whether there is a market for segregated non-GM canola and, if so, the size of the non-GM market relative to the total market and whether the market was domestic or export.

So, where else could sampling and testing occur in a GM/non-GM canola coexistence system, and how? To answer this question, this study has examined sampling and testing from a practical and scientific perspective and also considered if approaches developed overseas could be adapted to meet the Australian canola grain and oilseed industry needs.

Importantly, from the 2008 canola growing season onwards in Australia, the 'Canola' standard will be defined as a combination of GM and non-GM canola grain. If the market requests differentiation, 'non-GM canola' grain will be identified as a distinct commodity. If, or where, there is a need to provide non-GM grain, sampling and testing practices along the supply chain would need to be sufficient to confirm that the presence of GM material above the threshold in non-GM grain can be detected.

As noted above, there is routine sampling and testing for GM events at the canola seed breeder stage. Seed industry stakeholders have indicated that the optimal point for sampling and testing for AP of GM events at the breeder stage is the point at which the seed breeding flowchart (Figure) splits into the 'breeder seed' and 'field trial' pathways, as this represents a 'testing gateway' where both the number of lines being tested and the volume of seed is small. Sampling and testing for AP of GM events is most practical at this point, especially for checking that GMOs not approved by the Regulator and/or by FSANZ are absent, so that the GM status of all seed exiting this point can be confirmed.

The relevant screening package is shown in Table 2.12. Screening would need to be followed by more specific testing to distinguish approved and unapproved events. Such specific tests are outside the scope of this report.

Furthermore, if unapproved GMOs have not been detected in either imported seed used in early breeding or at the seed increase stage for seed-for-sowing, the need to test for unapproved GMOs further down the supply chain is greatly reduced and, we suggest, eliminated. Hence subsequent screening activities could be simplified because they could focus on the AP of approved GMOs in non-GM commodities (where there is market demand).

To date, there has been no need for sampling and testing to be conducted on-farm by growers, or at later stages in the supply chain, for AP of approved GMOs. Nor would on-farm sampling and testing in non-GM crops be needed in farming systems growing both GM and non-GM canola, provided farmers can be confident of the certified non-GM seed supply (above) and provided farmers comply with industry-developed crop management plans durinon-farm production so that the threshold of 0.9 per cent of GM grain would be where a particular grain bulk handler(s) decided to require documentation of testing from farmers.

Marketers and exporters may in the future require documentation of testing of supplied grain from bulk handlers, and so the potential need for sampling and testing post-farm gate arises. Sampling and testing for a range of different quality characteristics of grain is already carried out routinely by bulk handlers, marketers and exporters. It would therefore be practical for any future sampling and testing for AP of GM events in canola to be integrated into the existing sampling and testing practices, that is, at grain receival at a silo and/or at grain outturn. The relevant screening packages are shown in Tables. Screening would need to be followed by more specific testing if there was a need to distinguish approved and unapproved events. Such specific tests are outside the scope of this report.

Cotton

Seed imported for breeding purposes is the key identifiable point for sampling and testing for events not approved by the Regulator. Imported seed could be tested using a simple pat gene screen to monitor for AP of unapproved events. Confirmation of presence of the specific unapproved GMO would require additional testing, preferably using a validated event-specific method for conclusive evidence.

Exported non-GM cotton could be tested for all GM events approved by the Regulator using a single DNA screen to detect the *CaMV35s* 5' DNA sequence (Table), in order to confirm inon-GM status. The relevant screening package is shown in following Table. Screening would need to be followed by more specific testing if there was a need to distinguish approved and unapproved events. Such specific tests are outside the scope of this report.

Soybean and Maize

No GM soybean or maize lines are approved for commercial release in Australia and therfore no GM events should be present in any imported soybean or maize seed. Sampling and testing (for any GM events at all), or at any stage before, the breeder seed/field trial 'testing gateway' would confirm imported seed was non-GM. Relevant screening packages are shown in Tables. Screening would need to be followed by more specifictesting if there was a need to distinguish FSANZ-approved and– unapproved events. Such specific tests are outside the scope of this report.

In the case of GM soybean or maize grain imported for processing, a DNIR licence is required from the Regulator and approval from FSANZ is required for use in food.

POTENTIAL FUTURE SAMPLING AND TESTING

Several points for sampling and testing in current supply chains have been identified which seem practicable (discussed in the previous section). In the case of canola, cotton, soybean, and maize seed imported into Australia as new germplasm for breeding purposes, the key point is at the early seed breeding stage and also, at least, at the breeder seed/field trial 'testing gateway'. Sampling and testing at these points eliminates the prospect that unapproved GMOs can enter domestic production streams for non-GM commodities or, therefore, exported commodities or domestically produced food streams, from varieties or lines bred in Australia.

In the case of imported shipments of these commodities for seed-for-sowing, sampling and testing of seed at some stage before it was sown, either in the originating country and/or in Australia, would confirm the non-GM status of the seed (or, in the case of GM canola varieties approved for commercial release in Australia, confirm the GM variety) and this would further confirm that GM events not approved by the Regulator are absent. A risk-based national strategy to manage the unintended presence of unapproved GMOs in imported seed-for-sowing is in place.

Because a threshold for the AP of a GMO in a non-GMO commodity in domestic supply chains has been set only for canola, sampling and testing for AP is relevant to non-GM canolagrain at bulk handling and/or grain supply stages, including supply for domestic food production and for export, to meet any non-GM market demand. In the case of cotton, although there is no domestic demand for a non-GM supply and therefore no need to sample and test for AP of GMOs; there could be a need for sampling and testing in the case where a niche overseas market required non-GM cottonseed.

In practical terms, the canola industry has indicated that bulk handling companies could monitor non-GM canola for the presence of GM grain at grain receival should markets require segregated product, as sampling and testing for other characteristics is routinely carried out at this stage. The initial step would be to determine the presence or absence of any GM grain in grain to be marketed as non-GM so that it can be appropriately unloaded at the receival point—this could involve a set of industry-designed protocols including declarations and/or testing. Segregations could then be tested at various points as determined by industry protocols and then tested again at grain outturn to meet customer requirements. Depending on these requirements, testing at some points of the supply chain could variously require sophisticated tests (including if there is a need to quantify GMO presence), or perhaps lateral flow test strips may be sufficient in some cases.

It is important to note that GM canola grain would be classed as Standard 'Canola' CSO1, and thus it would not be necessary to test every load of grain at receival points: only those that were to be segregated as CS01-a Standard ('Non-GM Canola').

MODEL SAMPLING AND TESTING SCREENING PACKAGES

The matrix of unapproved and approved GMOs in the four commodities under considerationis complex, and becoming more complicated as more GM varieties are introduced into commercial production. It is complicated because there may be approvals in the country from which we receive imports of seed and/or grain, but not in Australia—and even though approvals for commercial cropping may have been given in a country, the GM crop may never have actually been commercially grown. Further, approvals may be for food in Australia, but not for field release (commercial or trial), or there may be an AP threshold overseas but not in Australia (and *vice versa*).

In this report we have analysed: the current GM events which exist in canola, cotton, soybean and maize varieties in North America; their approval status in Australia (for food and for commercial field release); the production supply chains in Australia; thresholds in place in our major export markets; and, sampling and testing methods and technology. In this context, we have developed model sampling and testing screening packages for potential useacross the four crops at the identified sampling and testing points discussed above.

Whilst the specific screening packages provide feasible options for screening in the current context, it is important to note that they may not reflect what is needed and/or applied in the commercial or regulatory environment. Their currency will depend on which new GM varieties are introduced overseas or in Australia, and at what rate. The screening packages presented in this report could, however, be used as a model approach to ensure continued product integrity in the seed and grain supply chain. They also highlight the potential complexity of sampling and testing for specific purposes.

The sampling process described in Chapter 4 involves taking a number of primary samples from a seed lot, combining these to form a composite sample and reducing it (if it is too large) into a submitted sample to be sent to the laboratory. Key factors associated with this process are the confidence level and relative uncertainty. Understanding the confidence one can have that the results are correct and how far away the actual value could be from the calculated results plays a fundamental role when deciding a sample size. In regard to testing, qualitative PCR tests are the most reliable detection tests and so are to be recommended for determining presence/absence.

The sampling and testing screening packages below have taken the above factors into account when suggesting sampling and testing protocols, target confidence levels and the relative uncertainty (specified in each case).

Depending on the testing results, different decisions will need to be made. For example, if no GM events are detected in a certified non-GM seed or grain lot, it could continue to the next stage in the supply chain with no further sampling and testing requirements. For seed or grain lots, if the screen suggests that a GM event may be adventitiously present in a non-GM lot, further testing could be conducted to determine if the GMO(s) present is Regulator-approved and, if so, the level of GM presence (*i.e.* is it above or below the permitted AP threshold). Such further testing would require the availability of event-specific methods as discussed previously. The outcomes would determine subsequent actions: forexample the lot may no longer be classified as non-GM.

Canola

The following screening package (Table) has been developed for the situation where canola seed (for example, for germplasm enhancement or seed increase to commercial quantities) imported from the USA is tested to confirm that the seed lot does not contain AP of GMOs that have not been approved by the Regulator. This example uses the maximum permitted seed lot recommended by ISTA for canola of 10 tonnes. Since analytical testing to a zero presence level is not possible, this package is designed to confirm with a confidence level of 99 per cent that the seed lot contains less than 0.1 per cent GM seed which has not been approved by the Regulator for commercial release.

The following screening package (Table 2.12) has been developed for the situation where non-GM canola seed has been grown in Australia and is tested at grain receival to confirm that the seed lot (a 500 tonne silo lot) does not contain AP of Regulator-approved GM canola at a level above the 0.9 per cent threshold. The screening package has been tailored to take advantage of the current sampling and testing practices that are already occurring at the grain receival point and the canola supply chain. The latter makes this an attractive point for sampling and testing grain, allowing early detection of misidentified GM canola being added to non-GM grain.

Different sampling rates for current testing of bulk grain commodities are specified for each bulk road unit, varying depending on the bulk road unit size. In the package below, sampling at 3 × 1 litre probes per tonnes has been identified to cover this situation of varying bulk road unit sizes. The 500 tonne silo lot into which road unit lots are pooled is assumed to be highly heterogeneous. Excess sample material from that already collected for grain quality determinations is combined to form the basis of the composite sample required for this screening package. If the Australian grains industry were to adopt this type of sampling and testing screening package it would represent little extra sampling work as the grain is already being sampled at this point to ensure it meets quality parameters. Extra testing would be three DNA screening tests for each bulk sample (a 500 tonne silo lot).

Table 2.12 Sampling and Testing Screening Package for the Scenario of an Imported Shipment of Canola Seed from the USA

Scenario: Non-GM canola grain at receival into storage	
Purpose of testing:	Monitoring for adventitious presence of Regulator-approved GM canola in non-GM canola grain early in the grain supply chain (at grain receival)
Regulatory approval status:	Eight GMOs (and hybrids derived from some of these GMOs) approved for commercial release by the Regulator
Threshold level:	0.9%
Target confidence level:	99% confidence level that shipment contains less than 0.1% GM grain
Seed lot details	
Size of lot:	500 tonnes This is the maximum lot size recommended by ISO. Larger storage sites could be treated as multiple 500 tonne silo

Seed lot composition:	Assumed highly heterogeneity due to incorporation of one or more misidentified bulk road units of GM grain 95% of GM material localised in 5% of the lot
Target confidence level for sampling:	99% confidence level that laboratory sample is representative of the seed lot to within 10% of the true GM content
Sampling protocol	
Sample each bulk road unit at the rate of three probes per 10 tonnes of grain (minimum of three probes). Thoroughly mix the contents of the probes and, to produce a bulk sample representative of the silo, combine increments consisting of 100 g from each probe (a total of 1.5 kg for a 500 tonne silo). Thoroughly mix the entire bulk sample according to ISO 13690:1999 and reduce by means of a suitable divider to a laboratory sample of at least 0.3 kg	
Critical factors: Increments of equal size representing each probe on material added to the storage site Thorough mixing of bulk sample before dividing to minimum 0.3 kg (based on data from Figure and assuming an average canola grain weight of 5 mg)	

Analysis details	
Detection method:	Qualitative PCR detection of nos 3′, pat and cp4 epsps DNA sequences
Method LOD:	**One GM seed in at least 1 000 seeds**
Target confidence level for analysis:	99% confidence level that composite sample contains less than 0.81% GM seed (0.81% is the lower limit of sampling uncertainty for a sample with 10% uncertainty from a lot containing 0.9% GM)
Assay protocol	
Mix laboratory sample using a riffle box. Collect three working samples of 600 seeds each (Remund et al. 2005). Extract DNA from each sample and analyse each extract using the three DNA screening methods above. Two or more positive results for a given event constitute a positive finding	
Critical factors: Submitted sample mixed prior to splitting Method validation and LOD estimation determine based on the entire assay process Number of working samples required based on 5% false negative rates at the assay LOD	
Result	**Conclusion**
Neither *nos* 3′, *pat*and *cp4 epsps*detected in any working sample.	GM events not detected
Nos 3′, *pat* or *cp4 epsps* detected in at least two working sample.	Screen suggests sample contains a GM event. Approximately 40% of sample containing 0.1% GM will give a positive result. Confirmation required through identification, based on Figure, and quantification using event-specific method

An alternative or additional point for monitoring canola for AP of GM events is at the grain outturn from country storages. The following screening package (Table) has been developed for the situation where non-GM canola grain in a 200 tonne lot is tested to confirm that any AP of Regulator-approved GM canola is below the AP threshold level for GM canola grain of 0.9 per cent.

Table 2.13 Sampling and Testing Screening Package for the Scenario of Receival of Non-GM Grain into Storage by a Bulk Handling Company

Scenario: Non-GM Canola Grain at Outturn from a Country Storage Site	
Purpose of testing:	Monitoring for adventitious presence of Regulator-approved GM canola in non-GM canola grain at grain outturn from a country storage site
Regulatory approval status:	Eight GMOs (and hybrids arising from some of these GMOs) approved for commercial release by the Regulator
Threshold level:	0.9%
Target confidence level:	99% confidence level that shipment contains less than 0.9% GM grain
Seed lot details	
Size of shipment:	200 tonnes (this is within the maximum lot size recommended by ISO of 500 tonnes)
Seed lot composition:	Assumed highly heterogeneous 95% of GM material localised in 5%of the lot
Target confidence level for sampling:	99% confidence level that laboratory sample is representative of the seed lot to within 10% of the true GM content

Sampling protocol	
Use an automatic sampler according to ISO 6644:2002 to collect 100 equal sized increments of between 0.1–1 kg each from flowing grain. Combine all increments to produce a bulk sample. Thoroughly mix the entire bulk sample according to ISO 6644:2002 and ISO 13690:1999 and reduce by means of a suitable divider to a laboratory sample of at least 0.3 kg	
Critical factors: Sampling according to ISO guidelines with a large number of increments Thorough mixing of bulk sample before dividing to minimum 0.3 kg (based on data from Figure 4.2 and assuming an average canola grain weight of 5 mg)	
Analysis details	
Detection method:	Qualitative PCR detection of nos 3′, pat and cp4 epsps DNA sequences
Method LOD:	One GM seed in at least 1 000 seeds
Target confidence level for analysis:	99% confidence level that composite sample contains less than 0.81% GM seed (0.81% is the lower limit of sampling uncertainty for a sample with 10% uncertainty from a lot containing 0.9% GM)

Assay protocol	
Mix laboratory sample using a riffle box. Collect three working samples of 600 seeds each. Extract DNA from each sample and analyse each extract using the three DNA screening methods above. Two or more positive results for a given event constitute a positive finding	
Critical factors: Laboratory sample mixed prior to splitting Method validation and LOD estimation determined based on the entire assay process Number of working samples required based on 5% false negative rates at the assay LOD	
Result	**Conclusion**
Neither *nos 3′*, *pat*and *cp4 epsps*detected in any working sample.	GM events not detected
nos 3′, *pat* or *cp4 epsps* detected in at least two working sample.	Screen suggests sample contains a GM event. Approximately 40% of sample containing 0.1% GM will give a positive result. Confirmation required through identification, based on Figure, and quantification using event-specific method

The lot is assumed to be highly heterogeneous. Such heterogeneity means that bulk samples should be prepared from a high number of increments. The preferred sampling method is therefore to use automate sampling equipment operating on the flowing grain as it leaves the silo. A qualitative PCR test with the ability to detect one GM seed in one thousand is recommended as opposed to using lateral flow test strips, because PCR testing is more sensitive. Sampling of the grain in the package accords with ISO guidelines. From an industry perspective, the sampling at grain receival is unlikely to represent a significant extra sampling burden as sampling is carried out at this point to test for other grain characteristics.

Table 2.14 Sampling and Testing Screening Package for the Scenario of Outturn of Non-GM Canola Grain from a Country Storage Site

Scenario: Non-GM Canola Grain at Outturn from a Country Storage Site	
Purpose of testing:	Monitoring for adventitious presence of Regulator-approved GM canola in non-GM canola grain at grain outturn from a country storage site
Regulatory approval status:	Eight GMOs (and hybrids arising from some of these GMOs) approved for commercial release by the Regulator
Threshold level:	0.9%
Target confidence level:	99% confidence level that shipment contains less than 0.9% GM grain
Seed lot details	
Size of shipment:	200 tonnes (this is within the maximum lot size recommended by ISO of 500 tonnes)
Seed lot composition:	Assumed highly heterogeneous 95% of GM material localised in 5%of the lot
Target confidence level for sampling:	99% confidence level that laboratory sample is representative of the seed lot to within 10% of the true GM content
Sampling protocol	
Use an automatic sampler according to ISO 6644:2002 to collect 100 equal sized increments of between 0.1–1 kg each from flowing grain. Combine all increments to produce a bulk sample. Thoroughly mix the entire bulk sample according to ISO 6644:2002 and ISO 13690:1999 and reduce by means of a suitable divider to a laboratory sample of at least 0.3 kg	

Critical factors: Sampling according to ISO guidelines with a large number of increments Thorough mixing of bulk sample before dividing to minimum 0.3 kg (based on data from Figure 4.2 and assuming an average canola grain weight of 5 mg)	
Analysis details	
Detection method:	Qualitative PCR detection of nos 3′, pat and cp4 epsps DNA sequences
Method LOD:	One GM seed in at least 1 000 seeds
Target confidence level for analysis:	99% confidence level that composite sample contains less than 0.81% GM seed (0.81% is the lower limit of sampling uncertainty for a sample with 10% uncertainty from a lot containing 0.9% GM)
Assay protocol	
Mix laboratory sample using a riffle box. Collect three working samples of 600 seeds each. Extract DNA from each sample and analyse each extract using the three DNA screening methods above. Two or more positive results for a given event constitute a positive finding	
Critical factors: Laboratory sample mixed prior to splitting Method validation and LOD estimation determined based on the entire assay process Number of working samples required based on 5% false negative rates at the assay LOD	
Result	**Conclusion**
Neither *nos* 3′, *pat*and *cp4 epsps*detected in any working sample.	GM events not detected
nos 3′, *pat* or *cp4 epsps* detected in at least two working sample.	Screen suggests sample contains a GM event. Approximately 40% of sample containing 0.1% GM will give a positive result. Confirmation required through identification, based on Figure, and quantification using event-specific method

Other potential challenges which could be presented by adopting the above screening packages include:

- Delay in results could be a problem if outturned grain goes straight to the crusher, testing at grain receival, before storage, would therefore be better;
- Payment of farmers—if farmers are being paid a premium for non-GM grain (although, there is currently no indication in markets that there will be significant global demand for non-GM grain), but supply GM grain, this may not be known by the time farmer payments need to be made. Also, payments to farmers who actually supplied non-GM grain into the silo lot could be disadvantaged.

For some varieties, there is potential to avoid delays at the grain handling terminal by performing more rapid tests, either earlier in the supply chain or at the time of grain receival. Lateral flow strip tests are available for Roundup Ready® canola, and, while this remains the only commercially grown GM canola variety in Australia, these tests could form a part of a sampling and testing package.

However, the robustness of the Roundup Ready® lateral flow strip tests under field conditions would need to be verified as studies on the efficacy of other lateral flow strip tests in the field have indicated unacceptable levels of false positive readings and variances in the LOD between the laboratory and the field.

Cotton

The following screening package (*see table 2.15*) has been developed to meet the situation where non-GM cottonseed is exported to a niche market overseas. The seed lot is tested prior to export to confirm that any AP of GM cottonseed is present at a level of less than 0.1 per cent.

This example uses a 20 tonne lot size which is less than the maximum permitted seed lot recommended by ISTA for cotton of 40 tonnes. The screening package is designed to confirm with a confidence level of 99 per cent that the seed lot contains less than 0.1 per cent GM seed.

For the scenario of imported shipments of cottonseed, a simple pat screen could be applied to test for the presence of the two GM events not approved in Australia but approved and commercialised in the USA (Chapter). Such testing (for example, by pre-breeders) would give confidence that unapproved events are not entering the Australian cotton production system. A sampling and testing package has not been developed for this scenario.

Soybean and Maize

No GM soybean or maize varieties have been approved by the Regulator for field trials or commercial release in Australia. Six GM soybean lines (three derived from the same event) have been approved by FSANZ for use in food in Australia. FSANZ have also approved 13 GM maize lines for use in food. The import into Australia of GM soybean or maize for processing requires a DNIR licence from the Regulator.

The following screening package (Table 2.16) has been developed to meet the situation where imported non-GM soybean in bulk is tested to confirm that it does not contain GM soybean. This example uses a 25 tonne seed lot which is less than the maximum permitted seed lot recommended by ISTA for soybean of 40 tonnes. Since analytical testing to a zero presence level is not possible (Chapter), this package is designed to confirm with a confidence level of 99 per cent that the seed lot contains less than 0.1 per cent GM seed.

The screen also provides the basis for further sampling and testing (beyond the scope of this report) to distinguish between GMOs which have FSANZ approvals as GM foods and those which do not.

Table 2.15 Sampling and Testing Screening Package for the Scenario of Export of Non-GM Cottonseed for a Niche Market

Scenario: Export of non-GM cottonseed for a niche market	
Purpose of testing:	Monitoring for presence of Regulator-approved GM cotton in non-GM cottonseed for export
Regulatory approval status:	Five GMOs approved for commercial release by the Regulator
Threshold level:	0.1% tolerance level for adventitious presence
Target confidence level:	99% confidence level that shipment contains less than 0.1% GM seed
Seed lot details	
Size of shipment:	20 tonnes (this is within the maximum lot size recommended by ISTA of 40 tonnes)
Seed lot composition:	Assumed low level of heterogeneity
Target confidence level for sampling:	99% confidence level that submitted sample is representative of the seed lot to within 20% of the true GM content at 0.1% GM seed
Sampling protocol	
Collect forty primary samples of 0.4 kg each. Combine primary samples to produce a composite sample of 16 kg. Thoroughly mix and reduce by means of a suitable divider to a laboratory sample of sufficient size for assay protocol (suggested size at least 1.5 kg)	
Critical factors: Sampling according to ISTA guidelines with a minimum composite sample of 15 kg (based on data from Figure and assuming an average cottonseed weight of 110 mg) Thorough mixing of composite before dividing to submitted sample	

Analysis details	
Detection method:	Qualitative detection of*CaMV35s* 5′ DNA sequences
Method LOD:	One GM seed in at least 1 000 seeds
Target confidence level for analysis:	99% confidence level that composite sample contains less than 0.08% GM seed (0.08% is the lower limit of sampling uncertainty for a sample with 20% uncertainty from a lot containing 0.1% GM)
Assay protocol	
Mix submitted sample using a riffle box. Collect seven working sample of 1 000 seeds each. Extract DNA from each sample and analyse using the above DNA screening method	
Critical factors: Submitted sample mixed prior to splitting Method validation and LOD estimation includes entire assay process Number of working samples based on 5% false negative rates at the assay LOD A positive result may indicate presence of the Cauliflower Mosaic Virus itself, and not a GM event, so should be confirmed with additional testing	
Result	**Conclusion**
Neither result for all assays	GM events not detected
Positive results on at least one working sample.	Screen suggests sample contains a GM event. Confirmation required to identify the GM event(s) present using event-specific method

Table 2.16 Sampling and Testing Screening Package for the Scenario of an Imported Shipment of Non-GM Soybean from the USA

Scenario: Imported shipment of non-GM maize from the USA	
Purpose of testing:	Monitoring for presence of GM maize in non-GM maize
Regulatory approval status:	No GMOs approved by the Regulator
Threshold level:	No threshold (any presence level of unapproved GMOs is illegal)
Target confidence level:	99% confidence level that shipment contains less than 0.1% GM seed
Seed lot details	
Size of shipment:	25 tonnes (this is within the maximum seed lot size recommended by ISTA of 40 tonnes)
Seed lot composition:	Assumed low level of heterogeneity
Target confidence level for sampling:	99% confidence level that submitted sample is representative of the seed lot to within 20% of the true GM content at 0.1% GM seed
Sampling protocol	
Collect forty primary samples of 0.9 kg each. Combine primary samples to produce a composite sample of at least 34 kg. Thoroughly mix and reduce by means of a suitable divider to a submitted sample of sufficient size for assay protocol (suggested size at least 3 kg).	
Critical factors: Sampling according to ISTA guidelines with a minimum composite sample of 34 kg (based on data from Figure and assuming an average maize kernel weight of 250 mg) Thorough mixing of composite before dividing to submitted sample	

Analysis details	
Detection method:	Qualitative PCR detection of*CaMV35s* 5' and *cp4 epsps*DNA sequences
Method LOD:	One GM seed in 1 000 seeds
Target confidence level for analysis:	99% confidence level that laboratory sample contains less than 0.08% GM seed (0.08% is the lower limit of sampling uncertainty for a sample with 20% uncertainty from a lot containing 0.1% GM)
Assay protocol	
Mix laboratory sample using a riffle box. Collect seven working samples of 1 000 seeds. Extract DNA from each sample and analyse using both DNA screening methods	
Critical factors: Laboratory sample mixed prior to splitting Method validation and LOD estimation includes entire assay process Number of working samples based on 5% false negative rates at the assay LOD	
Result	**Conclusion**
Neither *CaMV35s5'* nor *cp4 epsps*detected in any working sample.	GM events not detected
Either *CaMV35s* 5' or *cp4 epsps* or both detected in at least one working sample.	Screen suggests sample contains a GM event. Confirmation required through identification, based on Figure, of GM event present using event-specific methods

The following screeing package (Table 2.17) has been developed to meet the situation where non-GM maize is imported. Since there are no GM maize varieties approved by the Regulator for commercial release in Australia, the seed lot is tested to confirm that it does not contain any GM maize.

This example uses a 25 tonne seed lot which is less than the maximum permitted seed lot recommended by ISTA for maize of 40 tonnes. Since analytical testing to a zero presence level is not possible, this package is designed to confirm with a confidence level of 99 per cent that the seed lot contains less than 0.1 per cent GM seed. The screen also provides the basis for sampling and testing to distinguish between GMOs which have FSANZ approval as GM foods and those which do not, in maize shipments for food and feed.

Table 2.17 Sampling and Testing Screening Package for the Scenario of an Imported Shipment of Non-GM Maize from the USA

Scenario: Imported shipment of non-GM maize from the USA	
Purpose of testing:	Monitoring for presence of GM maize in non-GM maize
Regulatory approval status:	No GMOs approved by the Regulator
Threshold level:	No threshold (any presence level of unapproved GMOs is illegal)
Target confidence level:	99% confidence level that shipment contains less than 0.1% GM seed
Seed lot details	
Size of shipment:	25 tonnes (this is within the maximum seed lot size recommended by ISTA of 40 tonnes)
Seed lot composition:	Assumed low level of heterogeneity
Target confidence level for sampling:	99% confidence level that submitted sample is representative of the seed lot to within 20% of the true GM content at 0.1% GM seed
Sampling protocol	
Collect forty primary samples of 0.9 kg each. Combine primary samples to produce a composite sample of at least 34 kg. Thoroughly mix and reduce by means of a suitable divider to a submitted sample of sufficient size for assay protocol (suggested size at least 3 kg).	

Critical factors: Sampling according to ISTA guidelines with a minimum composite sample of 34 kg (based on data from Figure and assuming an average maize kernel weight of 250 mg) Thorough mixing of composite before dividing to submitted sample	
Analysis details	
Detection method:	Qualitative PCR detection of*CaMV35s* 5′ and *nos* 3′ DNA sequences
Method LOD:	One GM seed in 1 000 seeds
Target confidence level for analysis:	99% confidence level that laboratory sample contains less than 0.08% GM seed (0.08% is the lower limit of sampling uncertainty for a sample with 20% uncertainty from a lot containing 0.1% GM)
Assay protocol	
Mix laboratory sample using a riffle box. Collect seven working samples of 1 000 seeds each. Extract DNA from each sample and analyse using both DNA screening methods	
Critical factors: Laboratory sample mixed prior to splitting Method validation and LOD estimation includes entire assay process Number of working samples required based on 5% false negative rates at the assay LOD	
Result	**Conclusion**
Neither *CaMV35s*5′ nor *nos* 3′detected in any working sample.	GM events not detected
Either *CaMV35s* 5′ or *nos* 3′ detected in at least one working sample.	Screen suggests sample contains a GM event. Confirmation required through identification, based on Figure, of GM event present using event-specific methods

TESTING CAPABILITIES

Three laboratories in each of Australia, North America and the EU were surveyed for this study to give an indication of the

GM testing capabilities in these countries. Australian laboratory testing capabilities identified in this report include event-specific testing capacity for all GM cotton and GM canola varieties approved by the Regulator for commercial release in Australia. While capabilities do not appear to include capacity to test for all GM events approved overseas, capabilities may exist in overseas and Australian laboratories not surveyed for this study.

The difference in cost for GMO testing between Australia, the USA and the EU is significant. For example, the cost of a qualitative PCR assay in the USA can be as little as US$12.75-209 (AUD$19.03–312), whereas in Australia and the EU it could cost between $400-680 and 109–222€ (AUD$209–426) respectively. This cost differential in testing for AP of GM events is a major reason why Australian seed breeding companies currently send their seed samples for testing to accredited USA and European laboratories. It is also a reason why the bulk handling companies look towards using the lateral flow test strips as opposed to qualitative PCR testing. At about AUD$6–7 per strip test, using lateral flow test strips is significantly cheaper than engaging an accredited Australian laboratory to perform the testing.

Event-specific PCR primer sequences for the GM events are often held as Commercial-in-Confidence by the technology providers and only made accessible to a limited number of accredited laboratories around the world. This could explain why industry may not be able to undertake much qualitative PCR testing in-house. If the cost of testing for AP of GM events in accredited Australian laboratories could be reduced, this could lower overall costs to Australian industry of maintaining product integrity in a GM/non-GM canola coexistence framework, should such segregation be required in the market.

In issuing a licence for dealings involving an intentional release of a GMO into the environment (DIR licence), the Regulator can impose conditions. For DIR licences issued to date, the Regulator has required that 'the licence holder must provide a written instrument to the Regulator describing an experimental method that is capable of reliably detecting the presence of the GMOs and the presence of the genetic modifications described in this licence in a recipient organism.' This testing methodology constitutes intellectual property of the licence holder and as such cannot be shared with commercial testing laboratories.

The International Experience

Approaches to the coexistence of approved GM and non-GM crops in different countries essentially fall into three groups. Some countries, for example the USA, Canada and Australia have adopted a non-legislative approach to coexistence. A second group, such as some EU countries, take a legislative approach (Chapter), and a third group comprises the many countries that are still in the process of considering, developing, or formalising their approach to coexistence.

Coexistence experiences overseas could be instructive aabout how to address sampling and testing for AP of GM events in non-GM seed and grain. In this study, we therefore looked for sampling and testing components in existing and proposed coexistence strategies in the USA, Canada, EU27 countries and the countries to which Australia exports significant volumes of canola and cottonseed.

With the exception of the EU, we found few sampling and testing components that formed part of legislation-based strategies. As highlighted in Chapter, strategies often focus mostly on managing physical admixture through handling methods and gene flow at the on-farm level though physical isolation (or separation) distances between GM and non-GM crops; sampling and testing for GM events is not a common requirement. Whether the coexistence approach is legislative-based or non legislative-based, the specific sampling and testing protocols and methods to be employed are not prescribed, consistent with the approach by, for example, ISTA. However, principles and/or guidance may be provided and international standards referenced, and, if in a legislated framework context, there may be a recommendation or a statutory requirement to comply with them.

Contrasting approaches are exemplified by the following two documents. First is the EC Recommendation on technical guidance for sampling and detection of GMOs and material produced from GMOs in seed, food and feed products (2004/

787/EC), which fulfils requirements set out in Regulation No. 1830/2003 on the traceability and labelling of GM organisms and the traceability of food and feed products produced from GMOs. Second is the SVGA Principles—and associated technical documents, particularly the ASF Best Practice Guidelines.

The first document illustrates an approach that is statute-based, with detailed reference in a guidance document to strategies, standards and processes relevant to sampling and testing. The latter documents illustrate an industry-based self-regulatory approach, which also includes detailed reference to strategies, standards and processes. In both these examples, the guidance/recommendations are detailed. The essential difference in approach is whether or not there is associated government intervention through legislation. The industry self-regulated approach relies on breeding programmes and seed companies to have in place quality management systems to ensure compliance and so meet any market demand for segregated product.

The international experience with coexistence models and sampling and testing for GM events can help inform Australia's needs, but does not provide any 'off-the-shelf' approach that can or should be adopted. This is because approaches to coexistence are determined and constructed around two drivers—market-specified demands and statutory regulatory requirements; these vary by commodity and by country, and so sampling and testing needs can become commodity-and country-specific. The sampling and testing needed is that which delivers the commodity which meets the market-specified and/or legally-specified requirements.

In the case of coexisting approved GM crops (approved both for commercial field release and for food) and non-GM crops, the sampling and testing issue is not one of ensuring that some safety threshold has not been exceeded or that an unapproved GMO(s) is absent. One view is, therefore, that the market should determine whether or not there is a need for a coexistence strategy, industry should be responsible for any strategy, and AP thresholds themselves should be what are realistically practical. AP thresholds for approved GM events in non-GM effectively set a zero presence threshold, while acknowledging it is not possibleto sample and test to zero presence.

The sampling and testing packages presented in this report are examples of the kinds of best practice packages that can be constructed. However, packages need to be tailored to the specific combination of the following: the AP threshold to be met; the target confidence levels for the test accuracy, representativeness of the sample, and analysis; the seed lot size; and, the particular commodity (taking into account grain size and weight).

In the case of the sampling and testing that is needed to determine the absence of unapproved GMOs or the absence of any GMOs, the AP threshold is presence. However, analytical testing to zero is not possible, because methods are limited by their sensitivity. Sampling and testing packages for any given commodity therefore need to acknowledge the limits of detection of the methods to be used and to specify the number of seeds to be sampled in a test working sample. A realistic testing plan would specify at least 99 per cent confidence that any AP is below 0.1 per cent.

As described in Chapters, both non-government (ISTA and ISO) and government (for example, the USDA GIPSA and the European JRC and CEN) standard setting bodies already produce comprehensive relevant rules and standards and accredit and certify laboratories.While sampling theory and methodology are well established, testing methodology continues to evolve. More efficient, effective and economic testing methodology is continually being developed. Any organisation or laboratory involved in testing therefore needs tobe aware of current testing methods and select the most appropriate test to meet the purpose required.

SEED AND GRAIN INDUSTRY

The SVGA process resulted in the grains industry agreeing to the*Principles for process management of grain within the Australian supply chain: a guide for industry in an environment where GM and non-GM grain is marketed*. This document underpins the Australian grains industry approach to coexistence, describing the Principles that the industry will adopt in order to maintain their product integrity and meet domestic and export customer requirements in any grains commodity. This document contains the standards, quality assurance practices and sampling and testing regimes which supply chain participants may use to meet customer requirements.

Reference to specific sampling and testing regimes in the SVGA document is currently limited, due to the desire not to impose a specific sampling and testing regime across the entire industry. This approach acknowledges the fact that a sampling and testing regime that works in one sector of the industry may not necessarily be practical in another.

The sampling and testing screening packages for AP of GM events presented in this report provide a level of detail and transparency that may be of benefit to the grains industry, their customers and others. They could also serve as models or be adapted or refined, as appropriate, for use by industry (for example the sampling and testing screening package for canola grain at the grain receival or grain outturn points). Successful development of packages now, when there is no significant GM canola production in Australi to warrant extensive testing of non-GM canola grain, could position industry for a potential future need, should markets require ongoing segregation.

The need to work towards harmonisation of sampling and testing protocols for GM events was also raised earlier in this report. Harmonisation stems from the need to judge that results are reliable and comparable. Appropriate reference materials are required in order to verify that testing methodologies used in different laboratories are able to produce accurate and comparable results. For example, in an ideal harmonised system, the sampling and testing carried out by an Australian bulk handling company at its grain receival points should be comparable with, and use the same testing methodologies as, the sampling and testing carried out on the grain received at port by an importing country. This would help ensure consistency in results when testing the same seed lot.

In addition to establishing consistency through harmonisation, sampling and testing practices will need to be adapted as future GM crops enter the marketplace. The points in the supply chain where seed and grain should be tested for AP may need to be reassessed in a given commodity, and procedures for sampling may also need to be changed accordingly, with changed characteristics of the seed and grain.

Concluding Statement

In an environment of growing global trade in GM commodities, understanding the sampling and testing protocols of other countries and their diverse contexts, and appreciating the varied systems and standards and levels of harmonisation that exist, will become an increasingly important aspect of the sampling and testing approaches that need to be applied within the Australian seed and grain supply chain. The sampling and testing screening packages presented in this report could be used as a model approach to continue maintaining product integrity in the seed and grain supply chain.

In regard to coexisting GM and non-GM varieties of a crop in a farming system, the sampling and testing needs of the Australian seed and grain industry for AP of GM events in non-GM seed and grain will ultimately depend on the market demand for differentiated products.

3

Seed Sampling

INTRODUCTION

Tests of the quality and other characteristics of seed need to be made at several stages during its progress from the parent tree to the seed bed. Tests for maturity and soundness of seed before and during collection in the forest have been described on pp. 34–36 and are usually associated with surveys of the abundance of the seed crop; they are intended to ensure that both the quantity and the quality of seed justify the effort and cost of collection.

Several tests may be required at the seed processing depot, after extraction and cleaning and before the seeds are despatched to the nurseries or placed in storage. Testing of moisture content is essential for many species before they are stored for a long time, but is usually unnecessary if the seed is to be sown immediately in the nursery; on the other hand, partial drying may be needed before despatch of seed to a distant forest station, to reduce the risk of deterioration in transit, and any deliberate drying operation must be accompanied by the testing of moisture content. Testing of germination or viability should be repeated at the end of the storage period if this is more than a few months and, in the case of long-term storage for conservation of genetic resources, testing should be done at intervals throughout the storage period.

Efficiency and success in raising plants in the nursery and in their subsequent establishment in forest plantations depend to a great extent on the quality of the seeds used. It follows that foresters, nurserymen, seed dealers and others need accurate estimates of the quality of the seeds in which they deal or which form the basis of their afforestation projects. This is particularly important when seeds are bought and sold, or move between countries in international trade.

The example of estimating seed demand which is shown in Table 3.1 and 3.2 estimates of the number of germinated seeds per kg of Pinus kesiya and Tectona grandis which are averages for the species. In practice, the number varies considerably from year to year and from seed lot to seed lot, so that it is necessary for the forester to have an accurate estimate of germination for every individual seed lot which he receives, if he is to fulfil planting targets while at the same time avoiding the waste of valuable seed caused by sowing too much. Similarly the nurseryman must have a good estimate of germination if he is to adjust sowing rates to produce the optimum spacing of seedlings in the seedbed.

Justice has defined the following objectives for developing rules for seed testing:

- To provide methods by which the quality of seed samples can be determined accurately;
- To prescribe methods by which seed analysts working in different laboratories in different countries throughout the world can obtain uniform results;
- To relate the laboratory results, insofar as possible, to planting value,
- To complete the tests within the shortest period of time possible, commensurate with the above-mentioned objectives; and
- To perform the tests in the most economical manner. For the practising forester, the most important object of seed testing is the provision of an accurate estimate of the capacity of a given seedlot to produce healthy, vigourous plants suitable for field planting. In the present context, seed 'quality' refers to the physiological vigour of the seed rather than its genetic quality.

The essence of good seed testing is the application of reliable standard methods of examination to ensure that uniform and reproducible results are obtained. Standardization has been greatly facilitated through the adoption by a number of countries of the International Rules for Seed Testing formulated by the International Seed Testing Association (ISTA).

ISTA was founded in 1921, drew up its first set of Rules in 1931 and made major revisions of the Rules in 1953, 1966 and 1976. In the early stages ISTA's primary concern was for agricultural seeds, but trees and shrubs have gradually assumed greater importance and the 1976 Rules give (firm) 'prescriptions' or (more tentative) 'suggestions' as to testing methods appropriate for 61 different genera of these, compared with 26 in the 1953 Rules. The Rules are published in English, French and German.

Although tree species and genera from the tropics and southern hemisphere (notably eucalypts) have begun to figure in the ISTA lists, the balance is still overwhelmingly weighted towards north temperate species. Thus important species such as Tectona grandis, Pinus patula, P. oocarpa and P. kesiya are listed, but only in the list of 'suggested' (non prescriptive) seed testing methods, while a recent survey has shown that 20 other important tropical species are not included at all; they include Cupressus lusitanica, Gmelina arborea, Cordia alliodoraand the genera Albizzia, Araucaria, Casuarina, Swietenia, Terminalia and Triplochiton. Their omission simply reflects the lack of reliable information from research on the best methods of testing these species and genera.

ISTA testing methods involve the maintenance of controlled laboratory conditions and the use of some items of equipment which are relatively expensive. They are therefore well suited to large, well-equipped seed laboratories but are impracticable for small forest stations which have no laboratory and must carry out germination tests in the nursery or the office. Lack of equipment is no reason to omit seed testing altogether. For example simple germination tests carried out in the nursery can produce results which are perfectly satisfactory for local use. But precise details of method should always accompany results whenever this is not standardized, so that the seed user can interpret the results in relation to his own nursery conditions.

An up-to-date guide to the range of equipment available for seed testing is contained in the 'Survey of Equipment and Supplies' published by ISTA. It lists equipment by type, use, model specification and supplier. The earlier directory, 'Equipment and supplies for collecting, processing, storing and testing forest tree seed' includes seed testing equipment and gives the addresses of user laboratories as well as suppliers.

Van der Burg *et al.* give a description of how a seed testing station in tropical or subtropical areas could be established. Two alternatives are described: Seedlab 2000, that can test about 2000 samples per year and Seedlab 5000 that can test at least 5000 samples per year. Directives and general considerations concerning the staffing, the organization of the work, the lay-out of the building, and the equipment needed are given. Forty-six figures and two tables give an impression of the equipment and administrative forms used. Equipment which in the experience of the authors has been found suitable for the work is recommended and detailed descriptions and company addresses are mentioned. Some equipment that is not commercially available is described and plans for construction are included. A list of books and journals for a basic seed testing library is appended.

The tests which may be required are purity, authenticity, seed weight, germination, indirect testing of viability, moisture content, and seed health and damage. A prerequisite for all testing is good sampling, which is described in the following section.

SAMPLING

When seed is tested, the sample on which the test is made has to be representative of the whole. No matter how accurate the technical work in the test, the results can only show the quality of the sample submitted for analysis. Therefore, every effort must be made to ensure that the submitted sample accurately reflects the composition of the whole seed lot. This is equally applicable, whether a whole series of tests is to be made in a laboratory, or a simple nursery test carried out to determine number of germinated seeds per kg of uncleaned seed. Time spent testing carelessly drawn samples may be time wasted.

Completely homogeneous seed lots would be easy to sample, but they do not exist. Common sense measures can be taken to reduce heterogeneity as much as possible, for example seed lots of the same species should not be mixed if they come from different origins (provenances), differ greatly in age or, in the case of the same introduced provenances, if they come from plantations growing on very different site types in the introducing country. But a seed lot may be heterogeneous even if collected from a homogeneous stand. Paul has given the simple example of pine seed transported over bad roads in the back of a landrover.

The bumps and vibrations to which it is subjected will cause a settling out of different types of material. All the small and empty seeds and other light rubbish will eventually reach the surface layers and a sample taken from the top alone will give a completely false impression of the potential performance of the seeds as a whole.

MIXING

If the seed lot is a small one consisting of only a few kg of seed, it is possible to improve its homogeneity by thorough mixing of the whole lot before taking a sample. In the case of very large seed lots transported and stored in many different containers, mixing of the whole seed lot is impracticable. Instead, a number of different samples are taken, and it is these samples which are thoroughly mixed together to form a homogeneous 'composite' sample for testing. The methods of mixing which are quoted below from Paul (1972), are equally applicable to small entire seed lots or to composite samples. 'Methods of mixing.

There are two simple ways in which seed may be thoroughly mixed:

1. *Mixing with the aid of a mechanical divider*: Mechanical dividers are used to reduce the size of seed lots or

samples by repetitive halving. Their operation is described below. The divider has the added advantage that it can also be used to mix seed in the following manner:

- Pass entire seed lot through divider;
- Take the two equal portions and feed them simultaneously into the divider;
- Repeat operation No. 2;
- Repeat operation No. 2 once more.
- Take the two equal portions and pour them simultaneously into the storage container.

2. *Handmixing*: It is surprising how difficult it can be to achieve a homogeneous seed lot using this method. The entire seed lot must be spread out on a sheet of paper or some other suitable smooth surface and mixed by scooping the seed from side to side and from top to bottom. After thoroughly mixing, spread the seed out evenly and divide the lot into four equal parts. Place these separately in four containers and with the aid of an assistant pour them simultaneously into the storage container. Repeat the spreading, quartering and pouring process another two times."

USE OF SEED TRIERS

For a large seed lot contained in a number of different containers, seed triers are used to take small sub samples from different parts of the lot. All of these 'primary' samples are mixed together to form a 'composite' or bulk sample, which is later reduced in size by successive dividings until it is small enough to form the 'working' sample on which the various tests are carried out.

As described by Turnbull, a seed trier is a probe, long enough to reach all areas of the seed bag and designed to remove an equal volume of seed from each area through which it travels. Most commonly used is a sleeve-type trier which consists of a hollow brass tube inside a closely fitting outer sleeve. The tube and sleeve have open slots in their walls so that, when the tube is turned or slid, the slots in the tube and the sleeve coincide and seeds can flow into the tube; when the tube is given a half turn or slid in the opposite direction, the openings are closed. Seed triers should have a series of separate compartments and not just a single long tube with several openings. Tubes are available in varying lengths and diameters to cater for different sizes of container and kinds of seeds. Triers known as 'thief' triers, with a single open slot, should be avoided, as they can damage the seeds.

Ideally, the primary samples should be distributed proportionally to the volumes of the different parts of the seed lot. For example, if a lot is contained in ten 10-kg containers and ten 20-kg containers, the 20-kg containers should contribute two thirds of the composite sample and the 10-kg containers only one third. For seed lots in containers of uniform size, ISTA has detailed prescriptions as to the number of primary samples appropriate for varying numbers of containers, *e.g.* for 6–30 containers at least one in three containers is to be sampled and never less than five.

Large seeds and others that are not free-flowing are not suitable for sampling by seed trier. They should be sampled by thrusting the hand into the seeds and removing small portions. The hand should be inserted flat with the fingers extended together. The fingers should be kept together as the hand is closed and withdrawn. It is difficult to sample with this method deeper than about 40 cm and containers may have to be partially emptied to facilitate sampling.

REDUCING THE SIZE OF COMPOSITE SAMPLES

The following description of the reduction of the size of the composite sample is taken largely from Turnbull.

Usually the composite or bulk sample for testing needs to be reduced to a working sample of standard weight. Whenever possible the sample should be subdivided by a mechanical divider to reduce any operator bias in the dividing. The non-mechanical halving method is described here for use if a mechanical divider is not available, but it is the least desirable method for most types of seed. Manual methods must, however, be used for seeds which are not free-flowing.

NON-MECHANICAL METHODS OF DIVIDING

Halving method. The sample is placed on a clean surface and thoroughly mixed by hand; it is then divided into quarters with a sharp-edged spatula and opposite quarters discarded. The process is repeated until a final sample of the approximate weight required is obtained.

Random cup method. A series of small cups or thimbles are arranged on a tray in a definite pattern and the sample is poured systematically over this area. The working sample is obtained from randomly selected containers. A modification of this method uses a tray divided into an equal number of square compartments, every alternate one of which has no bottom.

MECHANICAL METHODS OF DIVIDING

Most mechanical dividers are designed to split the sample into two approximately equal parts. The working sample is obtained by repeatedly dividing the bulk sample until it reaches the required weight. ISTA recommends three types of dividers as being suitable equipment. They are the conical divider (Boerner type), the soil divider, and the centrifugal divider (Gamet type). They are briefly described as follows:

Boerner Sampler. This divider is made in different sizes. The essential parts consist of a hopper, inverted cone, and a series of baffles directing the seeds into two spouts. The baffles form alternate channels and spaces of equal width. They are arranged in a circle at their summit and are directed inward and downward, the channels leading to one spout and the spaces to an opposite spout. A valve or gate at the base of the hopper controls the seed flow. When the valve is opened the seeds fall by gravity over the inverted cone where they are evenly distributed to the channels and spaces; then, they pass through the spouts into the seed pans below.

In Zimbabwe a similar arrangement on a larger scale is used for dividing and mixing large seed lots. From the inverted cone there are 8 outlets which pass the seed into buckets, and a battery of 8 buckets is available for each outlet. The buckets hold 6 kg of pine seed each, so that a seed lot of up to 384 kg can be handled in any one dividing and remixing operation.

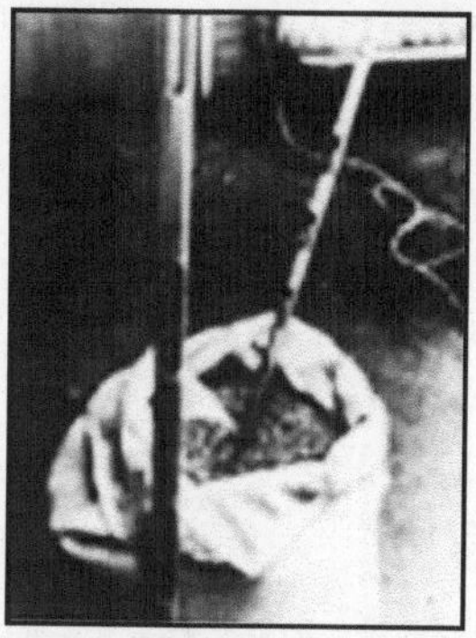

Fig. 3.1 A Seed Trier. (DANIDA Forest Seed Centre)

Fig. 3.2 Random cup Divider. (DANIDA Forest Seed Centre)

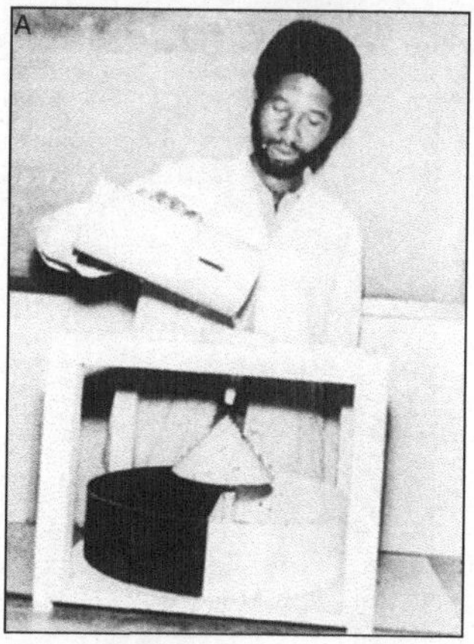

Fig. 3.3 Inverted Cone Dividers Used in Zimbabw for small

Fig. 3.4 For Large Quantities of Seed. (Forestry Commission Zimbabwe)

Fig. 3.5 Seed Dividers Boerner

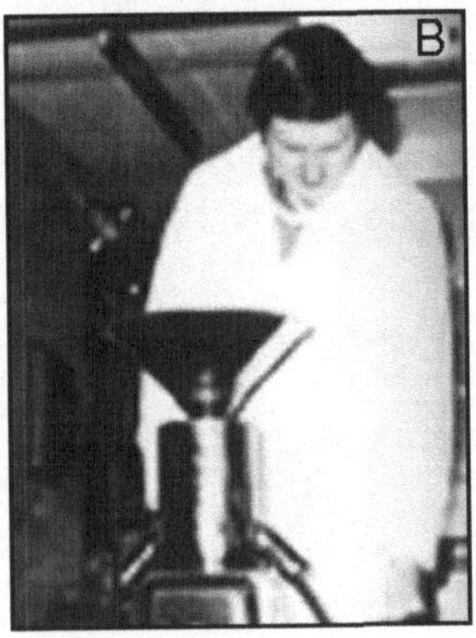

Fig. 3.6 Gamet. (Division of Forest Research, CSIRO)

Fig. 3.7 Two Types of Weighing Scales Used in Seed Laboratories. (DANIDA Forest Seed Centre)

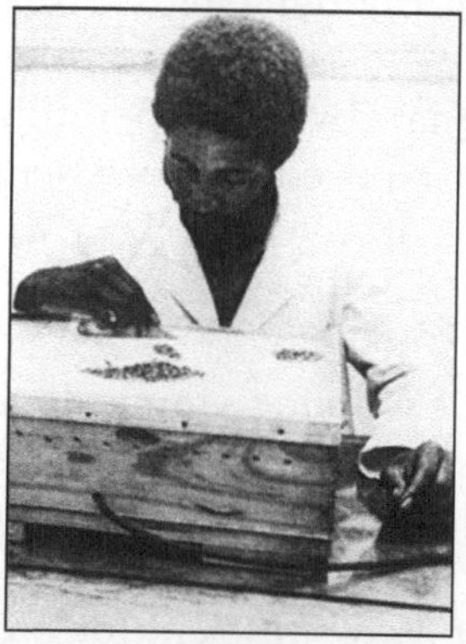

Fig. 3.8 An Opaque Glass Screen, Illuminated from Below, Used in Zimbabwe for Purity tests and Determinations of the Number of Seeds per kg. (Forestry Commission Zimbabwe)

Soil Divider. A simple divider, built on the same principle as the conical divider, is the so-called soil divider or riffle divider. The channels are here arranged in a straight row instead of a circle as in the conical divider. The soil divider consists of a hopper with attached channels or ducts, a frame to hold the hopper, two receiving pans and a pouring pan. In using the divider the seed is scattered fairly evenly in a pouring pan and poured in at approximately equal rates along the entire length of the hopper. The divider is suitable for large-seeded and chaffy species, but suitable types for small-seeded species can also be made.

Gamet Divider. The Gamet divider makes use of centrifugal force to mix and scatter the seeds over the dividing surface. The seeds flow downward from a hopper onto a shallow rubber cup below. Upon rotation of the rubber cup by an electric motor the seeds are thrown out by centrifugal force and fall downward. The circle or area where the seeds fall is equally divided into two parts by a sharp-edged, stationary baffle so that one-half of the seeds fall in one spout and the other half in the other spout. In using this divider care must be exercised in dividing very small samples as it is possible that a majority of seeds may be thrown out in one spout. Hardin *et al.* compared the effectiveness of the Boerner and Gamet dividers and concluded that if used correctly, the Gamet divider yields a slightly more accurate subsample.

Magini warns that dividers operating on the centrifugal principle should not be used for seed sensitive to damage by vibration as are those of Abies species.

Weight of Sample

The weight of the working sample depends on the seed size of the species in question. The ISTA rules are intended to provide a minimum of 2500 seeds for all except the very large-seeded species, for which a minimum of 500 seeds is prescribed. These quantities are considered sufficient for most of the usual tests (purity, authenticity, seed weight, germination or viability), but an additional 10 g of most species is needed if moisture content is to be determined. Among tropical species listed by ISTA the range of prescribed minimum size of working sample is from 2 g for Eucalyptus deglupta, which averages 4,000 viable seeds per gm of 'seed plus chaff' to 1 kg forTectona grandis which averages 2,000 fruits per kg. When seed is despatched to an independent seed laboratory for testing, ISTA recommends that the weight of the submitted sample be double that of the working sample.

PURITY ANALYSIS

Tree seed samples can contain impurities such as weed seeds, seeds of other tree species, detached seed structures, leaf particles and other material. The object of purity analysis is to determine the composition by weight of the sample being tested. To do this the sample is separated into component parts. When purity analysis is done, it is the first test to be carried out because subsequent tests are made only on the pure seed component.

Pure seed refers to the species under consideration and in addition to mature, undamaged seed includes: undersized shrivelled, immature and germinated seeds, provided they can be definitely identified as the species under consideration; and pieces resulting from breakage that are more than one-half their original size (ISTA 1976). Seeds of Leguminosae and Coniferae with the seed coats entirely removed are regarded as inert matter.

Other components of the sample may include Other seeds of all species except that under test and Inert matter. Inert matter consists of pieces of broken or damaged seeds less than half the original size, wings of coniferous species, leguminous and coniferous seeds with the seedcoat entirely removed and other matter such as fragments of leaves, twigs, stones, soil. In Coniferae (except Chamaecyparis,Cupressus and Thuja) any remaining seed wings not already removed in cleaning should be detached and classed as inert matter.

The working sample containing all the impurities is weighed and then the pure seed is removed and weighed separately. ISTA rules prescribe that weighing be done in gms to the minimum number of decimal places necessary to calculate the percentage of its component parts to one decimal place.

The percentage of pure seed is calculated as follows:

$$\text{Purity \%} = \frac{\text{Weght of 'Pure' Seed}}{\text{Total Weight of Original Sample}} \times 100$$

When a laboratory is testing a large number of samples for purity, the purity analyst usually examines and separates seed samples on a 'workboard' placed on top of a desk or table. The workboard can be adjusted to a desired height, usually 7–15 cm above table height. The analyst's equipment should permit him to do his work with a minimum of effort and time, and also with a minimum of eye strain.

Equipment required for making purity analysis is as follows: forceps and spatula for handling, separating, and pushing seeds over a surface; wide-field hand lens of 5× to 7×magnification; reading magnifiers relatively free of curvature and distortion, wide-field stereoscopic microscope with a range of magnifications from 10× to 75×; scale with capacity up to 1000 g and sensitive to 0.5 g; torsion balance with capacity of 120 g and accurate to 0.01 g; rapid-acting chemical balance accurate to 1 mg; small seed containers to hold separations; and seed blower. An assortment of small sieves can help in eliminating many impurities.

Analyses of many samples can be facilitated by removing the lightweight material with the aid of a seed blower. Seed blowers are described in Chapter.

Other methods reported by Turnbull (1975 d) as reducing hand labour are specific gravity separation by differences in density, separations by electrostatic charges, a vibrating table working on the basis of seed weight, surface texture and shape, and an X-ray radiograph technique.

The pure seed component from the purity analysis can be subsampled for the germination test, as well as for the determination of seed weight. Since the germination test is based on pure seed, it can be readily seen that the purity analysis and germination test are complementary to each other. The production potential of a seed lot can be determined only when the purity analysis and the germination tests are considered together.

SEED WEIGHT

Measurement of seed weight is made on the pure seed component separated by the purity test. Weight is normally expressed as the weight of 1000 pure seeds. This figure can be readily converted to number of pure seeds per g or per kg as required. Weight may be determined simply by counting out 1000 seeds and weighing them, but the use of several smaller samples enables the analyst to estimate variation within the sample. ISTA prescribes 8 replicates of 100 seeds each, from which the standard deviation and coefficient of variation may be calculated, as well as the mean. If the co-efficient of variation is less than 4, the mean is accepted, but, if it is more, 8 additional replicates are prescribed, a new standard deviation for the 16 replicates calculated and any replicate that diverges from the mean by more than twice the standard deviation is discarded before calculating the final mean for the sample.

The counting of seeds for weight may be done by hand or with the assistance of counting boards or vacuum or electronic counter. The following description of the essential features of seed counting devices is taken mainly from Magini.

Counting boards are useful for relatively large seeds of a regular shape, such as Pinus pinea or some leguminous species. The counter consists of two boards, a stationary top board with perforations and a thin solid board below, which serves as a false bottom.

In operating the counter, a quantity of seed is placed at the corner, the board tilted and moved so that one seed goes into each perforation. The board can then be emptied and the known number of seeds from it weighed. Alternatively, if the seeds are being counted in preparation for a germination test, the counter can be placed on the substrate and the bottom is withdrawn permitting the seed to fall through at a uniform spacing. In some types there is a second set of perforations in the bottom board. By slipping the top section about one centimetre, the seed falls through both boards onto the germination bed. In other types, the counting apparatus is perforated by holes too small to allow the seeds to pass through but suitable to allow a flow of air to suck the seeds into position.

In connection with tests on soil trays, a simple counting perforated board can also be employed. The board is first placed over the tray. The seeds are placed in the perforations and the board is lifted leaving the seeds on the tray.

Vacuum counters can be used with seeds of various sizes and shapes. For very small and irregularly shaped seeds some difficulties may occur. They are not suitable for very large seeds, such as many nuts.

A vacuum counting device has three essential parts: a vacuum system including pipes; counting heads; a quick release valve. A small house vacuum cleaner with a home-made head may be used, but special power units are generally preferable (1/4 to 1/2 hp electric motors). Perforated heads, with evenly spaced holes (generally 100) to house the seed, hold the seed by suction.

When suction is switched off, the seeds are released for weighing or onto the substrate for germination testing. Counting plates or heads are of a square, rectangular or circular form, according to the shape of the substrate employed. Espacement and diameter of holes should be proportionate to the seed size. Heads can be of plastic, chromium, brass or aluminium. The face plate should be relatively opaque and of a colour which contrasts with the seeds being counted, thus making it easier to check that all holes are properly filled.

A good valve is needed to allow a quick release of seed, as well as to avoid sucking up too large a proportion of the lightest seeds. The risk of picking up an excessive proportion of light, empty seeds in the counted sample may be reduced by inverting the head so that the holes are upwards and then pouring a large sample of seeds over it. Operation of vacuum counters with plastic heads may be adversely affected by static electricity.

In the modern types of electronic seed counters a vibrating feed bowl moves seeds past an electric eye in single file. The machine can be programmed to count a certain sample size, then cut itself off. Reservations have been expressed about the accuracy of vacuum and electronic counters on the grounds that they select a biassed sample. Manual counting boards, combined with careful random sampling, are likely to be more accurate, although considerably slower.

The 1000 pure seed weight can be converted to seeds per g or per kg as follows:

$$\text{Number of Seeds per g} = \frac{1000}{\text{Weight in g of 1000 Seeds}}$$

or,

$$\text{Number of Seeds per kg} = \frac{1000 \times 1000}{\text{Weight in g of 1000 Seeds}}$$

If the sample counted is other than 1000 seeds, the appropriate formula is:

$$\text{Number of Seeds per g} = \frac{\text{No. of Seeds in Sample}}{\text{Weight in of Sample in g}}$$

or,

$$\text{Number of Seeds per kg} = \frac{\text{No. of Seeds in Sample} \times 1000}{\text{Weight of Sample in g}}$$

Within a given species full seeds have a higher specific gravity and a higher germination rate than seeds of the same size but empty or partially filled. Large seeds weigh more per seed than small ones of the same specific gravity and, because they contain larger food reserves, they are likely to germinate better and produce initially more vigourous seedlings. Goor and Barney have reported that large seeds of Eucalyptus citriodora had a higher germination rate than medium-sized seeds which in turn had a higher rate than small seeds. Number of pure seeds per unit weight is therefore not in itself a good guide to potential for plant production and must be complemented by germination tests or indirect tests of viability. The effect of seed size on the growth of germinated seedlings of eucalypts usually persists for 8–14 weeks after sowing, thereafter other factors may become more important.

GERMINATION TESTING

Of all the quality measurements of seed lots, none is more important than the potential germination of the seeds. The main aim of a laboratory germination test is to estimate the maximum number of seeds which can germinate in optimum conditions. The use of standardized ideal conditions in the laboratory such as those prescribed by ISTA ensures that results obtained from a given seed lot in one laboratory should be identical with those obtained from any other laboratory in the same or in other countries.

A common standard for assessing germinative potential is very valuable for seed moving in international trade. On the other hand, it is clear that results obtained under ideal controlled conditions in the laboratory are not directly applicable in the field nursery, where only limited control over environmental conditions is possible. Each nurseryman should apply his own correction factor, derived from experience over the years, to convert the germination potential of a seed lot, as determined from laboratory tests, to the actual field germination he can expect under his own local conditions.

At the other extreme, a nurseryman may prefer to carry out his own germination test in his own nursery in advance of large scale sowing. The results of the test should be directly applicable to the later sowings of the same seed lot in the same nursery, but would not be applicable to other nurseries. However, there is sometimes insufficient time for germination tests in advance of the main sowing and managers of large operational nurseries may be reluctant to involve themselves in small scale research.

Between the two extremes lies the case of the small silvicultural research station which lacks the laboratory facilities to comply with ISTA prescriptions for testing, but which carries out germination tests in the nursery on bulk seed supplies before distributing them to afforestation projects throughout the country. Here again the local forester or nurseryman must apply his own correction factor to convert actual germination figures from the research nursery to expected germination figures in his large operational nursery. The following account is largely based on that of Turnbull. It is in conformity with ISTA rules, but some of the principles are equally applicable if lack of equipment or trained staff makes it necessary to use simpler methods.

Germination is defined as the emergence and development from the seed embryo of those essential structures which are indicative of the seed's capacity to produce a normal plant under favourable conditions. Germination is expressed as the percentage of pure seeds which produces normal seedlings or as the number of seeds germinating per unit weight of the sample.

In the laboratory the environmental conditions, including moisture, temperature, aeration and light, must not only be specific enough to initiate germination but also favourable for the development of the seedlings to a stage where interpretation of normal and abnormal types may be made.

With a few exceptions, all germination tests should be made with pure seeds separated by the purity test. The pure seed must be well mixed and counted at random into replicates. The seeds should then be spaced uniformly on the test substrate. Normally one test consists of 400 seeds in 4 replicates of 100 seeds each, but if 100 seeds overcrowd the test substrate, the replicates may be broken down into a larger number of smaller replicates of 50 or 25 seeds each. A general recommendation is to leave 1.5 to 5 times the normal seed width or diameter between seeds, in order to discourage the spread of fungal moulds.

The exceptions are very small-seeded species in which it is impossible (some species of Eucalyptus) or very difficult (Alnus, Betula, Populus,Salix) to separate the seeds from the accompanying inert matter or chaff. In these cases the test is made with the same number of replicates but the replicates are of equal weight rather than an equal number of seeds.

Counting of seeds for germination tests can be facilitated by the use of counting boards, as described.

GERMINATION EQUIPMENT

The kind of germinator can be selected according to the type and amount of seeds being tested and it is acceptable providing it can give good control of prescribed temperature, moisture, and light conditions.

Germinators range in size from small or portable individual units through cabinets of various sizes and large germination tables of the Jacobsen Copenhagen type, to walk-in germination rooms. The major types recommended by ISTA are as follows:

Jacobsen and Rodewald apparatus. In Europe, a germinator called the Jacobsen apparatus or Copenhagen tank is commonly used. It consists of a bath containing water, the temperature of which may be controlled by thermostats. The seeds are distributed on top of paper and placed on metal or glass strips suspended about 5–7 cm above the bath; paper or cotton wicks lie beneath the substrate and pass through slots into the water below. The moisture content of the substrate may be adjusted by altering the water level, and so increasing or decreasing the distance between the seed bed and the water.

High humidity is maintained around the seed either by covering the entire tank with a transparent lid or placing an inverted plastic funnel with a hole in the conical end over each germination pad. The apparatus may be exposed to natural daylight but artificial light is usually desirable.

One of the disadvantages of the standard Copenhagen tank is the absence of direct temperature control at the seed bed. In the tropics it tends to overheat. Improved models have been developed, such as the one by Overaa which uses hollow stainless-steel strips, through which the water for heating and cooling is circulated.

Other disadvantages are that the equipment requires a large amount of floor space for the number of tests accommodated. Also, the handling of covers and substrata appears to be more cumbersome than moving a lightweight tray with paper substrate.

The Rodewald apparatus consists of a zinc box covered with glass in which the seeds are exposed to direct or diffuse light. The bottom of the apparatus contains water over which a layer of moist sand is placed on a tray. The seed bed consists of unglazed porcelain dishes placed in the moist sand, or the dishes may be placed directly in the water. The temperature of the water is controlled thermostatically and the sand is moistened through wicks reaching into the water bath. A sand substrate is not desirable for species requiring alternating temperatures because of its slow adjustment to a change in temperature.

Germination cabinet. Another common type of apparatus is the closed chamber for germinating seeds in darkness, diffused light, or direct light. This type of germinator often consists of a double walled cabinet, suitably insulated against temperature changes by an air jacket or layer of insulating material. It is equipped with appropriate tray slides to accomodate the type of germination trays preferred by individual laboratories.

The modern germination chamber has provision for both heating and cooling. Usually, water is chilled and passed between the walls of the chamber or through cooling pipes placed along the inner walls of the chamber. Either the air or a reservoir of water in the bottom of the chamber may be heated. In such cabinets the temperature can be regulated at any desired setting between approximately 8°C and 40°C. Inexpensive germination cabinets are sometimes constructed locally. Gupta and Kumar describe the low cost germinators in use in the Seed Testing Laboratory in Dehra Dun, India. The outer wall of the cabinet is constructed of teak, the size 195 × 70 × 40 cm, and the electric controls include a thermostat, hot air blower, a separate air circulator and a time switch to control illumination. Glass wool is used for insulation between the inner and outer walls. Satisfactory performance is obtained at temperatures varying from room temperature up to 45°C (± 1°C).

A germination cabinet should meet as far as possible the following requirements:

- *Air humidity*: As high as possible but preferably never lower than 90 per cent, to prevent the seed substrate from drying up;
- *Air temperature*: Adjustable between 10°C and 35°C, the temperature all over the working section of the cabinet over a number of days to be uniform in each of the temperature regimes, within plus or minus 1°C;
- *Light*: Uniform illumination of the trays, intensity 750 to 1250 lux at the level of the seed;
- *Air movement*: As low as possible to prevent the seeds from drying up;
- *Fresh air supply*: Small, of the order of one air change per hour, which should be sufficient to remove the carbon dioxide produced by the germinating seeds;
- *Day and night cycling*: A rapid initial temperature drop to be achieved in 30 minutes during the day to night change, reaching the ultimate night temperature in one hour, a similar requirement to hold for the night to day change;
- *Condensation*: Not allowed.

However, when cabinets operate with alternating temperatures it is very difficult to maintain the high humidity and the substrates dry out; this necessitates frequent watering, which adversely affects the germination results and adds to the manhours spent on the test.

There are many modifications of the germination cabinet and for detailed descriptions of some of them. Room germinator. When large numbers of tests are made, whole rooms may be used as germinators, with temperature, humidity and light controlled.

The room germinator is a modification of the cabinet. It is constructed on the same principle as the cabinet, but is large enough to permit workers to enter it and place the tests along either side of a central passageway. Usually, fans are required to prevent stratification of temperature and special equipment is necessary to maintain a high relative humidity. Another modification is the combination room-cabinet germinator. The temperature of the entire room is kept as low as the lowest temperature required. Germination cabinets are placed in this room and heated, individually, by electricity to maintain the various temperatures required. Either constant or alternating temperatures may be obtained by this type of germinator.

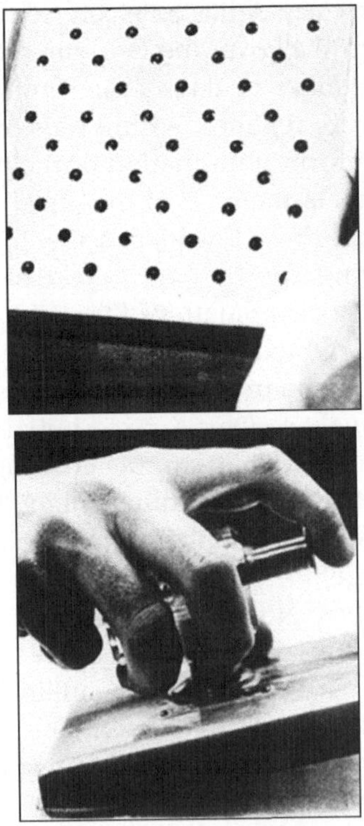

Counting board with seeds of *Celtis laevigata*. Seeds are spread on the top board to place one seed in each hole. The spring-held top board is then moved to the right until its holes line up with another set in the bottom board; the seeds then drop through. Counting head on a vacuum seed counter. A pump pulls a vacuum through the line and the hollow counting head that has 50 or 100 tiny holes on its bottom surface. When one seed per hole is attached, the vacuum can be released with the finger plunger to drop the seeds.

Fig. 3.9 Seed Germination Equipment at the Division of Forest Research, CSIRO Canberra *(A)* Open Seed Germination Cabinet *(B)* Group of Cabinets

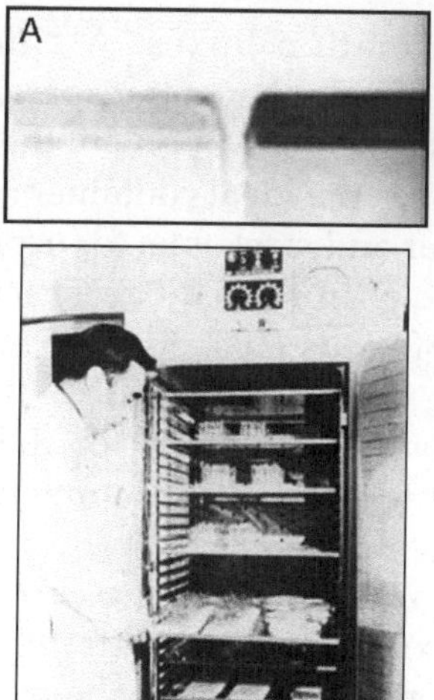

Fig. 3.10 Conviron G30 Germinator, with over 95 per cent Relative Humidity and Programmable Temperature and Photoperiod within 24 Hours, as Used at Petawawa National Forestry Institute, Canada

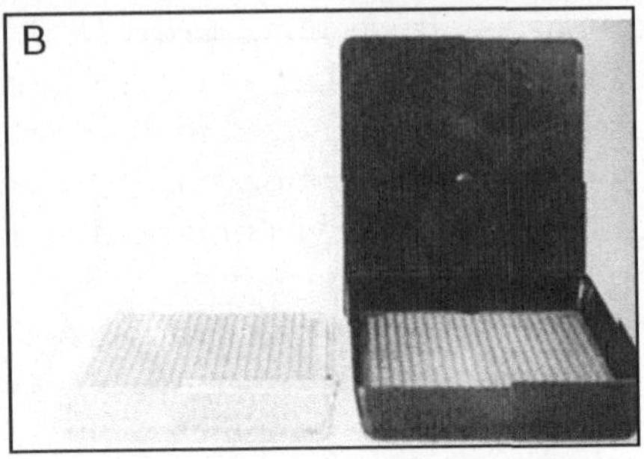

Fig. 3.11 Clear and Black Germination Boxes Developed for Seed Testing in Canada, Shown Closed (top) and Open (Bottom)

Fig. 3.12 Copenhagen Tank and Rolled Filter Paper for Germination Tests

Portable germination boxes. A simple and versatile germinator consists of a number of transparent plastic boxes with lids, which can be stacked one upon another.

Robbins describes the ideal container as being

- Rectangular and stackable, for economomy of space;
- Large enough for adequate spacing of at least one replicate of seeds (100, 50 or 25 seeds, depending on seed size);
- Sufficiently deep to allow for the required substrate depth and to permit development of the seedling for proper assessment;
- Provided with a wellfitting lid, to maintain a high moisture content of the substrate and surrounding air;
- Easy to sterilize by heat or chemical treatment;
- Transparent (at least the lid), to allow light if required for germination and subsequent development of the seedlings.

In Honduras the size of box used is 178 × 117 × 72 mm deep and each box contains one replicate of 100 pine seeds. This leaves a space of at least the width of one seed between each seed. For larger-seeded species there are fewer seeds per replicate box. Any of the common substrates described later in this chapter, *e.g.* filter paper, sand, may be used. By adding a suitable quantity of water to the substrate at the beginning of the test and then keeping the boxes covered with their lids at all times except during assessment and removal of seedlings, it is possible to maintain a high and constant moisture content in the substrate and the air inside the boxes, without the need for further additions of water or for control of humidity in the atmosphere outside the boxes. Where filter paper or blotting paper is used as the substrate, it can be kept permanently moist by placing it on a raised platform over a reservoir of water which is fed to the substrate by wicks.

This arrangement resembles, in miniature, the Jacobsen tank. The boxes may be placed inside an incubator where temperature and light can be controlled in accordance with *e.g.* ISTA recommendations or, if no incubator is available, they can be stored in ambient room conditions of temperature and light. In either case the closed boxes should provide optimum humidity conditions for the germinating seeds.

Researchers at the Petawawa National Forestry Institute in Canada have developed a germination box, moulded out of light, unbreakable and heat-resistant polycarbonate plastic, which is large enough to contain 4 replicates of 100 seeds each of pines or similarly sized seeds. The box is 28 cm long × 24 cm wide. The base is 5 cm deep and the lid 1 cm deep, but the special universal locking mechanism makes it possible to fit two bases together; alternative combined depths of 6 and 10 cm are thus available for use according to the characteristics of the species under test.

A perforated false bottom on eight legs 1 cm long supports the germination substrate and the space below can be used as a water reservoir if desired. The material is available in either clear or black plastic for germination in light or dark conditions; to ensure complete darkness it is necessary to seal the junction between base and lid with opaque tape. Four aeration holes on the side wall of the bottom component are optional in the clear plastic type.

Tests of this germination box gave results closely comparable with those from the much smaller, and thus less convenient, petri dishes. It was found that loss of moisture over a four week period was least in boxes which had the water reservoir filled at the start of the test and which had no aeration holes. Both clear and black were equally good in this respect, but growth of mould was more severe in the (sealed) black than in the clear model. A substrate of blotting paper over Kimpak (cellulose paper) lost moisture more slowly than Kimpak alone.

Selection of a germinator. Most forest seed laboratories with a moderate through-put of samples use either the cabinet-type germinators or germination tables. A report by Boeke *et al.* recommends the exclusive use of cabinettype germinators for small seed testing laboratories. The advantages of using cabinets instead of germination tables of the Copenhagen type are a saving in space and, in well constructed cabinets, the more precise control of temperature and humidity. It should be noted that a single-level Copenhagen tank requires five to eight times the floor space occupied by a cabinet of equal capacity. Where research is being carried out on germination conditions, or where testing covers a wide variety of seeds, the flexibility provided by several cabinets operating at different temperatures and/or light conditions can be very advantageous.

For nurseries or small research institutes concerned with carrying out simple tests of germination without maintaining strict control of temperature and light, the flexibility, storability and cheapness of plastic germination boxes have much to recommend them. They can also be used in combination with incubators in which light and temperature are controlled.

GERMINATION CONDITIONS

The optimum conditions for different stages of germination and seedling growth are not identical and may even vary for different seeds within the same seed lot. The aim of much seed testing research has therefore been to determine a combination of conditions which will give the most regular, rapid and complete germination for the majority of the same species.

Substrate. Soil is rarely used as a substrate for germination tests because each sample will vary greatly in physical, chemical and biological properties. While the germination results might be more comparable with field conditions, the lack of reproducibility and difficulty in comparing tests of different seed lots render it unsuitable. Artificial media are much more easily standardized.

Most laboratory tests on small seeded species are made on paper. Other materials used include sand, granulated peat moss and expanded mica.

The main requirements for the substrate are:

- Non-toxic to the germinating seedlings
- Free of fungi and other micro-organisms
- Of porous texture to enable adequate aeration and moisture for the germinating seeds.

The choice of media on which the seeds are placed for germination depends on the equipment, the species, the working conditions and the experience of the operator. It is prescribed in the ISTA Rules for a number of forest trees.

Filter paper, heavy box paper, or any other absorbent paper may be linked with a filter paper or cotton wick dipped into water, or placed on top of a layer of sand or vermiculite. Cellulose paper is becoming more commonly used as a germination medium because it is easier to handle than sand, but still permits penetration of the radicle, thus providing for better evaluation of abnormal germination. Also moisture content does not tend to become stratified within the paper medium as it does with sand.

The best paper substrates are germination blotters, paper towelling, laboratory filter paper and creped cellulose paper wadding. Any paper substrates should be checked for presence of toxic chemicals. The 1976 ISTA rules give detailed specifications for paper and towels, including weight, bursting strength, capillary rise and acidity.

Seeds without a specific light requirement may be placed on top of paper or between folded paper. Folded paper increases the surface contact area between the seeds and the moisture supply. Large seeds may be rolled in paper towels which are then placed in an upright position; this allows the roots to grow downwards and avoids tangling of the roots. Rolled or folded paper packs may be kept moist without the necessity of a wick dipping into water. Rolled seeds may be stored on glass plates above, but not in contact with, a water bath and covered by a polythene sheet. Any rolls which show signs of drying out may be sprinkled with water. Use of rolled paper is a very rapid and convenient method but may cause curling of the radicles. This is of no concern if the germinated seeds are to be discarded after testing. For operational germination of large quantities of seed, however, the slightly slower folded paper method is preferable. This is used with success as standard practice for Pinus and Eucalyptus spp. in Thailand.

Sand is not suitable for very small seeds because they are difficult to locate, but it is widely used for larger seeds. Sand can be sterilized and fungi develop on it less freely than on paper. It also provides a good contact between the seed and moisture because the seeds can be pressed into the medium. A commonsense rule is to cover the seed with a thickness of sand not less than the length of the seed on its longest axis. ISTA (1976) recommends a thickness of 1–2 cm according to seed size and prescribes that sand particle sizes should be between 0.05 and 0.8 mm and pH between 6.0 and 7.5.

Sand as a germination substrate is preferred for tree species that have a longer germinative period, for instance, Rosa spp., Pinus caribaea, P. elliottii, and P. palustris, or with larger seeds, for example, P. pinea and Quercus spp. A sand-perlite medium permits leaching of the water which can be important when testing repellent-coated seed, but may be a disadvantage when testing seeds which are sensitive to drying. Moisture and Aeration. The moisture level of the substrate has been suggested as one of the major causes of variation in seed research results. The ISTA Rules specify that a sand substrate be moistened depending on its characteristics and the size of the seed to be tested and suggest that a moisture level of 50–60 per cent of the water-holding capacity of the sand is suitable for several groups of agricultural seeds. A paper substrate must not be so wet that a film of water forms around the seed. Belcher, working with Pinus spp., concluded that most species have considerable tolerance to diverse moisture levels and the major variations in germination were due to dry conditions. He found some species to be sensitive to dry conditions and others to very wet conditions.

As a generalization, the substrate must be moist enough at all times to supply the necessary moisture, but excessive moisture will restrict aeration. All tests must be examined daily to ensure that the moisture content of the substrate is near optimum. The water should be reasonably free of impurities. Temperature control. In laboratory seed testing the important temperature is that at the level of the seed. The temperature will vary for different species and appropriate values are listed for a large number of tree species in the International Rules for Seed Testing. Table is an extract of selected species from the much more comprehensive ISTA table, with emphasis on tropical and sub-tropical species. In addition to temperature, it indicates prescribed substrates, light, counting periods and pretreatment.

Temperature is one of the most critical factors in the laboratory germination of seeds and must be regularly checked. When alternating temperatures are required the test is usually held at the low temperature for 16 hours and at the high temperature for 8 hours each day. Temperature of 20° and 30°C alternating are commonly prescribed for tree species. Although natural fluctuations between day and night temperatures are less in lowland moist tropical forests than in other forest types, alternating temperatures may still affect germination of tropical species. In one experiment of Terminalia ivorensis in Nigeria, alternating temperatures of

34° C and 24° C gave 93 per cent germination in 41 days compared with 27 per cent at a constant temperature of 30° C, both with continuous light.

Light. Light is required for germination in many tree seeds. Fluorescent light is as effective as natural daylight and is preferred in testing, because the wavelength and intensity can be standardized, within limits. Cool white fluorescent lamps are recommended because of their light quality and low heat emission: Light should be evenly distributed over the tests, with an intensity within the range 750–1250 lux. Seeds should be subjected to light for only part of the test period, 8 hours in every 24 hours is usual but a longer or shorter period may be beneficial to seeds of some species. Cotrolling fungi in germination tests. Laboratory practices that will minimize the spread of fungi include proper spacing of seeds, control of temperature, removing decayed seeds, proper aeration, and keeping the substrate only just wet enough to permit germination. Sterilization of laboratory equipment and the periodic disinfection of germination cabinets and other apparatus will assist.

As a general rule, seed is not disinfected because seeds which decay are usually of poor quality. Magini states that a number of experiments carried out with different methods of disinfecting the seed just before or during germination have shown no reliable improvement in germination percentage. A small quantity of fungicide added to the water used to moisten paper rolls has, however, been found beneficial in testing conifer seeds in Denmark. In Australia spraying of Karathane fungicide at a concentration of 0.8 g in one litre of distilled water has also proved effective when testing eucalypt seed on moist filter paper over vermiculite.

GERMINATION CONDITIONS FOR SELECTED SPECIES

Conditions prescribed by CSIRO and ISTA for germination testing of selected tropical, sub-tropical and temperate species are tabulated in Tables 3.1 and 3.2.

Table 3.1 Data on Seed Viability and Recommendations for Testing of Selected Eucalyptus

Species	Mean No. of Viable Seeds per g of Seed and Chaff	Seed Testing Recommendations				Special Recommendations 2)
		Weight of Replication (g)	Temperature (°C)1)	First Count (days)	Final Count (days)	
E. brassiana	340	0.15	25	7	14	
E. camaldulensis	670	0.10	30	5	10	Light essential
E. citriodora	110	0.50	25;30	5	14	Vermiculite only
E. cloeziana	130	0.40	25	7	28	Vermiculite only
E. deglupta	4,000	0.01	35	5	14	Vermiculite only
E. globulus subsp. globulus	75	0.70	25	5	14	
E. grandis	650	0.10	25	5	14	
E. microtheca	380	0.15	35	3	14	Light essential, Vermiculite only or stratify 3 weeks, then 20°C
E. regnans	180	0.30	15	10	21	
E. saligna	540	0.10	25	5	14	
E. tereticornis	600	0.10	25;30;35	5	14	
E. urophylla	460	0.10	(25) 3)	5	14	

Notes for table:

- Temperature recommendations separated by a semi-colon indicate that the (constant) temperatures have been found satisfactory. Alternating temperatures are not necessary.
- Unless otherwise specified, normal substrate used for testing eucalypts by Division of Forest Research, CSIRO, Canberra is moist filter paper over vermiculite in a petri dish. Where 'vermiculite only' is recommended, the filter paper should be omitted.
- A temperature shown in parenthesis *e.g.* (25) indicates that satisfactory results have been obtained with that temperature but a full range of temperatures has not been tested.

Extracted from ISTA (1976) Table. Germination Methods. Part II Tree Seeds. (incorporates amendments made by ISTA 1978) This table indicates permissible substrates, temperatures, duration and additional directions, including recommended special treatments for dormant samples. For species in section 1, the methods in columns 2–6 are prescriptive and no others may be used. Where two figures are shown under temperature, *e.g.* 20–30, this indicates daily alternation of temperatures.

The lower temperature should be maintained for 16 hours and the higher for 8 hours, in each 24 hour period. For species in section 2, other methods may be used provided that the method is indicated on the International Analysis Certificate.

The abbreviations have the following meanings:

TP - Top of paper
BP - Between paper (including rolled towels and pleated aper)
S - Sand
TS - Top of sand
L - Light essential
TT - Topographical tetrazolium test

For certain species indicated in column 7, duplicate tests (with and without prechilling) are necessary; the germination phase of these should run concurrently. The less desirable methods are placed in brackets in the Table.

Table 3.2

	Species	**Prescriptions for:**						
		Substrata	**Temperature (°C)**	**Light**	**First Count (days)**	**Final Count (days)**	**Additional Directions Including Recommendations for Breaking Dormancy**	
	1	**2**	**3**	**4**	**5**	**6**	**7**	
	Section 1 (Prescriptive)							
	Acacia spp.	TP	20–30(20)	L	7	21	(1)	Pierce seed, chio or file off fragment of testa at cotyledon end and soak 3 hrs. or
							(2)	(Soak seed 1 hr. in concentrated

							H_2SO_4, wash seed thoroughly in running water after acid treatment).
	Ailanthus altissima	TP	20–30	-	7	21	Removal of pericarp after soaking for 24 hrs. may speed up germination.
1)	Alnus spp.	TP	20–30	L	7	21	(May be tested also by using 4 weighed replicates of 0.10 to 0.25 gm each, according to species)
	Cedrela spp.	TP	20–30	L	7	28	
	Cryptomeria japonica	TP	20–30	L	7	28	
	Cupressus sempervirens	TP	20	L	7	28	
1)	Eucalyptus camaloulensis	TP	30	L	3	14	Use 4 weighed replicates of 0.10 gm each
	Liquidambar styraciflua	TP	20–30	L	7	21	Sensitive to drying in test

	Nothofagus obliqus	TP	20–30	L	7	28		No prechill and prechill 28 days at 3–5 ° C. Double tests.
	Pinus caribaea	TP	20–30	L	7	21		
	P. elliottii	TP	22;20–30	L	7	28		
	P. pinaster	TP	20	L	7	35	(1)	No prechill and prechill 28 days at 3–5 ° C. Light for no more than 16 hrs. per day. Double tests.
							(2)	(Use TT)
	P. radiata	TP	20	L	7	28		
	P. taeda	TP	22;20–30	L	7	28		
	Quercus spp.	TS(S)	20	-	7	28		Soak seed for up to 48 hrs. and cut off 1/3 at scar end of seed and remove testa.
	Robinia pseudoacacia	TP	20–30	L	7	14	(1)	Pierce seed or chip or file off fragment of testa at cotyledon end and soak 3 hrs.

							(2)	(Soak whole seed 1 hr. in concentrated H_2SO_4 for as long as necessary to pit surface of testa. Wash seed thoroughly in running water.)
	Section 2 (Not prescriotive)							
	Pinus kesiya	TP	20–30	L	7	21		
	P. merkusii	TP	20–30	L	7	21		
	P. oocarpa	TP	20–30	L	7	21		
	P. patula	TP	20(20–30)	L	7	21		
	Tectona grandis	S	30	L	14	28	Soak in water and allow to dry for 3 days - repeat this 6 times.	

EVALUATION

A seed is considered to have germinated after the emergence and development from the seed embryo of those essential structures which are indicative of the seed's capacity to produce a normal seedling under favourable conditions. Abnormal seedlings are not included in the germination count because they rarely survive to produce plants.

The ISTA Rules recognize four groups of abnormal seedlings:

- Damaged seedlings;
- Deformed seedlings;
- Decayed seedlings;
- Seedlings with unusual hypocotyl development. These groups and their characteristics are defined in detail in the ISTA Rules. In a laboratory test the majority of the normal seedlings are usually removed at the interim counts, but the assessment of many of the doubtful and abnormal seedlings must be left until the end of the test, to ensure that slower growing but otherwise normal seedlings are not incorrectly classified.

For many species the initial count is carried out one week after starting the test and assessments may be carried out at weekly intervals until the test is ended. More frequent assessment is needed if a more precise picture is needed of the speed of germination. At the end of the test period, all remaining ungerminated seeds should be cut and examined, and the number of fresh, firm and possibly viable seeds recorded. At the same time observations may be made on the condition of unsound ungerminated seeds *e.g.* an abnormally high incidence of insect-damaged or mechanically damaged seeds which would indicate the need for improvements in seed hygiene or seed processing methods. The record of the germination test commonly shows the percentage of germinated and the percentage of ungerminated but apparently sound seeds separately, *e.g.*

Germination%	=	82%
Sound ungerminated seeds	=	6%
Viability%	=	82% + 6% (= 88%)

It can be seen from the above Tables that the duration of a test commonly lasts from two to five weeks, but this does not allow any period for pretreatment to overcome dormancy. Many species require no pretreatment and some types of seedcoat dormancy can be successfully treated in a matter of hours. But the prescribed pretreatment of Tectona takes 18 days and some prescribed prechilling treatments 3–9 months. When planning a testing programme it is necessary to take account of pretreatment as well as testing time. In extreme cases it may be necessary to replace the germination test by one of the indirect tests of viability described below:

Fig. 3.13 Acorns of Quercus Alba Germinating on Kimpak in USA. Note Spacing Between Seeds. (USDA Forest Service)

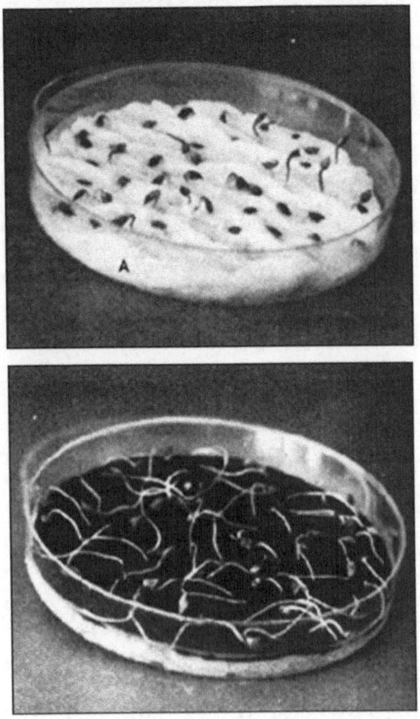

Fig. 3.14 **Germination of Douglas-fir and Lodgepole Pine Seeds On Kimpak (A left) and Blotter/Kimpak (A right) in Petridishes (A) and Canadian clear Germination boxes (B-C)**

GERMINATION ENERGY

Germination Energy has been defined in more than one way:

- The per cent, by number, of seeds in a given sample which germinate within a given period (defined as the energy period) *e.g.* in 7 or 14 days, under optimum or stated conditions or,
- The per cent, by number, of seeds in a given sample which germinate up to the time of peak germination, generally taken as the highest number of germinations in a 24 hour period.

In both the above definitions the length of the energy period is considerably shorter than the full test period prescribed by ISTA. Germinative energy is a measure of the speed of germination and hence, it is assumed, of the vigour of the seed and of the seedling which it produces. The interest in germinative energy is based on a theory that only those seeds which germinate rapidly and vigourously under the favourable conditions of the laboratory are likely to be capable of producing vigourous seedlings in field conditions, where weak or delayed germination is often fatal. Little experimental evidence has been published on this theory, but excessively delayed germinants must get eliminated automatically from the nursery, either because they are suppressed by older and more vigourous competitors or because, if transplanting has already been completed, they are not worth the trouble of a special supplementary transplanting.

Another method of comparing germination energy of different seed lots is to record 'Rate of Germination' *i.e.* the number of days required to attain 50 per cent of germination capacity. The shorter the period, the greater the germination energy. Yet another method is to evaluate the stage of development of germinated seeds and classify them into a number of development or vigour classes. For example Wang used seven classes for germinated normal seeds of Picea glauca, in addition to ungerminated and abnormally germinated seeds; they ranged from seedlings with healthy root, fully developed hypocotyl and seedcoat completely shed to seeds with seedcoat burst open but as yet no radicle emergence.

GERMINATION VALUE

The concept of Germination Value, as defined by Czabator, aims to combine in a single figure an expression of total germination at the end of the test period with an expression of germination energy or speed of germination. Total germination is expressed as (final) Mean Daily Germination (MDG), calculated as the cumulative percentage of full seed germination at the end of the test, divided by the number of days from sowing to the end of the test. Speed of germination is expressed as Peak Value, which is the maximum mean daily germination (cumulative percentage of full seed germination divided by number of days elapsed since sowing date) reached at any time during the period of the test.Germination Value (GV) can then be calculated from the formula.

$$\textbf{GV = (Final) MDG} \times \textbf{PV}$$

Germination Value, as an integrated measure of seed quality, has been used by several tropical seed workers *e.g.* for Terminalia ivorensis and for Pinus kesiya.

An alternative method of calculating Germination Value has been proposed by Djavanshir and Pourbeik, who found that it was more closely related to survival of plants in field nurseries than was Czabator's method, in the case of Pinus ponderosa and P. eldarica in Iran. The formula they proposed was:

$$GV = (\sum DGS/N) \times \frac{GP}{10}$$

where:

GV	=	Germination value
GP	=	Germination per cent at the end of the test
DGS	=	Daily germination speed, obtained by dividing the cumulative germination per cent by the number of days since sowing
ΣDGS	=	The total obtained by adding every DGS figure obtained from the daily counts
N	=	The number of daily counts, starting from the date of first germination.

The calculations required are somewhat lengthier than those of the Czabator method and, for many patterns of germination, the simpler method is likely to give sufficiently accurate comparisons between seed lots.

GERMINATION TESTING IN THE NURSERY

A good example of a suitable method for testing germination in the nursery is the procedure recommended for tropical pines in West Malaysia: "Take 400 pure seed and divide into 4 samples each of 100 seed. Take 4 wooden or plastic boxes (opaque flexible plastic sandwich boxes are very good) of dimensions 30 × 30 cm and of depth about 10 cm and fill them slightly overfull with sieved sand to the top of the sides.

Wet the sand by applying 0.5 litres of water to each box. Level the sand across the top of each box and make drills at 2.5 cm intervals and of depth 6 mm (for P. oocarpa the drills should only be 3 mm deep). Sow the seed (100) at intervals of 2.5 cm and gently press them on to the sand in the drill. Cover to a depth of 6 mm (3 mm for P. oocarpa) with sand which has been passed through a Mesh No. 12 (12/64" or 4.76 mm) but retained on a Mesh No. 8 (Size 8/64" or 3.18 mm). Lightly water with a fine mist spray. Cover with transparent polythene sheeting of 0.2 mm thickness mounted on the upper side of a square tight-fitting wooden frame of 5 cm thickness. Within 24 hours condensation of moisture will appear on the inside of the polythene cover.

If moisture disappears at any time during the ensuing 7 days then give a light mist spray and close lid once more. Germination will usually begin by the 7th day and the cover can be removed. Keep sand moist. A seed is recorded as having germinated when it has reached a height of 1 cm complete with seed coat enclosing the cotyledons. Record all germination from 7th to 28th day separately for each of the four boxes. Remove seedlings as soon as they are recorded plus any diseased ones which may not yet have reached 1 cm height as they may infect others.

On the 28th day after sowing sieve the top layer of sand in each box through a No. 12 mesh screen (mesh size 12/64" or 4.76 mm) and record the number of full seeds which have not yet germinated. (Use cut test.)"

TESTING HOMOGENEITY OF GERMINATION RESULTS

The use of 4 replicates in a germination test enables the tester to measure the degree of variation in the sample. A simple method is to calculate the range of difference in germination per cent between the highest and the lowest of the sub-samples. The range can then be compared with the table published by ISTA, reproduced here as Table 3.3 (it is applicable to replicates of equal numbers of seeds, not of equal weights). Provided that the actual range is less than the maximum in the table, the sample can be regarded as homogeneous and the average of the four replicates is accepted.

If the actual range exceeds the maximum in the table, then a new sample must be drawn and tested. Common causes of such situations are non-homogeneity of seed and, in nursery tests, fungal or insect damage in one or more of the replicates. Retesting is also necessary when an extremely high percentage of full, ungerminated seeds are left at the end of the test. In this case retesting should be done with a different pretreatment to try to overcome dormancy and improve total germination.

Table 3.3 indicates the maximum range (*i.e.* difference between highest and lowest) in germination percentage tolerable between replicates, allowing for random sampling variation only at 0.025 probability. To find the maximum tolerated range in any case calculate the average percentage, to the nearest whole number, of the four replicates: if necessary, form 100-seed replicates by combining the sub-replicates of 50 or 25 seeds which were closest together in the germinator. Locate the average in column 1 or 2 of the table and read off the maximum tolerated range opposite in column 3.

Table 3.3 Maximum Tolerated Ranges between Replicates

Average Percentage Germination		Maximum Range	Average Percentage Germination		Maximum Range
1	2	3	1	2	3
99	2	5	87 to 88	13 to 14	13
98	3	6	84 to 86	15 to 17	14
97	4	7	81 to 83	18 to 20	15
96	5	8	78 to 80	21 to 23	16
95	6	9	73 to 77	24 to 28	17
93 to 94	7 to 8	10	67 to 72	29 to 34	18
91 to 92	9 to 10	11	56 to 66	35 to 45	19
89 to 90	11 to 12	12	51 to 55	46 to 50	20

PURITY AND GERMINATION TESTS

Purity tests of most commercial seed lots of Eucalyptus are not made because it is difficult or impossible to separate the seed from the chaff of some species. Species in which seed and chaff are extremely similar in size, weight and colour include E. cloeziana, E. regnans and E. delegatensis. other small-seeded genera in which separation of pure seeds is difficult are Alnus, Betula, Populus and Salix. Even when separation is possible in these species, it is very time-consuming. In the seed laboratory in Canberra it takes only 6–7 minutes to set up a test of eucalypt seed with 4 weighed replicates, but to carry out a purity separation and set up a 4 × 100 seed test takes from 20 to 50 minutes, depending on the degree of difficulty in separating out the chaff.

The small size of seed also precludes a cutting test to determine the number of full but ungerminated seeds at the end of a test. For these reasons tests are best made on replicates by weight and results recorded as numbers of germinated seeds per unit weight of the impure mixture of seed and inert material. A squash test may also be used to give a rough estimate of viability.

Where seed is sown broadcast, the practising forester is primarily interested in the number of plants he can expect to get from a given weight of the seed lot he receives. Provided he is told that 1 kg of 'impure' seed should produce 36,000 germinated seedlings, he is not worried whether this is caused by a combination of 90 per cent purity × 80 per cent pure seed germination or 80 per cent purity × 90 per cent pure seed germination. For local tests, therefore, if seed laboratory staff is insuffient, there is no objection to omitting the purity test even on species for which it would be practicable. In the case of direct sowing into individual containers, however, there are obvious advantages in having separate figures for purity and germination, since sowing is by numbers of (one to several) seeds per container rather than weight of seed per m^2 of bed or tray.

INDIRECT TESTS OF VIABILITY

Estimating the germination potential of a seed lot by actually germinating a sample of it is often the method most relevant to practical forestry. But the tests take several weeks to complete and for some species pretreatment may take some additional weeks or months. For this reason much research has been conducted to find other methods by which seed viability can be estimated accurately but much more rapidly than by germination testing. The following account of these methods closely follows that of Turnbull.

The objects of quick viability tests are:

- To determine quickly the viability of seeds of species which normally germinate slowly or show dormancy under the normal germination methods;
- To determine the viability of samples which at the end of the germination test reveal a high percentage of fresh ungerminated or hard seeds.

Only two methods, the topographical tetrazolium test and the embryo excision test were previously accepted by the

International Seed Testing Association as official methods for some species of seeds. ISTA has recently accepted the X-ray method as a valid alternative to the cutting test for the detection of empty and insect-damaged seeds. The following tests can be applied depending on the circumstances:

CUTTING TEST

The simplest viability testing method is direct eye inspection of seeds which have been cut open with a knife or scalpel. If the endosperm is of normal colour with a well developed embryo, the seed has a good chance of germinating. This test is not very reliable. Seeds with milky, unfirm, mouldy, decayed, shrivelled or rancid-smelling embryos and abortive seeds that have no embryo can be judged as non-viable without much difficulty. But it is not possible to distinguish moribund, recently dead or recently injured seeds which still appear the same as sound ones. The cutting test, as already mentioned, is used at the end of a germination test to determine the apparent viability of ungerminated seeds; it is also a useful tool in estimating the size and maturity of the seed crop before collection and the efficiency of methods used in processing.

In the philippines good correlation has been found between cutting and germination tests in fairly large-seeded species such as Leucaena,Intsia bijuga and Lagerstroemia speciosa, but germination per cent was consistently 10–20 per cent less than the percentage of sound seeds on cutting test.

TOPOGRAPHICAL TETRAZOLIUM TEST

The tetrazolium method is only one of a number of biochemical tests which have been developed for seed testing. The various tests have been briefly reviewed by Moore (1969). The tetrazolium test was introduced in 1942 by G. Lakon in Germany.

In this method living cells are stained red by the reduction of a colourless tetrazolium salt to form a red formazan. The method emphasizes the need for a knowledge of the soundness of individual embryo parts for predicting the development of embryos into countable seedlings.

The testing procedure is described in detail in the ISTA Rules which approve the test for some species of hardwoods and conifers which germinate slowly by regular germination methods. Normal practice is to soak the seeds in water for about 20 hours, then cut or puncture the seed coat to facilitate entry of the 1 per cent aqueous solution of tetrazolium (TZ) and immerse the seeds in the dark for 48 hours. The process can be greatly speeded up by cutting through the seed at a distance of one third from the micropyle and placing it in a Vitascope vacuum machine for only half an hour. This method gives satisfactory results in Denmark but interpretation of results requires more experience in the operator than the method of seed immersion followed by excision of the stained embryo. The test is done on 4 replicates of 100 seeds each.

Justice states that, while the tetrazolium procedure is good in principle, its practical use in routine testing is limited by many problems, including: difficulty in staining of some seeds; necessity of cutting of dissecting seeds to permit observation of stained parts; poor agreement with results of germination tests in some cases, especially for seed of low germination capacity; lack of uniform interpretation of staining and difficulty in interpreting the significance of different degrees of staining; and an increase in man-hours required to test 400 seeds compared to regular germination tests.

The necessity for an experienced analyst for the successful use of this 'common sense test' is admitted by Moore. There is little doubt that the test can be useful for testing the viability of certain species, providing trained staff are available to prepare the seeds and evaluate the results.

EXCISED EMBRYO TEST

By this method, the seeds are soaked for 1–4 days and the embryos are then excised from the seeds and placed on moist filter paper or blotter discs in petri dishes. The tests are placed in the light at a constant temperature of 20°C. The condition of the embryos is examined daily. Depending upon the species and lot differences, the tests can be terminated after only a few days, up to a maximum of 14 days, or as soon as distinct differentiation into viable and non-viable embryos can be made.

The excised embryo test is similar to germination tests in that it measures the quality of the seed by their actual germination. In addition it allows some measure of the embryo dormancy to be made, by counting those seeds which, although not growing normally, have grown slightly, remained firm and have kept their colour for the test period. The test is not valid for previously germinated seeds and must not be applied to samples which contain any dry germinated seeds. The success of the test requires considerable skill and experience in the operator and the ISTA rules restrict it to only a few species.

In a comprehensive study, Schubert compared the excised embryo method with the tetrazolium method for determining the viability of dormant tree seeds. He concluded that the tetrazolium method should receive preference over the embryo excision method but that improvements in the tetrazolium test should be made by providing for the use of bactericides and stronger reducing solutions to resolve doubts in weakly stained tissues.

Radiographic Methods

Radiography was first used to determine seed quality over 70 years ago. The studies of Simak and Gustafsson highlighted the X-ray technique as a diagnostic method of tree seed analysis. The X-ray contrast method which uses various contrast or radiopaque agents was developed and applied successfully to species of Pinus and Picea.

The X-ray method permits the detection of empty seeds, mechanical damage and abnormally developed internal seed structures, measurement of the thickness of the seedcoat and assessment of the seed viability when combined with a contrast agent.

The X-ray contrast method is based on the principle of semipermeability. When seeds are treated with a contrast agent, for example aqueous $BaCl_2$ or vapourous $CHC1_3$, their living tissues are able to prevent its entry due to their semi-permeability, but the dead tissues become impregnated. The impregnated tissues absorb X-radiation more intensively than the unimpregnated ones and thus appear lighter on the film than the unimpregnated ones. The contrast permits living and dead tissue to be located in the seed and an estimation of its viability. There are now possibilities of using non-toxic water, instead of toxic $BaCl_2$ or $CHC1_3$, as a contrast agent for testing seed viability.

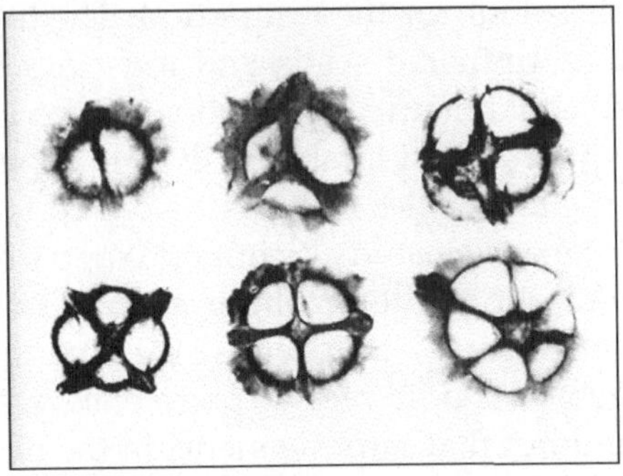

Fig. 3.15 X-ray Radiograph of Teak Fruits Showing the Variation in the Number of Locules (two to six)

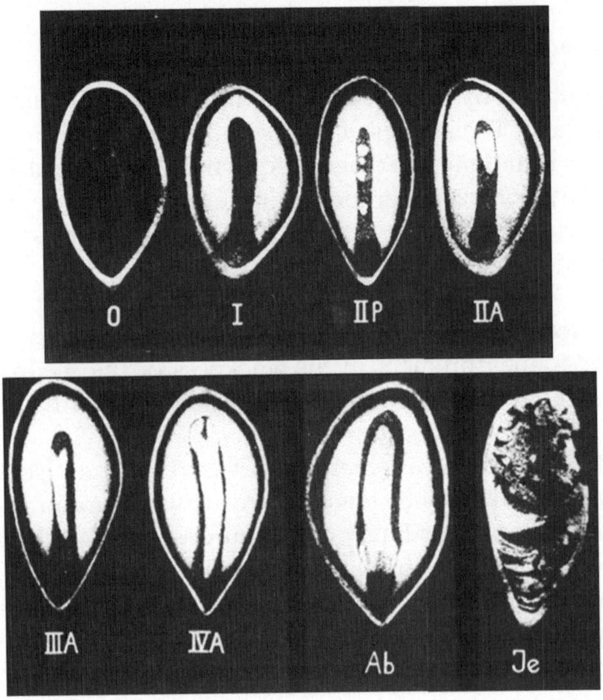

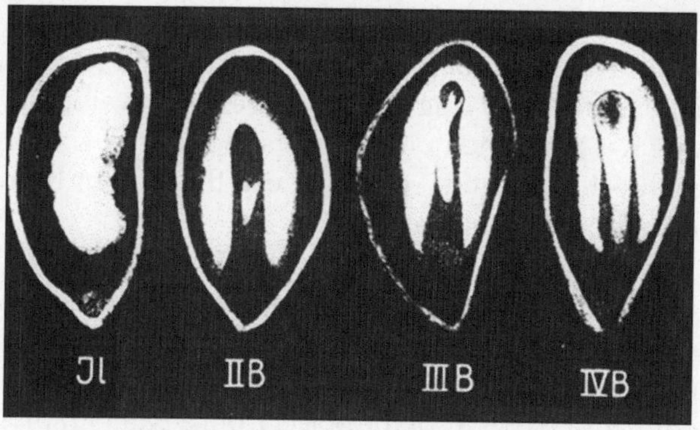

Fig. 3.16 X-ray Radiographs Showing Embryo and Endosperm Classes in Coniferous Seeds

O	Neither embryo nor endosperm (= empty seed)
I	Endosperm, embryo cavity developed but no embryo observed.
IIP	Endosperm, one or more small embryos the length of which does not exceed their breadth ('point embryos').
II	Endosperm, and one or several embryos, none of which is longer than half of the embryo cavity.
III	Endosperm, and one or more embryos, the longest of which measures between half and three quarters of the embryo cavity.
IV	Endosperm, with one fully developed embryo, completely or almost completely occupying the embryo cavity. Diminutive embryos rarely occur.
A	The endosperm almost fills the seed coat to capacity and easily absorbs the x-rays.
B	The endosperm fills the seed coat incompletely and is often shrunken or otherwise deformed. The x-ray absorption is inferior to that of class A.
Ab	Seed with abnormally developed endosperm or embryo.
J	Seeds damaged by insects, containing larvae (JI) or their excrement (Je).

The development of soft X-ray equipment has greatly simplified the operation. Complicated photographic equipment is not necessary and pictures can be made with polaroid film which provides clear and detailed radiographs within 30 seconds.

X-ray radiography has been successfully applied in determining the number of seeds in fruits of teak (Tectona grandis) and for studying their degrees of development. The technique has been tried on the fruits or seeds of sixty tropical forestry species and the results show that it can be reliably applied in processing such seeds.

A technique of stereoradiography as a supplement to the X-ray contrast method for use in seed quality testing has been developed by Kamra, Meyer and Wegelius. The chief advantage of stereoradiography is that it is possible for the observer to have a three-dimensional view of the object from a pair of radiographs. In this way, the exact topographical location of the contrast agent in the seed can be reliably determined. This increases the information which can be obtained from radiographs and adds to the analytical accuracy.

The X-ray method is a useful one and is likely to play an increasing role in seed testing. Earlier models of X-ray machines were expensive, but recent models, particularly from Japan are much cheaper and now cost less than a cabinet germinator. Improvements in photographic films and paper have speeded up the process and simplified the interpretation, so that technicians can be trained easily to produce consistent results. ISTA has accepted the method as a valid alternative to the cutting test for the detection of empty and insectdamaged seeds. It also shows considerable promise for distinguishing between viable and non-viable seeds among 'full seeds'.

For certain temperate conifers it has been possible to obtain good correlation between the Development Class (DC) of seeds, based on the development of both embryo and endosperm, and their germinability. Figure 3.16 illustrates the DCs which have been defined for conifers, and Table 3.4 illustrates the germinability corresponding to each class, for Pinus sylvestris and Picea abies. (Material: Widespread seed samples from the whole of Sweden. Germination test: Jacobsen's apparatus, temperature 23°C constant, light 1000 lux 8 hours/day).

Table 3.4 Germinability of Fresh Collected, Undamaged Seeds (in%) Belonging to Different DCs, Selected by Radiography

Species	DC							
	I A	II A	III A	IV A	II P	II B	III B	IV B
Pinus sylvestris	0	50	88	99	0	5	43	68
Picea abies	0	36	82	97	0	15	71	92

HYDROGEN PEROXIDE

Hydrogen peroxide (H_2O_2) has a stimulating effect on seed germination and has been used in a rapid test for germination of several conifers in the western USA. Seeds are soaked overnight in 1 per cent H_2O_2. The seedcoat is then cut open to expose the radicle tip and the seeds put back into 1 per cent H_2O_2 in the dark at alternating temperatures (20° and 30°C). Counting and refreshment of H_2O_2 is done after 3 or 4 days and final assessment after 7 or 8 days. Radicle growth of 5 mm or more is scored 'evident', 0–5 mm 'slight' and no growth means a nonviable or empty seed. The test is quicker but less reliable than a normal germination test (usually producing a more rapid and higher final germination), slower but simpler to perform than excised embryo and easier to interpret than TZ.

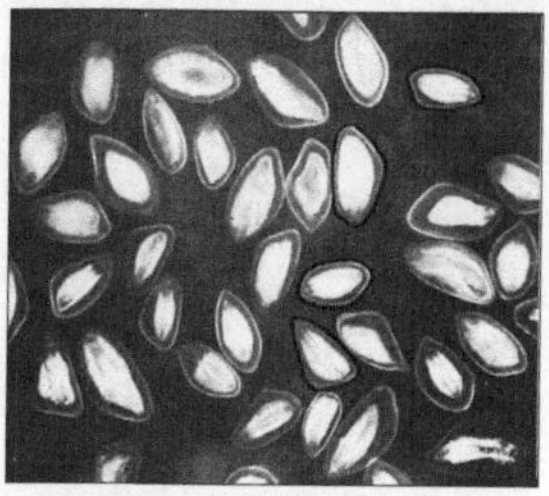

Fig. 3.17 X-ray Radiograph of Pinus Caribaea Seed. Most Seeds Have Very Poorly Developed Gametophyte and Embryo and are Dead. A Few Germinable are Indicated by the Black Outlines

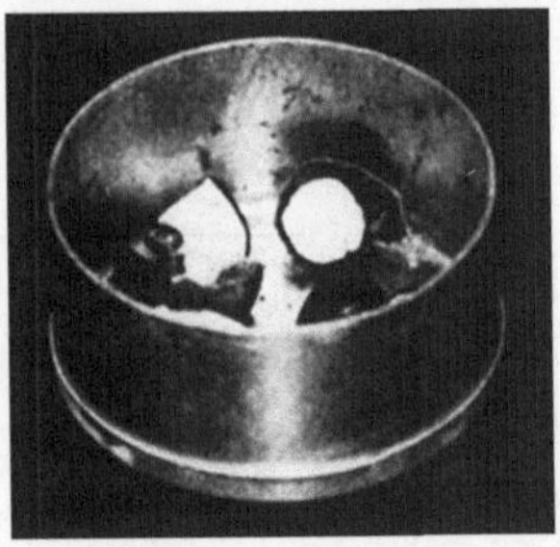

Fig. 3.18 Quercus Seeds cut in Halves for Oven Drying in Moisture Determination. (USDA Forest Service)

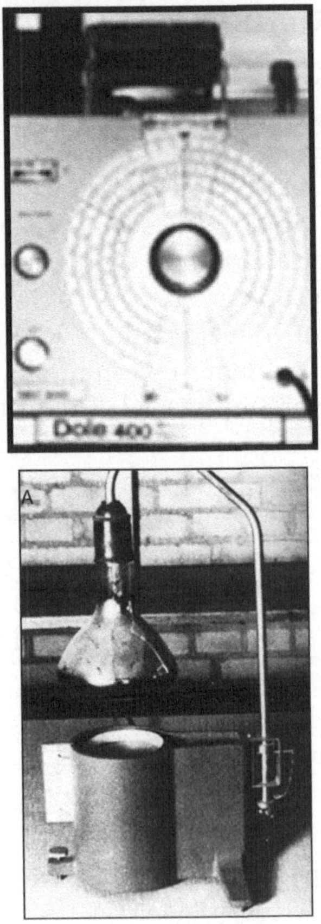

Fig. 3.19 Dole Electric Seed Moisture Meter Used in the USA. (USDA Forest Service)

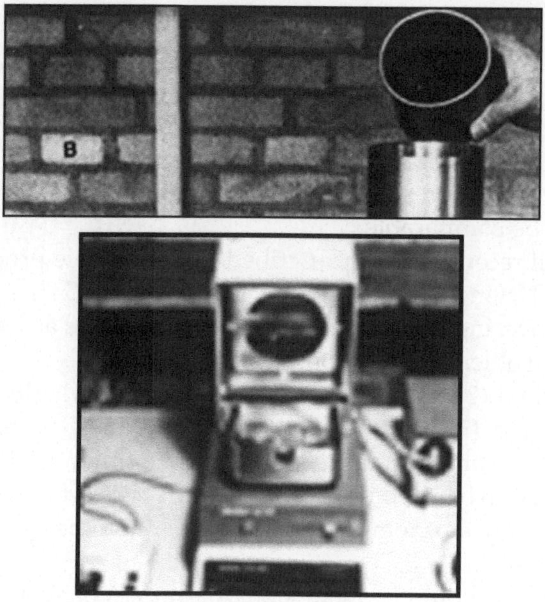

Fig. 3.20 Electric Moisture Meters Used in Denmark. *A:* Jacoby's Infrared. *B:* Super-matic. *C:* Mettler. (DANIDA Forest Seed Centre)

MOISTURE CONTENT

The importance of moisture content in affecting the longevity of seeds in storage has been stressed in Chapter. In order to control the operations of drying (or moistening) of seeds in preparation for storage and to check the stability of moisture content during storage, it is clearly essential to have reliable methods of measuring the amount of moisture in a given sample.

Methods of determining moisture content of seeds have been classified by Justice into:

- Basic methods in which the moisture is driven out of the seeds by heat and measured by the loss of weight of the original material, or the weight or volume of the condensed moisture, and
- Practical methods designed for rapid routine work and standardized against one or more of the basic methods. Probably all the moisture cannot be driven out of seeds

without driving out small amounts of other volatile constituents or causing chemical changes in the material which would result in weight changes. In applying any method, therefore, it is necessary to adhere closely to the prescribed procedure in order that the results of all tests made by that method will be comparable.

Until recently ISTA prescribed three possible procedures:

- Drying in an oven for 17 hours at 103°C
- Drying in an oven for one to four hours at 130°C and
- Toluene distillation.

Method (2) is applicable only to certain agricultural seeds and method (3), previously used for Abies, Cedrus, Fagus, Picea, Pinus and Tsuga, has now been eliminated because it had ceased to be used in practice. This leaves only method (1)- the 'Low constant temperature oven method' as applicable to forest trees.

The test should be made on two samples of about 5 g each, drawn from the working sample including impurities, not on pure seeds. Large seeds should be ground, broken or cut into small fragments to facilitate drying and a good rule of thumb is that any seeds that average over 10 mm in diameter or length should be broken. The samples should be weighed and placed in metal containers, well-spaced to facilitate air circulation, within an oven which is maintained at a temperature of 103° ± 2°C for 17 ± 1 hours. At the end of that period the seed should be placed in a desiccator to cool for 30–45 minutes and then reweighed.

The relative humidity in the laboratory where the final weighing is done should be less than 70 per cent, to avoid rapid re-absorption of moisture. The difference in MC of the two samples should not exceed a stated tolerance per cent. If it does, a further pair of samples should be tested; otherwise the mean of the two samples is the final result. The tolerance earlier prescribed by ISTA for all species was 0.2 per cent but, as pointed out by Gordon and Bonner, a single tolerance figure is not applicable to all species. At the 1983 ISTA Congress in Ottawa, the tolerances approved for moisture tests in tree seeds were agreed as follows:

Sample Condition	Tolerance per cent
Small seeds, moisture <12%, *e.g.* Picea, Alnus	0.3
Large seeds, moisture <12%, *e.g.* Carya	0.4
Small seeds, moisture >12%	0.5
Large seeds, moisture 12 to 25%	0.8
Large Seeds, moisture > 25%, *e.g.* Quercus	2.5

For tropical tree seed laboratories wishing to conform to ISTA rules, this relaxation of tolerances will be a considerable help.

The calculation of moisture content should be made on a wet weight or fresh weight basis.

$$\text{Moisture Content \%} = \frac{\text{Original Weight} - \text{Oven Weight}}{\text{Original Weight}} \times 100$$

Although wet weight basis is prescribed by ISTA and is becoming increasingly the standard form for expressing moisture content, it is not yet universal. To avoid any doubt, the method of calculating moisture content should be stated explicitly on any certificate or statement of results.

As explained by Gordon and Rowe, provided that the initial fresh weight of a seed lot is measured and the initial moisture content (wet weight basis) calculated by oven-drying a sample, any new MC reached as a result of drying (or wetting) can be calculated directly from the new weight of the seed lot; there is no need for further oven-drying of samples at the new MC. The desired weight of the seed lot to be achieved through drying (or wetting) can be calculated by multiplying its initial weight by the initial dry matter percentage and dividing by the desired dry matter percentage.

e.g.	(1)	If initial wet weight of a seed lot = 50 kg and the MC (wet weight basis), determined by oven-drying a sample, is 25%, the oven-dry weight = 75% of wet weight = 37.5 kg.
	(2)	If a period of drying reduces the wet weight to 46.5 kg, the new MC [illegible]
	(3)	If it is desired to reduce the MC (wet weight basis) to 10%, then desired oven-dry weight will be 90% of new wet weight and the seed lot must be further dried until its wet weight [illegible]

Electric moisture meters give rapid estimates of seed moisture but they are not considered accurate enough for official seed testing. Their rapid operation does make them very useful in certain situations, for example they should be accurate enough to check tree seed moisture as a guide to drying seeds for storage. Meter readings are converted to seed moisture content by means of charts supplied by the manufacturer or developed from calibration curves in the laboratory for the species in question. Most meters will not measure moisture above 15–20 per cent and require a minimum of 90–100 g of seeds for a test. A locally made, cheap and portable electric moisture meter has been used successfully in Thailand for several years to measure the MC of rice grains and could be used for tree seed of similar size. It measures electric capacitance and uses a 9-volt battery as the source of power.

Electric moisture meters are well suited to small seeds, but cannot be used for large seeds such as Juglans or Quercus; winged seeds such as Fraxinus are also difficult to measure. Large or winged seeds can be rapidly dried in a microwave oven. If the oven is preheated, drying can be completed in 5 minutes and weighing in 6 minutes immediately afterwards if in an electronic balance, or after 30–45 minutes' cooling in a desiccator if weighing is done in an ordinary balance.

Results can be expected to be within 7 per cent at a probability of 0.05 in the case of large seeds of high MC such as Quercus, and within 2 per cent in Fraxinus and Carya, as compared with the more accurate results of the slower conventional methods.

A simple and cheap method of drying seeds quickly is to use an infra-red lamp. A weighed sample is subjected to heat from an infra-red lamp with such an intensity that it loses all its moisture, without being burnt, in about 20 minutes. When the loss of weight ceases, the new weight is measured and the percentage loss calculated. An up-to-date account of the measurement of tree seed moisture content has been published recently.

SAMPLING TESTS

Other qualitative tests or observations may be made as the

need arises, but do not call for detailed prescriptions. In many cases they can be combined with the purity test. They include:

AUTHENTICITY

There are several methods of determining whether the seeds are of the species stated.

They are:

- Positive identification of the parent trees and their certification preferably on the basis of herbarium samples.
- Identification of the seeds by use of an analytical key or by comparison with a reference collection.
- Identification of the seedling. This may be the only way of determining if the seedlot is contaminated by hybrids or a mixture of two or more species with similar seed characteristics. A key and reference collection of seedlings will assist in identification.

Authenticating seeds as to provenance is not possible for most species, but some progress has been made in this field for Pseudotsuga andAbies and the use of isoenzyme techniques may open new possibilities.

DAMAGE, HEALTH

During the purity test, the operator should be alert to the incidence of mechanical damage and pathogenic infestation, which may indicate the need to improve the methods of transport or processing in use.

CALCULATION OF RESULTS

The following examples indicate the type of calculations required in the various stages of seed testing.

Purity

Weight of Full Working Sample		62.52 g
Weight of Pure Seed		56.89 g
[illegible]	=	91 %

Seed Weight

The weight of 1000 seeds may be calculated as follows:
Either

- Seed weight determination carried out on 8 × 100 seeds from the pure seed component of the purity test.

Replicate No.	1	2	3	4	5	6	7	8	Total	Mean
Weight (g)	3.81	3.69	3.75	3.79	3.82	3.72	3.71	3.79	30.08	3.76

$$\sqrt{\frac{n(\sum X^2)-(\sum X)^2}{n(n-1)}}$$

$$=\sqrt{\frac{8(113.118)-904.806}{8\times 7}}=0.0496$$

$$\text{Coefficient of Variation} = \frac{0.0496}{3.76}\times 100 = 1.32$$

Since this is considerably less than the maximum of 4.0 prescribed by ISTA, the sample is judged to be homogeneous and no further sampling is needed.

Weight of 1000 seeds = 3.76 × 10 = 37.6 g

Or

- Seed weight determination carried out on 1000 seeds from the pure seed component of the purity test, without replication.

Weight of 1000 seeds = 37.6 g

The number of seeds per unit weight may be derived as follows:

$$\text{Number of seeds per g of Pure Seed} = \frac{1000}{37.6} = 26.6$$

$$\text{Number of seeds per g of Pure Seed} = \frac{1000\times 1000}{37.6} = 26,600$$

Germination

Test made on 4 × 100 seed replicates from the pure seed component of the purity test.

Replicate No.	1	2	3	4	Total	Mean
No. Germinated on completion of test	79	85	76	88	328	82
Sound seeds on cutting test	4	3	6	3	16	4

The range in number of germinated seeds from the largest to smallest of the replicates is 88-76 = 12. Reference to Table shows that the maximum tolerated range for a mean germination of 82 per cent is 15. Since the actual range is less, the sample is accepted as homogeneous.

Germination%	=	82%
Viability%	=	82 + 4 = 86%

Viable seeds per unit weight. A combination of the Viability per cent and weight of pure seed will give a figure for the number of viable seeds expected per unit weight of pure seed, while use of the germination per cent will indicate the number of germinable seeds. Incorporation of a factor for purity per cent will express the numbers in terms of the number of viable or germinable seeds per unit weight of 'impure' seed.

	Pure Seed	
	Per g	**Per kg**
No. of viable seeds	26.6 × 86 ÷ 100 = 22.9	22,900
No. of germinable seeds	26.6 × 82 ÷ 100 = 21.8	21,800
	Impure Seed	
	Per g	**Per kg**
No. of viable seeds	22.9 × 91 ÷ 100 = 20.8	20,800
No. of germinable seeds	21.8 × 91 ÷ 100 = 19.8	19,800

In the case of very small-seeded species for which the purity test is impracticable, the number of germinated seeds per unit weight of impure seed is determined directly by test. Figures for numbers of pure seeds per unit weight are not obtainable for this type of seed. Although usually expressed as 'viable seeds per g', it should be noted that a cutting test is also impracticable for these small seeds, so strictly speaking the figures refer to germinable seeds. As an example:

Weight of replicate of impure seed (E. grandis) 0.10 g

Replicate No.	1	2	3	4	Total	Mean
No. germinated on completion of test	65	73	63	71	272	68

No. of germinable ('viable') seeds per g = 680
No. of germinable ('viable') seeds per kg = 680,000

Germination energy. Calculation of germination energy and energy period depends on the criterion used to define this. Table gives an actual example extracted from paul. As mentioned above, the energy period may be arbitrarily defined in advance but is normally much less than the full period of the test. A single assessment is sufficient in this case. If, in the present example, the energy period had been defined as 12 days, then,

$$\text{Germination Energy} = \frac{29+31+44+36+23}{400} \times 100 = 41\%$$

Energy period = 12 days

If, on the other hand, the energy period is taken as that up to the day of peak germination, then daily assessment is necessary as shown in the table and,

$$\text{Germination Energy} = \frac{29+31+44}{400} \times 100 = 26\%$$

Energy period = 10 days

Table 3.5 Germination Test Sheet (Extracted from Paul 1972)

Days after Sowing	Sub-Samples (4 × 100 Seeds)				Daily Total	Cumulative Total	Cumulative Total as % of Total Seeds	Mean Daily Germination %.	Daily Total as % of Germinable Seeds.	Cumulative Total as % of Germinable Seeds
	A	B	C	D						
1	–	–	–	–	–	–	–	–	–	–
2	–	–	–	–	–	–	–	–	–	–
3	–	–	–	–	–	–	–	–	–	–
4	–	–	–	–	–	–	–	–	–	–
5	–	–	–	–	–	–	–	–	–	–
6	–	–	–	–	–	–	–	–	–	–
7	–	–	–	–	–	–	–	–	–	–
8	6	8	7	8	29	29	7.25	0.91	12	11
9	5	9	9	8	31	60	15.00	1.67	12	23
10	10	11	13	10	44	104	26.00	2.60	17	40

11	9	8	10	9	36	140	35.00	3.18	14	54
12	6	5	7	5	23	163	40.75	3.40	9	63
13	3	5	6	4	18	181	45.25	3.48	7	71
14	5	3	2	3	13	194	48.50	3.46	5	75
15	4	2	1	3	10	204	51.00	3.40	4	79
16	2	4	2	4	12	216	54.00	3.38	5	84
17	2	1	1	1	5	221	55.25	3.25	2	86
18	1	2	2	3	8	229	57.25	3.18	3	89
19	2	–	–	1	3	232	58.00	3.05	1	90
20	2	1	2	–	5	237	59.25	2.96	2	92
21	–	1	1	–	2	239	59.75	2.85	1	93
22	2	1	2	-	5	244	61.00	2.77	2	95
23	2	–	1	1	4	248	62.00	2.70	2	97
24	–	1	1	1	3	251	62.75	2.61	1	98
25	1	2	–	–	3	254	63.50	2.54	1	99
26	–	–	–	–	–	254	63.50	2.44	–	99
27	–	–	–	–	–	254	63.50	2.35	–	99
28	1	–	1	–	2	256	64.00	2.29	1	·100
Totals	**63**	**64**	**68**	**61**	**256**				**100**	
Cut test	5	2	4	5	16					

$$\text{Mean Germination \%} = \frac{63+64+68+61}{400} \times 100 = 64\%$$

$$\text{Viability \%} = \frac{256+16}{400} \times 1000 = 68\%$$

Inspection of the pattern of germination suggests that rejection of all seeds germinating after peak germination would result in the rejection of an excessive proportion (60 per cent) of the potentially germinable seeds, while acceptance of all germinable seeds would unduly prolong the period of test and probably result in the inclusion of some seedlings of very poor vigour. A sensible rule of thumb applicable to the type of germination pattern in this example would be to define the energy period as lasting until daily germination falls to less than 25 per cent of peak. With this definition,

$$\text{Germination Energy} = \frac{29+31+44+36+23+18+13+10+12}{400} \times 100 = 54\%$$

Energy period = 16 days.

Percentage of total germinable seeds which germinate within the energy period = 84%.

Another commonsense measure of germination energy, used in Zimbabwe, is the percentage of germination when mean daily germination (cumulative germination divided by time elapsed since sowing date) reaches its peak. In the present example (Table) the peak of mean daily germination per cent is 3.48 per cent, the energy period 13 days and the germination per cent is,

$$\frac{29+31+44+36+23+18}{400} \times 100 = \frac{181 \times 100}{400} = 45.25\%$$

Percentage of total germinable seeds which germinate within the energy period measured in this way $= \frac{181}{256} \times 100 = 71\%$

Germination Value. Calculation of germination value, by the methods of Czabator and Djavanshir and Pourbeik, is shown in Table, using the data from Table.

(Methods of (1) Czabator and (2) Djavanshir and Pourbeik)

(1) Czabator method

Germination value = Final DSG × Peak Value DGS = 2.29 × 3.48 = 7.97.

(2) Djavanshir and Pourbeik method

Germination value = (Final ΣDGS (N) × (Final Cumulative Germination%/10) = 2.78 × 6.4 = 17.79.

Table 3.6 Calculation of Germination Value

Days since sowing	Daily Germination Percent	Cumulative Germination Percent	Daily Germination Speed (or Mean Germination) (Col. 3 ÷ Col. 1)	Σ DGS	Number of Counts	Σ DGS/N (Col.5 ÷ Col.6)
1	2	3	4	5	6	7
8	7.25	7.25	0.91	0.91	1	0.91
9	7.75	15.00	1.67	2.58	2	1.29
10	11.00	26.00	2.60	5.18	3	1.73
11	9.00	35.00	3.18	8.36	4	2.09
12	5.75	40.75	3.40	11.76	5	2.35
13	4.50	45.25	3.48	15.24	6	2.54
14	3.25	48.50	3.46	18.70	7	2.67
15	2.50	51.00	3.40	22.10	8	2.76
16	3.00	54.00	3.38	25.48	9	2.83
17	1.25	55.25	3.25	28.73	10	2.87
18	2.00	57.25	3.18	31.91	11	2.90
19	0.75	58.00	3.05	34.96	12	2.91
20	1.25	59.25	2.96	37.92	13	2.92
21	0.50	59.75	2.85	40.77	14	2.91
22	1.25	61.00	2.77	43.54	15	2.90
23	1.00	62.00	2.70	46.24	16	2.89
24	0.75	62.75	2.61	48.85	17	2.87
25	0.75	63.50	2.54	51.39	18	2.86
26	0.00	63.50	2.44	53.83	19	2.83
27	0.00	63.50	2.35	56.18	20	2.81
28	0.50	64.00	2.29	58.47	21	2.78

Indirect Tests of Viability

Similar methods should be used as for germination tests *i.e.* 4 replicates should be used, the results tested for homogeneity and the mean number of apparently sound full seeds (cutting test) or stained embryos (tetrazolium test) expressed as a percentage of the total pure seeds tested.

Moisture Content (Example of Small Seeds <12% MC)

	Original weight	Oven-dry weight	Difference = moisture content	% MC (wet wt. basis)
	(g)	(g)	(g)	
Sample 1	5.65	5.14	0.51	
Sample 2	4.92	4.47	0.45	

Difference between samples (0.12 per cent) is less than the 0.3 per cent prescribed by ISTA, so no further sampling is needed.

RESULTS

It is important that results of tests should lead to decisions and action. For example an abnormally low purity per cent may indicate a further cleaning operation for an organization which collects, processes and stores its own seed; or it may lead to a contested account if the seed was bought and the purity is less than that specified by the seller. Determination of moisture content is necessary before deciding whether a seed lot is suitable for immediate storage or should be subjected to further drying.

Most important of all are the various measures of germination potential and of the numbers of plants which can be produced from a unit weight of seed. This affects both nursery management and the achievement of afforestation targets, because it enables the somewhat crude estimates of average requirements shown in Table to be refined in the light of more precise data on the actual seed lots being used in a given year.

The results of the seed tests approved by ISTA make no forecast of survival and mortality after the stage of germination. Germination energy is the only measure which attempts to do this but it is entirely dependent on the subjective choice of an appropriate criterion by which to define the Energy Period. Extrapolation of seed testing results to nursery management is, strictly, outside the scope of this manual, but it is worth brief discussion here because it is of vital importance to treat seed management as part of a continuous chain of operations including plant production, plantation establishment and plantation management, and not as an end in itself.

The factors which the nurseryman needs to consider in converting seed testing results to nursery production include the following:

- Field germination in an operational nursery will often differ from test germination. It may be considerably lower than that in the ideal conditions of a laboratory test and somewhat lower than that in a research nursery. It should differ very little from a test carried out in the same nursery in advance of the main sowings. Observations on the differences between laboratory and nursery germination in trials in the Sudan have been reported by Wunder. Differences varied with species and in some cases speed of germination was affected more than the final numbers germinated.

Species	**Laboratory germination % in days**		**Nursery germination % in days**		**Pretreatment**
Acacia albida	76	60	70	60	
Cedrela odorata	100	3	85	18	
Prosopis chilensis	100	15	79	38	2 minutes in conc. H_2SO_4
Acacia raddiana	100	3	30	4	60 minutes in conc. H_2SO_4

- Variation between nurseries may be associated with a number of different climatic, soil or cultural factors. As an example Roney and Brown found that germination of Pinus ponderosa was 38 per cent better if the seeds were covered with a depth of 1.5 cm of grit than if covered with a depth of 0.4 cm. Frequency of watering also has a significant effect on germination.

- Some losses may occur in the seed beds.
- Some losses may occur during pricking out or transplanting.
- Some losses may occur in the transplant beds.
- Some of the least vigourous surviving plants may be culled at planting time.

All of these factors together combine to make the number of plantable plants raised per unit weight of seed much less than the number of germinated seeds indicated by testing. The nurseryman must make an equivalent increase in the quantity of seed sown. The term 'plant per cent' or 'tree per cent' is frequently used to combine these factors. It is defined by Ford-Robertson as 'The per cent, by number, of seeds in a given sample that develop into seedlings at the end of a given period, generally the end of the first growing season'. Bonner specifies 'plantable seedlings' and this is commonly understood, since it adds the important concepts of usefulness and vigour to mere survival.

For practical purposes it is preferable to broaden the usage to cover the whole period in the nursery *i.e.* 'the per cent, by number, of seeds that develop into plantable plants (transplants or seedlings) at the end of a given period, generally the end of the nursery period at the time of field planting". This is much more appropriate for tropical conditions where many species are pricked out within a week of germination and spend a further 6–12 months in transplant beds.

In practice, the record of plant yields obtained in past years from any given nursery provides the most useful basis for estimating future production from that locality. Records based on production on other soil types or in other climatic conditions are very little help.

Where experience is lacking, as in the early years of new nurseries, only rough 'guesstimates' are possible. In Zambia a reduction factor of 20 per cent was allowed for the difference between laboratory and field germination in both pines and eucalypts, *i.e.* if laboratory tests indicated that 1 kg of seed produced 100,000 germinated seedlings, it was assumed that only 80,000 germinated seedlings would be obtained in the nursery; a further reduction factor of 10 per cent was made for pricking-out losses in pines and 15 per cent in eucalypts.

Some additional, but unspecified, allowance would be needed for later culling. Paul proposed a 20 per cent allowance for seedbed losses plus 15 per cent for pricking-out and transplant losses and culls. The nursery recovery factor, which converts test germination per cent to plantable plant per cent, varies considerably with species, seed lot and year. In Zimbabwe a nursery recovery factor of 70 per cent has been provisionally adopted for pines and of 25 per cent for eucalypts, equivalent to 30 per cent and 75 per cent nursery losses respectively have shown that, in Pinus kesiya, the lower the germination per cent the greater the gap between the proportion of seeds which germinate and those which grow into plantable plants.

	Seed Lot 1	Seed Lot 2
Number of pure seeds per liter	30,000	30,000
Purity %	95	95
Germination %	90	60
Plant %	60	30
Nursery recovery factor %	[illegible]	[illegible]
Number of plantable plants/ liter of seed	30,000 × 0.95 × 0.60 = 17,100	30,000 × 0.95 × 0.30 = 8,550

For Pinus patula Wormald reports that a survey of a number of countries raising the species in large quantities indicated a plant per cent of about 33 per cent compared with an average of 80 per cent for germination tests, a recovery factor of about 45 per cent. He remarks that 'From these figures it would appear that one usable plant is obtained for about every 3 seed that are sown. This compares well with the British Forestry Commission who have, over the last 15 years, improved their seedling recovery from one in ten to one in four".

It confirms the statement in Goor and Barney that "Actually, in nursery and direct seeding practice, this amount (quantity of seed needed based on germination tests) would be doubled or tripled to compensate for seedling losses in the first few years". The nursery recovery factor must be based on personal experience but, because of vagaries in weather, seed lots etc., it can never be very precise. Because of this there is a limit to the precision to be demanded from routine (as opposed to research) testing in the laboratory.

Using the example shown on, plant per cent may be calculated as follows:

	Nursery Recovery Factor	**Germination %**	**Plant %**	**Germinable Seeds per kg**	**Plantable Plants per kg**
Nursery 1 Many years' experience in raising the species	0.65	82	53	19,800	12,900
Nursery 2 New, on difficult site, without experience in raising the species	0.33	82	27	19,800	6,500

On the assumption that both nurseries were required to raise 500,000 plants, nursery 1 would need,

$$\frac{500,000}{12,900} = 38.76, \text{ Say 39 KG of Seed}$$

while nursery 2 would need,

$$\frac{500,000}{6,500} = 76.92, \text{ Say 77 KG of Seed}$$

If seeds are to be sown into seed beds for later transplanting (rather than direct into pots) in addition to calculating the total amount of seed to be sown, the nurseryman will need to calculate the weight of seed to be sown per seed bed. For example if,

Size of one seed bed = 10 × 1 m	**= 10 m²**
Desired final stocking of seedlings Number of seeds/kg of pure seed Purity per cent Germination per cent Expected seedbed recovery rate (Seedlings which survive until transplanting as a proportion of germinated seeds reported by test)	= 2400/m² = 26,600 = 91% or 0.91 = 82% or 0.82 =0.65

then the required sowing rate,

$$= \frac{10 \times 2400}{26,600 \times 0.91 \times 0.82 \times 0.65} = \frac{24,000}{12,900} = 1.86 \text{ Kg Per Bed}$$

In the case of nursery 2 above, the number of seedbeds needed,

$$\text{Would Be } \frac{77}{1.86} = 41.4 \text{ Beds}$$

The concept of 'effective kilogram' of seed, which is in use now in several countries, has been found useful in planning sowing programmes and in calculating seed prices. The 'effective kilogram' is defined as the weight of seed of any particular seed lot which can be expected to produce the same number of viable seeds (as used in UK) or of plantable plants (as used in Zimbabwe) as would be produced by one kilogram of standard seed; this number is determined for each species from the average of previous experience. In Zimbabwe separate standard seedling recoveries have been established for *(a)* Orchard seed *(b)* Select and ordinary seed *e.g.* for Pinus elliottii the standard seedling recovery (= plantable plants per kg of seeds) is 15,500 for orchard seed and 14,500 for select or ordinary seed.

The Kilogram Effective Factor (KEF) is the ratio of standard seedling recovery to actual seedling recovery of a given seed lot. It can be calculated from the equation:

$$\text{KEF} = \frac{\text{Stabdard Seedling Recovery}}{\left(\frac{\text{No. of Pure}}{\text{Seeds/kg}} \times \frac{\text{Purity}}{\text{Factor}} \times \frac{\text{Germination}}{\text{Factor}}\right) \text{of Given seed lot} \times \frac{\text{Nursery Recovery}}{\text{Factor}}}$$

Using the previous example (26,600 pure seeds/kg, purity factor 91 per cent or 0.91, germination factor 82 per cent or 0.82 and nursery recovery factor 65 per cent or 0.65) and assuming a standard seedling recovery of 15,000/kg,

$$\text{KEF} = \frac{15,000}{26,000 \times 0.91 \times 0.82 \times 0.65} = \frac{15,000}{12,900} = 1.16$$

The KEF can then be used, in conjunction with standard seedling recovery, to calculate the weight of seed required to raise any given number of plants. The equation is:

$$\text{Seed Weight Needed} = \frac{\text{KEF} \times \text{No. of Plants to be Raised}}{\text{Standard Seedling Recovery}}$$

For example, to raise 1.5 million plants from the above seed lot,

$$\text{Seed Weight Needed} = \frac{1.16 \times 1,500,000}{15,000} = 116\,\text{kg}$$

The 116 kg actual seed weight is equivalent to 100 effective kilograms or 100 kg of standard seed. Only when KEF = 1.0 are actual and effective seed weights identical.

In the case of eucalypts and other small-seeded species in which purity analysis is not done, the KEF equation is modified as follows:

$$\text{KEF} = \frac{\text{Standard Seeding Recovery}}{\text{No. of Germinable Seeds / kg of Given Seed} \times \text{Nursery Recovery Factor}}$$

For E. grandis, the KEF of a particular seed lot might be,

$$\text{KEF} = \frac{150,000}{680,000 \times 0.25} = 0.88$$

and the quantity of seed needed to raise 1.5 million seedlings would be:

$$\frac{0.88 \times 1,500,000}{150,000} = 8.8\,\text{kg}$$

RETESTING

The main testing of a seed lot is done after processing and before storage or immediate despatch to nurseries. If a seed lot remains in storage for any length of time, it is essential to retest the germination or viability before use in case there has been any deterioration with time. Many seed centres retest annually, setting aside a representative sample of the whole seed lot in a small container in advance, so as to avoid recurrent opening of the bulk seed containers. Purity per cent does not need retesting and moisture content should be retested only if there is reason to believe that leaks have developed in sealed containers.

Special measures have been suggested for recurrent testing of agricultural seed in storage for long-term genetic conservation. The authors suggest that, in view of the high value of the stored germ plasm and the need to avoid unnecessary wastage of it in testing, a sequential sampling system may be more economic of material than the standard ISTA method of 4 ×100 replicates. The objective is to detect loss of viability in the early stages of ageing, *i.e.* as soon as it falls to below 80–90 per cent of the initial rate and to initiate rejuvenation by growing out the seed to produce a new generation.

The proposed method would be equally suitable for conservation of forest genetic resources although, because of the much longer generation cycle in trees, conservation as growing plants will be more important than in agricultural crops, as compared with conservation as seed.

SPECIAL CONSIDERATIONS FOR RECALCITRANT SEEDS OF TROPICAL RAINFORESTS

Many of the tests prescribed in this chapter depend for their usefulness on the ability to keep the bulk of the seed alive during the period while the sample is being tested. Seeds of most species in tropical rainforests are recalcitrant and lose viability at such a rapid rate that any certificate of quality is already obsolete at the time it is issued. In normal practice all recalcitrant seeds are sown in a nursery as soon as possible after collection.

For purposes of documentation, a germination record is usually maintained, based on a random sample of the seeds being sown. This sample (conveniently 50–100 seeds) is sown separately from the rest, in an enclosure protected by wire mesh, to keep out birds, rats and other pests. The medium (usually soil) should be the same as that used in germinating the bulk of the seeds. Germination should be monitored daily until no more seedlings emerge and the investigator is satisfied that all ungerminated seeds are decayed.

For most rainforest seeds, the end point is reached within a few weeks, nevertheless there may be a significant number of surprises. In view of the paucity of knowledge of rainforest seeds, it is desirable to record the progress of germination from beginning to end, regardless of time. Any arbitrary cut-off point *e.g.* 21 or 28 days, is too restrictive in this present exploratory phase of rainforest seed investigation.

4

Seed Pretreatment

INTRODUCTION

Seeds of many tree species germinate readily when subjected to favourable conditions of moisture and temperature. As mentioned in Chapter, many other species possess some degree of seed dormancy. Where dormancy is strong, some form of seed pretreatment is essential in artificial regeneration, in order to obtain a reasonably high germination rate in a short time. In experiments with Robinia, the best treatment gave a ten-fold increase in germination after 10 days compared with the control. In other cases the main difference may be in the speed of germination rather than the final total, *e.g.* in Pinus taeda and P. elliottii. Where dormancy is slight, the effect of pretreatment may be marginal. The benefits from pretreatment (savings in seed and seed-bed space, predictable and concentrated period of transplanting, more uniform nursery stock) need to be weighed against the cost and trouble of treating. The decision whether or not to pretreat the seed will vary not only in accordance with the species but also with provenance, seed year, local nursery conditions and length and conditions of storage.

Pretreatment to terminate dormancy and speed up germination is thus one important type of pretreatment. Another comprises various forms of seed dressing, pelleting or coating, designed to give the seed protection against pests, diseases or adverse conditions, to improve the uniformity of seeds or to render them more visible to the nurseryman.

CLASSIFICATION OF TYPES OF DORMANCY

Dormancy may be of several different types and sometimes more than one type occurs in the same seed.

The simplest grouping distinguishes between:

- Exogenous or seedcoat/pericarp dormancy;
- Endogenous or embryo dormancy; and
- Combined dormancy, in which both seedcoat and embryo dormancy occur at the same time.

More detailed classifications of dormancy have been published. That by Nikolaeva has been applied, in simplified form, to temperate broadleaved tree and shrub seeds by Gordon and Rowe. The types of dormancy differentiated by them are:

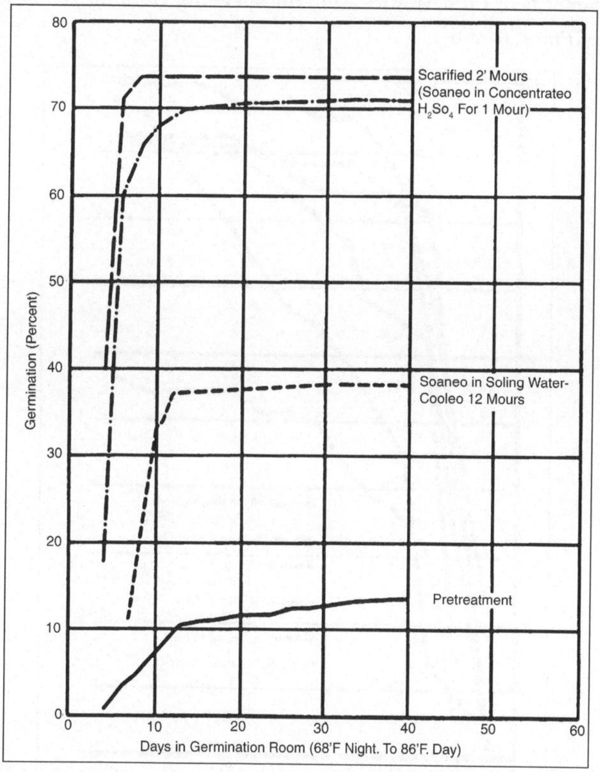

Fig. 4.1 Effect of Several Presowing Treatments on Germination of Black Locust *(Robinia Pseudoacacia)* a Hard-seeded Species. (USDA Forest Service)

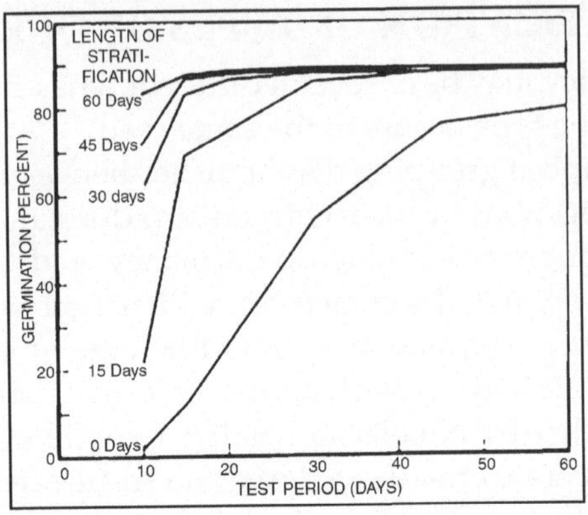

Fig. 4.2 Benefits of Cold Stratification for Speeding Germination of Loblolly Pine *(Pinus Taeda)*

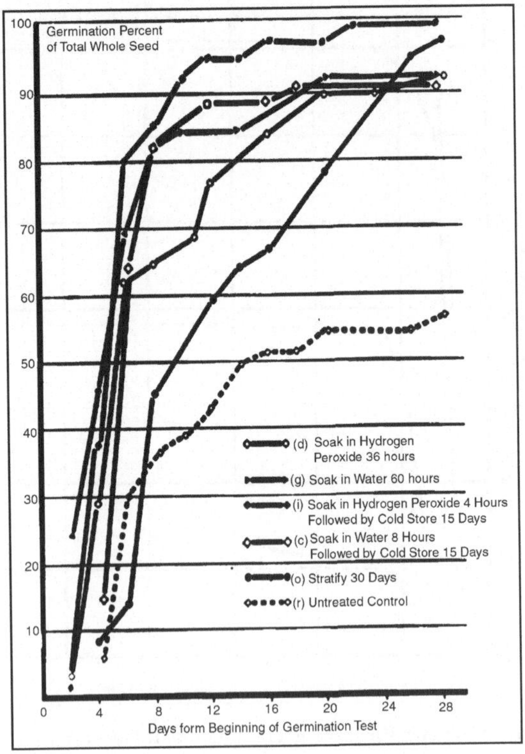

Fig. 4.3 The Effect of Various Pretreatments on Germination of Pinus Elliottii in New South Wales

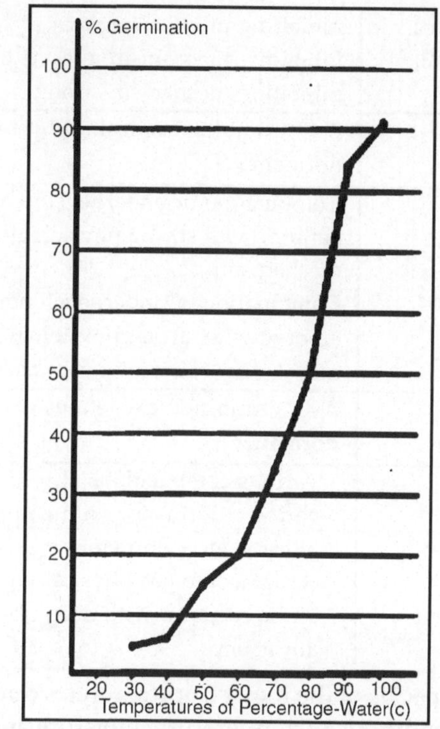

Fig. 4.4 Acacia Mangium. Percentage Germination, Mean of Seven Half-sib Seedlots, Pretreated with 10 Times Their Volume of hot Water for 30 Seconds, at Various Water Temperatures in Sabah.-Data derived from Bowen and Eusebio

		A. Exogenous dormancy
A ph	Physical	*i.e.* impermeability of seedcoat or pericarp to water
A ch	Chemical	*i.e.* inhibitors in pericarp or seedcoat
A m	Mechanical	*i.e.* Mechanical resistance of pericarp or seedcoat to embryo growth
		B. Endogenous dormancy (morphological)
B	Morphological	*i.e.* underdevelopment of embryo
		C. Endogenous dormancy (physiological
C	Physiological	*i.e.* germination prevented by physiological inhibiting mechanism

(Contd...)

C1 Shallow C2 Intermediate C3 Deep	Inhibiting mechanism weak Inhibiting mechanism intermediate Inhibiting mechanism strong
	B-C. Combined morpho-physiological dormancy
B-C3 B-C3e	Combination of underdevelopment of embryo with strong physiological inhibiting mechanism. Combination of underdevelopment of embryo with strong physiological inhibiting mechanism of epicotyl growth.
	A-C. Combined exogenous/endogenous dormancy
A-C	Various combinations of seedcoat or pericarp dormancy with endogenous physiological dormancy *e.g.* Tilia cordatacombines physical impermeability of the seedcoat with deep physiological dormancy.

In most species of the moist tropical forests dormancy is not a problem. Conditions of temperature, moisture and oxygen are almost invariably suitable for germination immediately on dispersal, so most species germinate within a matter of days or weeks and would not benefit from dormancy. In the drier tropics, on the other hand, seedcoat dormancy is common and some form of pretreatment is necessary to obtain rapid and uniform germination. Both physical dormancy, caused by hard seedcoats or pericarps with cutinised layers which are impermeable to water, and chemical dormancy, caused by inhibiting chemicals present in the seed covering, occur; it is likely that they sometimes occur simultaneously in the same seed. But it is often difficult to differentiate between them, since a treatment which softens the seedcoat, *e.g.* hot water, will automatically leach out inhibitors at the same time.

As pointed out by Gordon and Rowe, the covering of seeds which exhibit mechanical dormancy is thick, tough and resistant to embryo growth but, unlike the 'hard seeds' characteristic of physical dormancy, it is permeable to liquids. The severe treatments, such as boiling water or acid, which can be effective in overcoming physical dormancy, would penetrate the covers of the mechanically dormant seeds and kill the embryos. Mechanical dormancy occurs in a number of temperate genera *e.g.* Crataegus, Carpinus, Elaeagnus; it is not known whether it occurs in the tropics.

In temperate forestry, methods of overcoming the various types of endogenous dormancy have been investigated for a long period and the most important treatments are described later in this chapter. It is doubtful whether any of these methods will have application in the lowland tropics, but some of them may be applicable to species planted in the sub-tropics and tropical highlands; for example germination of Pinus taeda, an important species for afforestation in some tropical highlands and in the sub-tropics is known to benefit from cold moist pretreatment.

In general, however, the physical and chemical types of exogenous dormancy are likely to be of most concern to tropical foresters.

TREATMENTS DESIGNED TO BREAK EXOGENOUS OR SEEDCOAT DORMANCY

Seeds of some species have hard, cutinised seedcoats that completely prevent the imbibition of water and sometimes also the exchange of gases. Without imbibition and gas exchange renewal of embryo growth and germination are impossible. Physical seedcoat dormancy of this kind occurs most frequently in species adapted to alternating dry and wet seasons, including several leguminous genera such as Acacia,Prosopis, Ceratonia, Robinia, Albizzia, Cassia. In some species, *e.g.* Tectona grandis and Pterocarpus angolensis, the hard layer is formed by the pericarp or fruit. The unit of dispersal, storage and sowing in Tectona is the fruit, often referred to loosely as the 'seed', but for practical purposes the origin of the impermeable layer does not affect the choice of pretreatment.

Pretreatment to overcome physical seedcoat dormancy are designed to soften, puncture, wear away or split the seedcoat in order to render it permeable, without damaging the embryo and endosperm within. They include physical and biological methods, dry heating and soaking in water or chemical solutions. Any treatment which destroys or reduces seedcoat impermeability is commonly known as scarification. Destruction of impermeability at a single point in the seedcoat is normally sufficient to allow imbibition and gas exchange.

Chemical seedcoat dormancy, caused by the presence of chemicals located in the seedcoat but inhibiting germination of the embryo, can usually be overcome by some form of liquid treatment which leaches out the chemicals. The wet treatment methods described in this chapter should therefore be effective in breaking chemical, as well as physical seedcoat dormancy, and a combination of the two. Dry methods on the other hand, which are effective in overcoming physical dormancy, are unlikely to have any effect on chemical dormancy.

PHYSICAL METHODS

One of the simplest and most direct physical methods is to cut, drill or file a small hole in the coat of each seed before sowing. This method has been found appropriate in the Philippines for large leguminous seeds in the genera Afzelia, Albizzia, Intsia and Sindora and in Honduras for Acacia, Prosopis, Enterolobium and other legumes Intsia seed is nicked at each end and a third time in the area of the hilum and micropyle; the last area is the most important. In Tanzania the hard and bristly pericarp of Pterocarpus angolensis is chipped at one edge by knife or cracked by beating with clubs. In the Philippines the hard seedcoat of Eusideroxylon is cracked by hammer. In Calophyllum complete removal of the seedcoat has produced better germination than nicking. Sand-paper may also be used to reduce seedcoat thickness by abrasion.

In trials in Pakistan sandpaper proved the most effective treatment in increasing and accelerating germination in a number of hard-coated species. As an example Leucaena seeds had zero germination in the untreated control and after 24 hours' soaking in cold water. This was increased to 42 per cent in 26 days by 1 minute soaking in concentrated H_2SO_4, to 60 per cent in 13 days by 2 minutes in boiling water, and to 100 per cent in 3 days by sandpaper treatment. In laboratory trials in Sweden, sandpaper scarification followed by a three hour cold water soak, was the most effective treatment for Acacia farnesiana, yielding 88 per cent germination in 7 days and 100 per cent in 21 days, compared with 63 per cent, 23 per cent and 3 per cent in 21 days, respectively for soaking in concentrated sulphuric acid, absolute alcohol and hot water.

In six other hard-seeded species from Iraq tested at the same time, it was less effective than one or other of the soaking treatments. Manual treatment of individual seeds is slow but, with experienced workers, is safe and effective. It is best suited to the larger and more refractory seeds *e.g.* Delonix regia. The effect of physical scarification may be reinforced by soaking in cold water before sowing.

For treatment of large quantities of seed, mechanical scarification is more suitable than the manual method. Seed may be tumbled or churned in a concrete mixer with sharp gravel or sand, or in a special drum lined with abrasive material such as sandpaper, cement or crushed glass or incorporating rotating abrasive disks. If gravel or sand is used, it should be sieved to ensure that it can be readily separated from the seed by use of an appropriate mesh screen. The method is not suitable for seeds with abundant resin or pulp which may clog the machine. Care must be taken to avoid overtreatment causing damage that can reduce or destroy germinability of the seeds. Examination of the seedcoat surface, if necessary by hand lens, or testing the capacity of the seed to take up water, demonstrated by swelling, can be used to estimate effectiveness of scarification.

In India mechanical scarification is used successfully to overcome seedcoat dormancy in Acacia catechu, A. nilotica subsp. indica, Albizzia falcataria, A. lebbek, Cassia fistula, C. javanica, C. nodosa, Delonix regia, Dichrostachys cinerea, Santalum album, Terminalia arjuna and T. tomentosa. Horizontal shaking of seeds of Acacia farnesiana, bottled with crushed glass, for five hours gave a germination of 20.7 per cent plus additional imbibed seeds 10.7 per cent in 43 days, compared with 0.7 per cent + 0.7 per cent for the control in the same period. But this result was much inferior to that obtained with the same species by manual scarification with sandpaper.

SOAKING IN WATER

A number of treatments involve soaking seeds in water or other liquids. These wet treatments may combine the effects of softening hard seedcoats and leaching out chemical inhibitors.

Some seeds which have little resistance to germination may respond well to soaking for 24 hours in water at ambient temperature. This may be the result of a more rapid imbibition than can be achieved in a moistened nursery bed. It is recommended for some species after manual, mechanical or acid scarification. Matias *et al.* found that 48 hours' soaking of Pinus caribaea seed in water at room temperature gave more uniform germination than in the untreated seed.

In India soaking in water, for periods varying from two to 48 hours according to species, accelerates germination in Acacia mearnsii, A. melanoxylon, A. nilotica subsp. kraussiana, Adenanthera microsperma, Albizzia amara, A. procera, Grevillea robusta and Trewia nudiflora.

A more effective treatment, especially in hot climates, is alternate wetting and drying of seed. This has frequently been used for Tectona fruits. In Thailand, after scarification, alternate soaking and drying was applied, 4 times soaking and 3 times drying, each for 30–45 minutes. Elsewhere, if preliminary scarification is not applied, common practice is to spread the 'seed' out on a hard surface in the sun in a layer about 5 cm deep and to soak it thoroughly; then to turn it over from time to time, allowing it to dry out and bake in the sun for a day or two.

This process of alternate soaking, drying and baking is repeated a number of times, usually between five and ten cycles, until signs of germination appear. Each cycle of wetting and drying may be one day for soaking and 3–5 days for drying and baking. As soon as germination starts, the 'seed' should be sown in the nursery. In Tanzania the preliminary soaking is for 72 hours in full sacks in a stream or in large drums. It is then sown on the surface at the rate of 5 kg/m^2 and, after two days in the sun, is covered with about 2–5 cm depth of soil and watered daily.

Tectona grandis is one tropical species in which there is evidence that chemical dormancy caused by inhibitors in the pericarp may be more important than physical dormancy. Fairlamb and Davidson found that an aqueous extract, obtained by soaking T. grandis fruits for 4 days and used to moisten filter paper, inhibited germination of cress seeds. Germination was 11 per cent in 144 hours in the extract, compared with 76 per cent in tank water and 96 per cent in distilled water. On the other hand Pattanath could find no evidence for physical dormancy in T. grandis. She found that, after soaking the fruits in water for 24 hours, water had soaked right through to the locules where the seeds were attached. There is great variation in the degree of dormancy between provenances of teak.

Some require no pretreatment, some require alternate wetting and drying as described above, others respond to soaking for four hours in Sach's nutrient solution, which may indicate a nutrient imbalance in the seeds.

Chemical dormancy apparently occurs also in Terminalia ivorensis. Alternate daily soaking and drying of the fruits of this species for seven days was effective in producing 50–70 per cent germination, whereas germination of untreated seed is usually poor. In a later experiment the same author found that an aqueous extract from Terminalia ivorensis fruits had a slight inhibitory effect on germination of lettuce seeds but a more serious effect in the number of malformations in the germinated seedlings. He identified Coumarin as one of the more important inhibitants involved. Soaking in running water for one to two weeks has been used successfully to remove inhibitors in Atriplex spp.

Hot water treatment has given good results with a number of leguminous seeds. The seeds are usually placed into boiling water which is immediately removed from the heat source and left to cool gradually, the seeds remaining in the water for about 12 hours. They imbibe and swell as the water cools. The proper relationship of the volume of water to volume of seeds can be determined by experiment.

It may vary considerably according to species, ratios of 2–3 times, 4–5 times and 5–10 times (Seeber and Agpaoa as much water as seed have been suggested. Some species respond better to an initial temperature well below boiling *e.g.* Albizzia falcataria. An initial temperature of 90° C, cooled to ambient 20° C, has given good results with Parkinsonia aculeata and Ziziphus spina-christi. Of various initial water temperatures and periods of soaking and cooling tested forLeucaena leucocephala in the Philippines, one minute soaking from an initial temperature of 80° C gave the best result 90 per cent germination. The period of soaking and cooling appeared to have little effect, *e.g.* an initial 80°C and 6 hours' soak and cool gave 89 per cent germination. The initial water temperature had a big effect; germination was only about 30 per cent after an initial temperature of 100°C and only about 25 per cent after an initial 40°C.

Bowen and Eusebio found that in Acacia mangium seeds in Sabah there was a close correlation between the initial temperature of the water and the subsequent germination. Germination increased progressively from 5 per cent after immersion in water at 30°C to 91 per cent after immersion at 100°C. Prescribed treatment for this species is now to immerse seeds in 5 × their volume of water at 100°C, stir in the cooling water for 30 seconds, pour off hot water and soak overnight in 20 × their volume at room temperature.

For Albizzia falcataria a lower initial temperature of 80°–90°C is recommended. Some species of Acacia require more severe treatment. Larsen found that, whereas the standard treatment with boiling water improved germination of Acacia sieberiana, an exceptionally resistant species, from 2 per cent to 10 per cent, continuous boiling of the seed in water for 60 minutes achieved 60 per cent germination within two weeks.

Prescriptions for hot water treatment must be applied meticulously if seedcoat dormancy is to be removed without killing the seeds through excessive heating. It is often easier to ensure this at a central research laboratory than in a number of scattered field nurseries. In Sabah it was found possible to redry seeds of Acacia mangium and Albizzia falcataria after the initial 30 seconds' hot water treatment, package and despatch them to field nurseries and, after 3 days' storage, to give a simple cold water soak before sowing. Germination was just as good (c. 80 per cent) as when seeds were sown immediately after treatment. Drying was done in a current of dry air at 45°C for periods of 6–18 hours.

Hot water treatment is relatively easy and safe to apply, as well as being effective with some species. It is not well adapted to large lots because of the difficulty in handling and sowing the swollen seeds.

ACID TREATMENT

The chemical most commonly used to break seedcoat dormancy is concentrated sulfuric acid. For some species it is more effective than hot water treatment. Seed which has been kept for a long period in store may require a longer period in the acid than fresh seed, which could be severely damaged by the same length of treatment. Great care is needed in the handling of sulfuric acid and this method is not suitable for use by unskilled workers.

Detailed instructions for use of sulfuric acid are given by Bonner *et al.* and are reproduced below:

Materials and equipment required are as follows: commercial grade (specific gravity 1.84, 95 per cent pure) sulfuric acid; acid-resistant containers (thick plastic preferred); wire containers and screens for handling, draining, and washing the seeds; an abundant supply of running water; a safe place to drain the dilute acid resulting from rinsing the seeds; and facilities for drying the seeds after rinsing.

Safety precautions are a must! All workmen must understand and obey safety precautions in the use of acid. Seeds, containers, implements, and the acid itself must be handled with great care to avoid injury. Water must not be splashed into the acid, as a violent reaction will occur. All workmen should wear suitable safety clothing, gloves, and goggles or other eye protection.

Toughness of the seedcoat varies between lots and even between individual trees in most species. The optimum period of immersion in acid for each lot may be determined by treating a small sample for different periods and then soaking the lots in water at room temperature for 1 to 5 days (depending on species). The treatment period that yields a high percentage of swollen seeds (by water uptake) without visible injury is the right one. Oversoaking may pit the seed and even expose the endosperm.

Insufficient soaking leaves the seedcoats of most species glossy; coats of correctly treated seeds are dull, but not deeply pitted.

If tests reveal only small differences between lots, then all may be lumped together for treatment, unless there are other reasons for keeping them separate (such as seed source distinctions). Large differences between lots should occasion separate treatment.

The steps in acid treatment are as follows:

- Allow seeds to come to air temperature. If they have been removed from cold storage, do not open the container until temperature equilibrium is reached. Moisture will form on cold seeds exposed to warm moist air, and this moisture can react with acid to raise temperature to the danger point.
- Thoroughly mix seeds to be treated as one lot.
- Immerse seeds in the acid for the required period, making sure that all are covered. Treatment should be carried out at 65° to 80° F (18°–27°C), preferably on the upper end of the range. Lower temperatures require longer soaking times than do higher temperatures. Careful stirring will reduce the length of treatment necessary.
- Remove seeds from the acid and wash them promptly and thoroughly in cool, running water for 5 to 10 minutes to remove all traces of acid. Water should be applied copiously at the start, and the seeds stirred carefully during rinsing.
- Spread the seeds in a thin layer for drying, unless wet sowing is preferred.

Fig. 4.5 A Rinsing Trough for Washing Acid from Treated Seeds

Fig. 4.6 One Apparatus for Treating Large Lots of Seed With Acid

Fig. 4.7 Outdoor Stratification of *Juglans Nigra* in Sand in USA

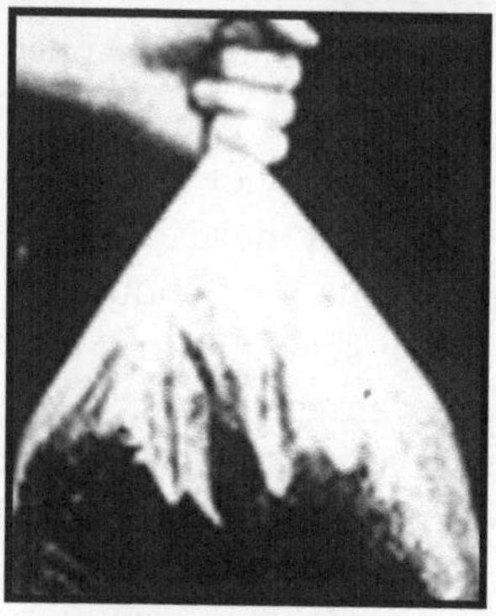

Fig. 4.8 Loblolly Pine (Pinus Taeda) Seed Prepared for Stratification in a Plastic Bag

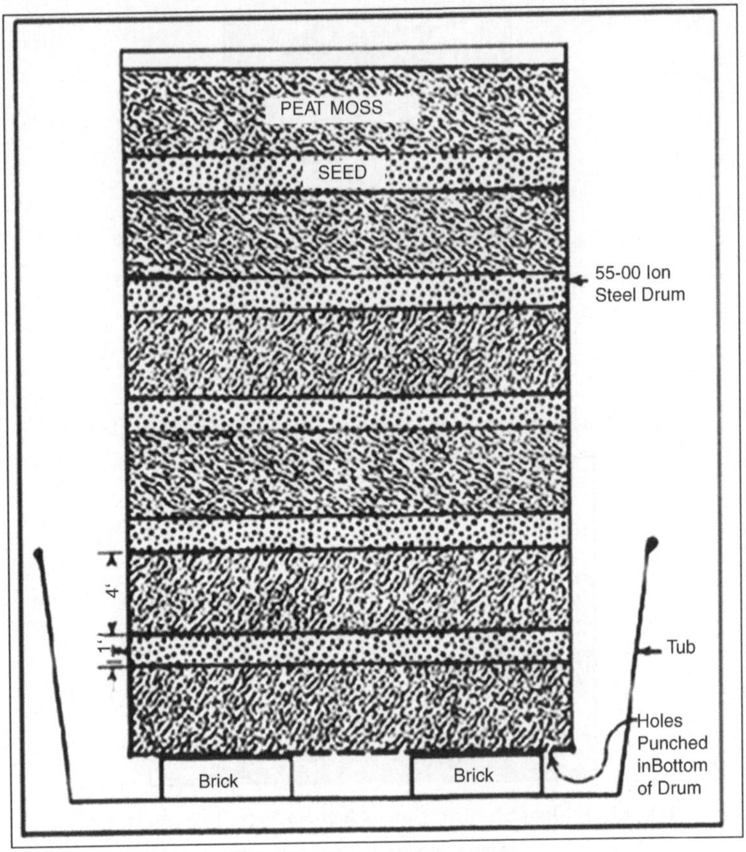

Fig. 4.9 Desired Arrangement for Stratification in a Large Barrel

Fifty-pound (20 kg) lots can be treated in screen-wire cylinders (reinforced with heavier wire) that can be lowered into the acid. In this way, most of the acid is retained for reuse. After a short draining period, the seed should be washed. Extra care must be taken in large-scale treatments to avoid excessive temperatures that can damage seeds.

There are several advantages of the acid treatment. It is effective for many species and requires little or no special equipment. Cost is reasonable. Most of the acid can be recovered and reused (unless the acid is poured on a pile of seed). Treated seeds can be held from a week to a month or more before sowing, without appreciable deterioration. Since the process leaves the seeds dry, firm and unswollen, they can be sown with mechanical seeders as well as by hand.

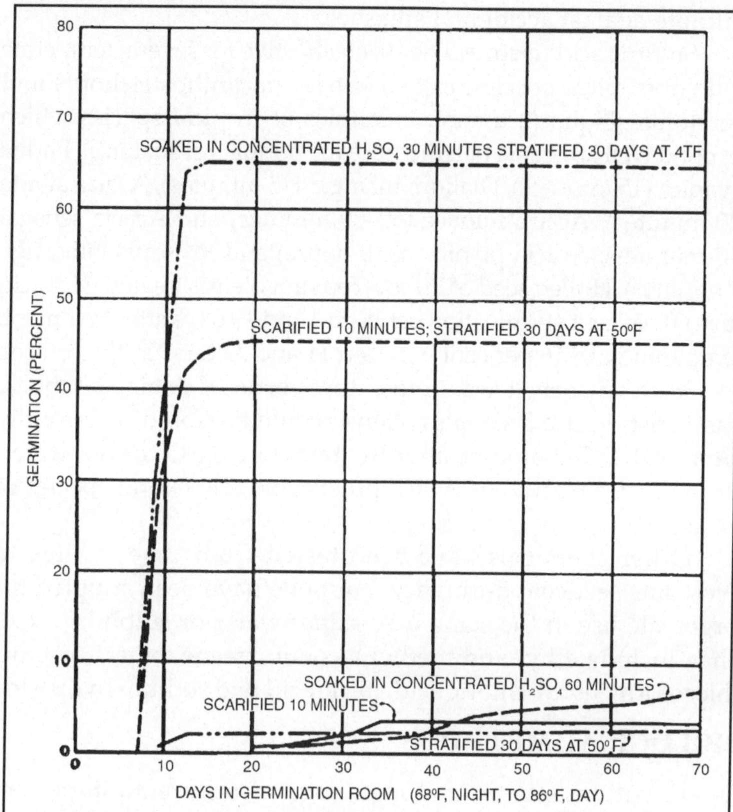

Fig. 4.10 Effects of Several Treatments to Overcome Double Dormancy in Eastern Redbud (*Cercis Canadensis*)

There are also disadvantages. Length of treatment must be carefully determined, and temperature must be carefully controlled, especially in large lots, to prevent serious injury to the seeds. Workmen also face a safety hazard.

If a large quantity of one seed lot is to be treated in several batches, it is desirable to standardise treatment as far as possible *e.g.* by using fresh acid of full strength and exactly the same volume (two volumes of acid to one volume of seed) for every batch.

In addition to protective clothing, a concentrated solution of sodium or potassium bicarbonate should be kept handy as an antidote against accidental splashes.

Sulfuric acid treatment has been effective for several temperate and subtropical species, *e.g.* Gleditsia triacanthos (1 hour) and Ceratonia siliqua (2 hours). Examples of tropical species which respond well are Intsia palembanica (60 minutes of soaking), Parkia javanica (15 minutes), Dialium maingayi (5 minutes), Acacia albida (20 minutes), Acacia nilotica (60–80 minutes) and Acacia senegal (40 minutes), Acacia planifrons (2 hours) and Prosopis tamarugo (7 minutes). Hulled seed of Pterocarpus angolensis treated with acid gave 60 per cent germination between 4 and 19 days after treatment, compared with 16 per cent between 11 and 37 days in the control.

In the Sudan it was found that seeds of Albizzia lebbek, Cassia fistula and Prosopis chilensis could be stored successfully for a further 3–4 months after treatment in H_2SO_4 or hot water. Storage after treatment is also practicable for several species of Acacia.

Other chemicals have been tested from time to time to overcome seedcoat dormancy, but none have been adopted for largescale use in the same way as hot water or sulphuric acid. They include ethyl and methyl alcohol, xylene, ether, acetone, chloroform, hydrochloric acid, nitric acid and sodium hydroxide

BIOLOGICAL METHODS

In nature animals and micro-organisms are an important factor in the breakdown of seedcoat impermeability. It is difficult to make use of these organisms as a controlled pretreatment of seed, but in a few cases successful results have been obtained.

Seeds of Acacia senegal and Ceratonia siliqua that have passed through the digestive tracts of goats germinate readily when placed in favourable conditions, because of the action of the strong digestive chemicals. Feeding the pods to penned goats and collecting the seeds from the droppings is a convenient pretreatment for these species. Seeds of some species are said to be regurgitated after partial rumination *e.g.* Gmelina arborea. Troup states that seeds of Acacia nilotica are ejected after rumination by sheep and goats but pass right through the digestive tract in cattle. In either case germination is improved by the digestive action.

Termites are an important agent for breaking down seedcoat dormancy in many parts of the tropics. In Thailand teak fruits were spread on the ground in a 5 cm thick layer immediately after collection and covered with cardboard. After about 5 weeks the termites had removed the exocarp and subsequent germination, after alternate wetting and drying, was significantly improved in comparison with fruits sown with intact exocarps. Termites have been used in a similar way to break down the tough winged and bristly fruit ofPterocarpus angolensis. Periodic inspection is essential to ensure that the process is not carried too far.

Partial fermentation, which is damaging to many seeds, can be beneficial in overcoming seedcoat dormancy in some. In the southern Sudan fruits of Tectona grandis are allowed to lie on the ground through the rainy season for partial fermentation.

They are then collected, stratified in a pit with layers of:

- Seed
- Organic matter
- Soil and watered daily for 10 days. Satisfactory germination results.

Dry Heat and Fire

Solar radiation is not used alone to promote germination but is an important component of the alternate soaking and drying treatment described above under 'Soaking in water'.

In the seasonal wet and dry tropics, fire is a powerful natural factor in the removal of seedcoat dormancy. A fierce fire will kill the seeds but a light to moderate fire, such as those associated with controlled early burning, will reduce seedcoat impermeability and stimulate germination. Fire has been used in a number of countries to stimulate germination of Tectona. The fruits may be spread thickly on the ground and covered with grass which is burnt off, or they may be lightly scorched by a flame gun. Adjusting the heat of the fire to achieve the maximum effect on the pericarp without damaging the seed embryo requires experience. Similar treatment is used for Aleurites moluccana in the Philippines. The nuts are spread evenly on the ground and covered with a 3 cm thick layer of dry Imperata grass which is set on fire. As soon as the grass is burned, the seeds are placed in cold water. The quick change of temperature causes the nuts to crack and they are ready for sowing. An alternative is to sow the nuts at correct spacing with only half their diameter in the soil. A layer ofImperata grass is spread over the seed bed and set on fire. After burning, the seedbed is sprinkled with water and the nuts are pushed 2 cm deep into the soil and watered thoroughly.

In Sabah Bowen and Eusebio found that ten minutes' exposure of Acacia mangium seeds to dry heat at 100°C was nearly as effective in overcoming dormancy as the immersion in water at 100° C described. Germination was 83 per cent compared with 92 per cent in the hot water treatment.

Special Treatments for Mechanical Dormancy

The thick, tough but water-permeable coverings of seeds exhibiting mechanical dormancy prevent embryo growth even when water can be freely imbibed. This mechanical obstruction to germination can be overcome by a period of 'warm moist' treatment the length of which varies according to species.

The treatment recommended by Gordon and Rowe for temperate species is:

- Soak seeds in several times their volume of cold water at approximately 3–5 ° C for 48 hours.
- Drain off the water and mix the seeds with two to four times their volume of a moistened, water-retaining medium such as sand, sand/peat mixture, vermiculite.
- Store at a warm temperature. A constant 20–25°C or alternating 20° and 30°C is suitable for many species.
- Open containers weekly, mix seeds and, if surfaces show signs of drying out, remoisten with water spray.

The period of 'warm moist' treatment can be shortened in some species by a preliminary treatment in sulfuric acid. This requires more care and expertise than the use of acid for physical dormancy. Seeds or fruits must be thoroughly dried before treatment and the process should be limited to the partial digestion of the outer layers only, leaving the final weakening of the inner layers to be done by the subsequent warm moist treatment. In most cases it is preferable to accept the safer but slower method of warm moist treatment alone. Periods of treatment vary from 2 weeks for some species of Prunus to 16 weeks for some species of Crataegus.

At the end of the appropriate period seeds which possess only mechanical dormancy are ready for sowing. Many species in this class also have physiological dormancy of the embryo and will need further treatment to remove this, as described.

It may be noted that the warm moist treatment which removes mechanical dormancy is identical with the warm moist treatment which removes morphological dormancy (underdeveloped embryos).

TREATMENTS DESIGNED TO BREAK ENDOGENOUS OR EMBRYO DORMANCY

Embryo dormancy is a prominent feature in some temperate genera. For example in the USA Rudolf noted that, of 400 species of woody plants studied, about 60 per cent required pretreatment to induce prompt germination. Endogenous dormancy occurs in both orthodox and recalcitrant seeds. Its occurrence in the lowland tropics is probably rare (most seeds in moist tropical forest germinate quickly or not at all and those in the dry tropics typically have seedcoat dormancy).

It could be of importance in the high altitude tropics and sub-tropics. Trials of prechilling on seed of the Zambales (Philippines) provenance of Pinus merkusii showed no improvement in germination; if anything germination was slightly depressed. Wunder mentions Cordia africana as a species suitable for prechilling for several weeks in moist sand at 5°C but does not give any comparative figures of germination from treated and untreated seeds. In Eucalyptus prechilling is effective in promoting germination in only a few species from the cold temperate region *e.g.* E. delegatensis and E. pauciflora; in the great majority of species it has no effect at all.

Endogenous dormancy includes the cases of embryos which are morphologically underdeveloped at the time of separation from the parent tree and which need a subsequent period for further growth before they can germinate. It also includes the cases of embryos which are morphologically mature at the time of seed dispersal or collection but are physiologically incapable of germination until certain biochemical changes, still little understood, take place.

MORPHOLOGICAL DORMANCY

Seeds with underdeveloped embryos at the time of dispersal or collection will not germinate until the embryos have had time to mature. In a few species maturation is possible during dry storage *e.g.* Gingko biloba. More commonly, a period of moist warm pretreatment is necessary before the embryos develop sufficiently for germination to take place.

The recommended treatment is the same as that for mechanical dormancy *i.e.*

- Soak seeds in several times their volume of cold water at approximately 3–5°C for 48 hours.
- Drain off the water and mix the seeds with two to four times their volume of a moistened, water-retaining medium such as sand, sand/peat mixture or vermiculite.
- Store at a warm temperature. A constant 20–25°C or alternating 20° and 30°C is suitable for many species.
- Open containers weekly, mix seeds and, if surfaces show signs of drying out, remoisten with water spray.

Most species which have underdeveloped embryos also have physiological dormancy, therefore warm moist treatment must be followed by cold moist treatment.

OVERCOMING PHYSIOLOGICAL DORMANCY-COLD STRATIFICATION

Far more common than morphological dormancy among temperate species are the cases where seeds are fully developed at dispersal or collection but are inhibited from immediate germination for physiological reasons. The pretreatment most effective in removing this physiological dormancy is that which approximates to the conditions of overwintering in nature *i.e.* a moist cold treatment, or cold stratification.

Cold stratification will not only overcome physiological dormancy but can also reduce the sensitivity of both dormant and non-dormant seeds to their optimum requirements for light and temperature, resulting in increased rate and uniformity of germination over a variety of conditions. If properly carried out, cold stratification does no damage to non-dormant seeds which are undamaged and have not deteriorated from excessive physiological ageing (Wang in press). It can therefore be safely used when different degrees of dormancy are expected in the same seed lot.

Stratification (sensu stricto) refers to the method of placing seeds in layers alternating with layers of a moisture retaining medium, such as sand, peat or vermiculite, and keeping them at a cool temperature for a period, which is commonly between 20 and 60 days but varies considerably from species to species. The combination of high moisture and low temperature appears to trigger off biochemical changes which transform complex food substances into simpler forms utilized by the embryo when it renews growth at germination. The use of the word 'stratification' has recently been extended to include all forms of cold, moist treatment whether or not the seeds are placed in layers.

The present section gives a brief description of stratification in the original sense (outdoor and indoor), while the following section on 'Other moist prechilling methods' describes non-layered methods of cold, moist treatment. The three main requirements for success in both stratification and moist prechilling are a renewable source of moisture for the seeds, low temperature and adequate aeration. Only imbibed seeds will benefit fully from cold, moist treatment, while good aeration is needed to supply oxygen for respiration and to dissipate heat and CO_2. Low temperature not only favours biochemical changes in the seed but reduces micro-organism activity and the risk of overheating and premature germination of the after-ripened seeds.

In temperate climates low enough temperatures to accomplish prechilling are experienced by overwinter stratification in outdoor pits. The method used in the UK is described by Aldhous.

Its main features are:

- The pit should be located in a cool, shady and well-drained site. The bottom 10 cm should be filled with either sand or gravel for drainage. Pit contents should remain moist during stratification, but should never become waterlogged.
- 60–80 cm is convenient for depth and width, the length can be adjusted to the volume of seed to be stratified.
- The pit should be lined at the bottom and sides with a frame carrying 6 mm mesh wire netting as a protection against mice. After the pit is filled, it should be covered by a lid of the same mesh netting.
- The seed to be stratified should be mixed with 4 times its weight of sand and the pit filled with the seed/sand mixture to within 15 cm of the surface. The top 15 cm should be filled with pure sand.
- The start of stratification should be timed in relation to the anticipated sowing date and the optimum period of stratification expected for the species. Seeds should be inspected periodically, starting a few weeks before the sowing date. They should be sown when most seeds are beginning to split and the tips of the radicles are visible but before the radicles have elongated. Delayed sowing leads to broken or injured radicles; hardwoods can sustain such damage without too serious ill effects, but it can cause severe losses in conifers.

Where cold-room facilities are available, stratification may be carried out indoors, where closer control of moisture and temperature can be achieved than with the pit method. A temperature of +1° to +5°C is commonly recommended. In the USA one method in common use is to place 10-to 25-pound (4.5–12 kg) lots of seeds in loosely woven bags which are flattened into disks no more than 3 inches (7.5 cm) thick and alternated with layers of moist medium. Boxes, trays, cans or drums make suitable containers but must have perforated bottoms to facilitate drainage and aeration. Soaking seeds overnight in water at room temperature is common practice with southern pines and hardwoods. Containers should be covered loosely to prevent the seed and medium drying unevenly. The seeds should be inspected periodically to prevent heating, poor aeration and excessive drying and to detect the first stages of germination.

Seeds should be sown soon after removal from stratification. Stratified but ungerminated seeds of some genera, *e.g.* Prunus, may undergo a secondary dormancy if subjected to extreme drying or to temperatures over 20°C. A new cold stratification is then needed to overcome the secondary dormancy.

OTHER MOIST PRECHILLING METHODS

Similar results to stratification in layers may be obtained with many species by storing the seeds moist in polythene bags. As with indoor stratification, seeds should be soaked in several times their volume of water before prechilling, a 48 hour soak at 3–5°C is suitable for many temperate broadleaved species. After soaking, the water is drained off and the moist seeds are then prechilled at 3–5°C for the period appropriate to each species. Prechilling may be 'naked' *i.e.* without any medium, or the seed may be mixed with 2–4 times its volume of a medium such as moist sand, moist peat or a mixture of the two Polythene bags of about 100 micron thickness make suitable containers since they are moisture proof but somewhat permeable to oxygen. They should be lightly tied and opened weekly when the seed should be mixed and, if necessary, remoistened. A smell of alcohol on opening a bag indicates that anaerobic respiration is taking place because of inadequate oxygen; in this case frequency of opening and mixing should be increased.

Naked prechilling has the advantage that it is easier to check the condition of the seeds throughout the prechilling operation and there is no need to separate seeds from medium at the end of treatment. On the other hand, there is evidence that germination in some species benefits from use of a medium. Gordon and Rowe reported less than 30 per cent germination in

50 days from seeds of Sambucus racemosa treated 'naked', compared with 60 per cent in 20 days from seeds in peat/soil mixture, other elements in the treatments being identical. These authors give detailed prescriptions for pretreatment of a large number of temperature broadleaved species; as a general rule 'naked' prechilling is satisfactory for species which need only a few weeks' prechilling, while use of a medium is advisable for those which need a longer prechilling period and for all species which need warm moist pretreatment.

Periods of prechilling vary considerably from species to species and, to some extent, from seed lot to seed lot within a species. For Abies a period of 3 weeks at 3–5°C has proved satisfactory. The same temperature and period is effective for most of the cold-temperate eucalypts, but some provenances of E. delegatensis need 4–8 weeks for fast, uniform germination. For Nothofagus obliqua and N. procera naked prechilling at 3°–5°C for six weeks, and surface drying before sowing, gave high germination (usually over 80 per cent in 28 days) under nursery conditions. But, as described later in this chapter, treatment with gibberellic acid was a reliable and simpler alternative. In species having deep physiological dormancy the prechilling period may be as long as 20 weeks *e.g.* Liriodendron tulipifera.

For Fagus sylvatica in Poland, after storage for several years at-5°C and 10 per cent MC, the following pretreatments are recommended:

- Allow to defrost.
- Moisten by sprinkling of water and thorough mixing of wetted nuts twice a day for 6 days, at 3°C, until MC rises to 31 per cent.
- Leave wet nuts in unsealed containers without any storage medium at 3°C for a period equal to two weeks longer than the minimum required to produce 10 per cent germination in a sample within two weeks of its transfer to a moist germinating medium. Recurrent sampling and germination testing is needed to estimate this period, which may vary considerably from seed lot to seed lot. MC of 31 per cent to be maintained meanwhile by periodic weighing of

containers and remoistening of nuts to restore loss of weight.

- Sow in moist germinating medium at 3°C and leave for two weeks. This should initiate germination of radicles.
- Transfer to temperature of 20°C to promote hypocotyl and epicotyl elongation and seedling emergence, which are inhibited in this species at 3°C.

For large-scale operational sowings, the ideal experimental conditions described above can be simulated to some extent in the nursery by timing the spring sowing so that the nuts experience an adequate period of cold temperature first, followed by the higher temperatures of late spring and early summer.

There is some evidence that steps (2) and (3) of the pretreatment described above can be carried out before, as well as after, storage. The advantage is that the nuts are ready for sowing as soon as they come out of store, without the need for a subsequent cold, moist treatment covering several weeks. Nuts pretreated before storage have been successfully stored for 15 months in France.

CHEMICAL TREATMENT OF PHYSIOLOGICAL DORMANCY

A wide range of chemicals have been tested experimentally in an attempt to overcome internal dormancy. They include gibberellic acid, citric acid, hydrogen peroxide and a number of other compounds. Some have given a degree of improvement, *e.g.* Bachelard found that the germination of dormant seeds of Eucalyptus delegatensis, E. fastigata and E. regnans could be improved by treatment with gibberellic acid (GA). 24 hours' immersion in either GA 3 or GA 4/7 of Nothofagus obliqua has given rapid and complete germination in 14 days, although this normally dormant species otherwise requires 28–42 days' stratification. Shafiq found that the strength of the gibberellic acid had only a small effect, 200 ppm giving 100 per cent germination in 8 days, 50 ppm the same germination in 12 days.

The best stratification treatment (42 days at 3–5°C) yielded 70 per cent in 14 days and 88 per cent in 28 days and the control

(24 hours' soaking in distilled water and no prechilling) only 20 per cent in 28 days. The saving in time effected by the GA treatment (1 + 12 days compared with 42 + 28 days) is considerable. Results reported later by Rowe and Gordon showed that GA 4/7 was more reliable than GA 3 as it was less sensitive to temperature during the germination period. Excellent germination was obtained throughout the temperature range 15–30°C, whereas GA 3 required temperatures over 21°C for comparable results.

These successes, however, are the exception. In general, for cheapness and reliability chemical treatments cannot compete with stratification or moist prechilling and they are unlikely to play a major role in normal nursery practice in the foreseeable future.

OTHER TREATMENTS FOR ENDOGENOUS DORMANCY

X-rays, gamma rays, light rays in the red region of the spectrum and high frequency sound waves have all been used experimentally to try to overcome dormancy and stimulate germination. Improvement has been reported in some species including Tectona but it has proved difficult to achieve consistent results and the treatments may induce chromosome damage and other abnormalities concluded that there was far more evidence of unfavourable effects from irradiation of seed than beneficial effects. None of these methods are suitable for practical application at the present time.

TREATMENTS DESIGNED TO OVERCOME DOUBLE DORMANCY

Some species combine more than one form of dormancy at the same time. Pretreatment to break one type of dormancy alone will be largely ineffective, unless it is followed by a second pre-treatment to overcome the other type.

Physical dormancy of the seedcoat may be combined with physiological dormancy of the embryo. In this case seedcoats should be treated first *e.g.* by scarification and cold moist prechilling applied afterwards to overcome embryo dormancy. Cercis canadensis provides a good example; single treatments gave less than 10 per cent germination in all cases, while successive applications of seedcoat and internal dormancy treatments gave rapid germination of 45 per cent (mechanical scarification) or 65 per cent (acid scarification). In a few cases treatment of the seed covering after stratification has proved effective.

Recent trials with Fraxinus pennsylvanica showed that cold stratification at 4° C for 88 days produced 35 per cent germination in 3 weeks, compared with 2 per cent in unstratified seed. But removal of the pericarp after stratification further increased germination to 56 per cent, while the best, but laborious, treatment of stratification followed by removal of embryos from pericarp and endosperm gave 88 per cent. Treatment to increase permeability of the pericarp in acorns after stratification benefits germination. Tuskan and Blanche found that 6 hours of mechanical shaking in distilled water, after 3 months' storage at 0° C and 30–40 per cent MC gave 90 per cent germination in Quercus shumardii, compared with 70 per cent from 6 hours' simple soaking after storage. The shaking treatment also increased MC over that from the soaking treatment, indicating increased permeability.

Fraxinus excelsior combines morphological dormancy (underdeveloped embryo) with physiological dormancy. Warm moist treatment to remove the morphological dormancy should be followed by cold moist treatment to remove the physiological dormancy. For UK conditions Gordon and Rowe recommend 8–12 weeks warm, followed by 8–12 weeks cold, while in Poland, Suszka recommends 16 weeks of each treatment.

A number of species, especially in the family Rosaceae, combine mechanical dormancy, caused by a tough, thick pericarp, with physiological dormancy. The same combination of warm moist followed by cold moist pretreatment is effective. In the case of a resistant species, Crataegus monogyna, the recommended periods are 4–8 weeks warm, followed by 12–16 weeks cold.

In some species, germination of the radicle takes place readily at warm temperature, but the epicotyl will not start to grow until:

- The radicle has already started to germinate and

- The seed has been exposed to a period of low temperature. Examples are Viburnum opulus andCarpinus caroliniana. Here again the same sequence of warm moist treatment at 20–25°C followed by cold moist treatment at 3–5°C should induce satisfactory germination.

Thus the same combination of warm moist plus cold moist treatments applied in that order is capable of removing several different combinations of double dormancy.

SEED DRESSING AND PELLETING

USES

In seed dressing or seed pelleting treatments, the surface of the seeds is coated with some inert material, the sticker, to which chemicals of various kinds may be added.

Some of the advantages claimed for pelleting and listed by Magini are:

- The incorporation of fertilizer material in the pellet furnishes the young germinated seedlings with needed nourishment.
- Plant growth regulators or stimulants may promote rooting or hasten emergence of the seedlings.
- Fungicides and insecticides are more effective when in direct contact with the seeds.
- Seeds may be protected against rodents by adding unpalatable, repellent or poisonous substances.
- Small seeds become larger and heavier and this improves the scatter pattern in aerial seeding.

Pelleting can also be used to incorporate a brightly coloured substance with the seed, which renders it more visible against the soil and thus facilitates uniform sowing rates. Coating with an anti-desiccant material such as alginate can preserve the seed against drying out, until adequate rain has fallen to permit safe germination.

Investigations have shown that some fungicides used in seed dressings may have an adverse influence on germination. The adverse effect was found to increase with temperature and this calls for extra caution in tropical countries. The cost of seed dressings is seldom justified when plants are raised in a nursery. Fertilizers, fungicides or insecticides can be applied more conveniently to the nursery soil than to the seeds, while good nursery hygiene coupled with presence of nursery staff through the day and periodic trapping or poison-baiting should be effective against birds and rodents. Pelleting is, however, sometimes used to improve the uniformity of seed for precision sowing in the nursery.

The main use of pelleting is for direct seeding, including aerial seeding. Protective measures to assist individual seeds after sowing are impracticable and pelleting is the only possible means of achieving some degree of protection. Most emphasis is now given to seed protection through incorporation of fungicides, insecticides and repellents; inclusion of fertilizers is seldom practised. One example of successful use was in aerial seeding of pines in the southern USA. The coating formulation consisted of endrin and arasan as the protectants, with a latex sticker to act as a bond.

The seedling yields in field studies comparing coated with untreated seed were 55 to 1 for Pinus palustris and 12 to 1 for P. taeda. Seed coating of eucalypts is practised for aerial seeding of cutover mountain forests in southern Australia, where an area of 8,000 to 12,000 ha annually has been regenerated by this method. Aerial seeding has been used very little in the tropics but some success was obtained in Indonesian trials in Central and Eastern Java on areas dominated by Imperata grass, using Leucaena leucocephala,Calliandra calothyrsus and Acacia auriculiformis.

MATERIALS AND METHODS

Latex, methylcellulose and hydrol emulsions are used as stickers. Flaked aluminium powder is sometimes incorporated, because its shining quality is effective in scaring off birds, or to hasten drying and prevent clumping of the treated seed. A variety of chemical protectants is available. Thiram or arasan, endrin and anthroquinone are among those commonly used. Thiram has been found effective against damping off. Red lead was long used as a dressing to protect seeds against birds and rodents but it is now considered to be valueless in this role.

It has reduced germination and growth in Larix and may sometimes be toxic to the operator in hand-sowing techniques. A more suitable dye which is equally effective as colouring and which has no apparent adverse effect on subsequent germination is a Waxoline dye such as Lithofar red or the later Waxoline red A. It can also be used as a marker for special certified seed batches in storage.

Magini describes one method of coating seeds through use of a small cement mixer. The seed is placed in the mixer (a batch of about 12 kg at a time is suitable) and moistened with a latex sticker solution of one part latex to nine parts of water at the rate of one eighth to one quarter of a litre per kg of seed. Enough treating powder is then added to dry the sticker, usually in a volume relationship of four parts powder to one part sticker. The thickness of the seed coating is dependent on the amount of sticker in relation to the amount of seed. The total mixing time should not exceed four minutes, since prolonged agitation damages seeds or chips off the pelleted coat.

The procedure described by Aldhous for coating seed with a Waxoline red dye is first to prepare a mixture of 1 part of dye to 19 parts of French chalk. The seed is mixed with a small volume of linseed oil and stirred gently until all the seed appears evenly covered. The freshly oiled seed should be mixed without delay with the French chalk/dye in a closed container until evenly coloured. The seed is then ready for sowing.

Fig. 4.11 Add 1 kg Animal Repellent (Endrin) to 1 kg Bird Repellent (Thiram)

Fig. 4.12 Stir

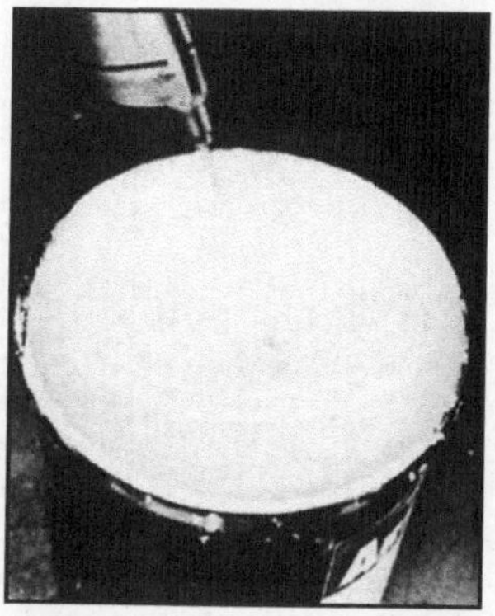

Fig. 4.13 Beat with Paint Stirrer

Fig. 4.14 Add 700 ml Latex Adhesive to another 1 kg Bird Repellent (thiram)

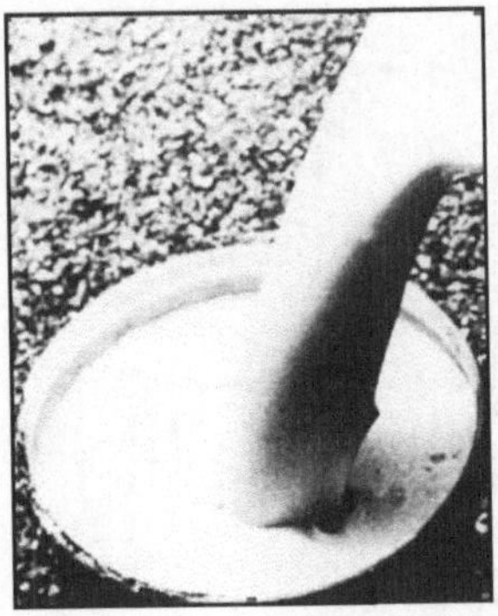

Fig. 4.15 Blend by Pouring from Can to can About 10 times

Fig. 4.16 Pour Finished Repellent Directly Onto 10 kg of Seed as Concrete Mixer is Turning. Tumble about 2 Minutes

Fig. 4.17 Add Aluminium Powder. Tumble for Another Minute

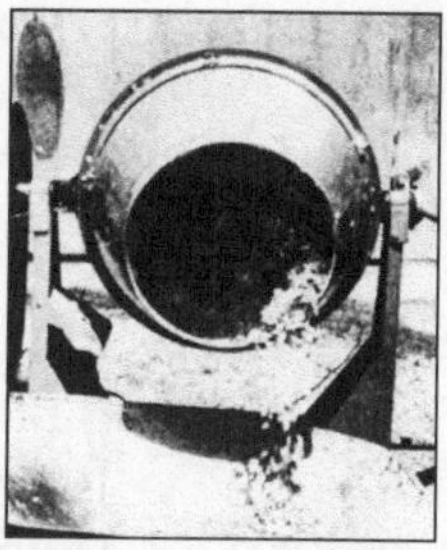

Fig. 4.18 Spread Out the Now Fully Coated Seed to Dry

8.11 The U.S. Forest Service recommendation for preparing repellent and applying it to seed of *Pinus elliottii*. (USDA Forest Service)

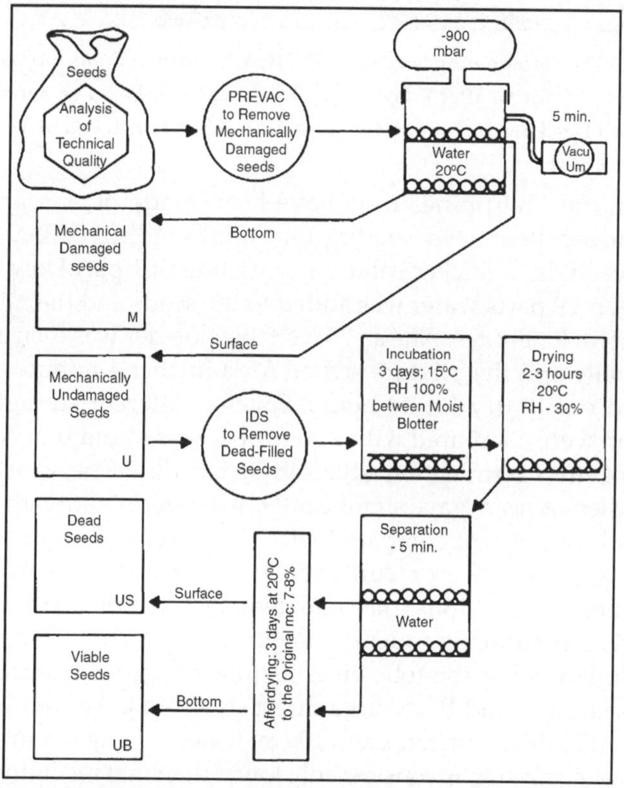

Fig. 4.19 Flow-scheme for the Removal of Mechanically Damaged and Filled-dead Seeds According to PREVAC-and IDS-methods

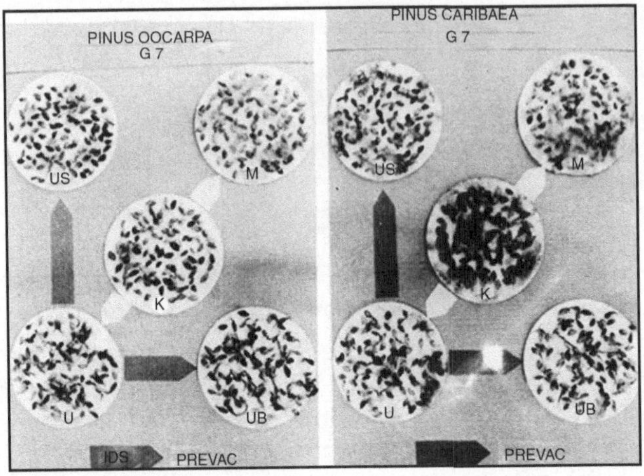

Fig. 4.20 The Germinating Seeds of IDS/PREVAC-treated *Pinus Caribaea* and *P. Oocarpa* after 7 days. Note Development of Fungi on Series with Dead Seeds. Fungi were Much More Abundant at end of Test (21 Days)

In the Philippines tests have been made of Arasan as a rodent-repellent seed coating for aerial seeding of Leucaena leucocephala. A sticker solution consisting of 1 part Dow Latex 512 R and 9 parts water was added to the seeds and the mixture stirred for 2 minutes. Arasan 75 wettable powder was then added gradually and the mixture stirred for a further 4 minutes, then spread out to dry for 14 hours. Several different strengths of Arasan were compared with a control. It was found that Arasan did not effect germination adversely, in fact the 7.5 per cent active ingredient Arasan gave significantly better germination than the control (74 per cent compared with 64 per cent). Results from 5 per cent and 10 per cent acid equivalent Arasan were intermediate. Previous trials had demonstrated that Arasan was effective in reducing rodent damage.

In Honduras the following mixture has proved suitable for Pinus oocarpa and P. caribaea direct sown: 60 g Arasan, 20 g 50 per cent Endrin, 5 ml latex and 100 ml water for 1 kg of pure seed. This concentration is considerably lower than that recommended for southern pines in the USA, since it was found that the higher concentrations caused some damage to these tropical specie.

TYPES OF PRETREATMENT

One pretreatment designed to separate viable full seed from non-viable full seed has been described by Simak. It involves a form of pregermination of the sound seed and is thus a treatment suitable for application between storage and sowing and not between processing and storage. It is appropriate in cases where seed must be sown after a long period of storage, either because of a long interval between good seed years-a decade or more sometimes in northern conifers—or because of storage for conserving gene resources. Seed stored for such long periods may contain a substantial proportion of full seeds which have lost the power to germinate and the separation of non-viable from viable seeds greatly facilitates subsequent nursery operations.

The method involves three stages:

1. The provision of conditions ideal for initiating the internal seed processes which lead to germination in viable seeds, especially the imbibition of water
2. Partial redrying of the seeds. The viable seeds retain more absorbed water after redrying than the dead filled seeds and their specific gravity is therefore greater.
3. Separation, *e.g.* by flotation, of the non-viable from the viable seeds. In one seed lot of Pinus sylvestris the treatments were
   - 16 hours' soaking in water, followed by 72 hours' storage in an incubator in a 2 cm thick layer at 15°C and 100 per cent moisture
   - 12 hours' drying at 15°C, 35 per cent RH and light of 800 lux
   - Separation into two fractions of 'floaters' and 'sinkers' by flotation in water. This method, applied to 10 kg of seed of 67 per cent germination, separated the seeds into one fraction of 7.3 kg 'sinkers' with 90 per cent germination and a second fraction of 2.7 kg 'floaters' with 13 per cent germination. The resulting component with the higher germination can be sown at the rate of a single seed per paper pot in the

nursery and germination is more rapid because of the pregermination treatment.

The method, known as the IDS (Incubation-Drying-Separation) treatment, requires very close control of temperature and moisture conditions if the desired differentiation between live and dead seeds is to be achieved without bringing the pregermination effect on the live seeds to the stage of radicle emergence. The optimum times of treatment may vary from seed lot to seed lot and it is necessary to carry out a preliminary trial on a small sample of each lot before treating it in bulk.

The method is likely to have most application in circumstances where:

- A substantial proportion of full but non-viable seeds is expected after storage
- Close control of temperature and moisture conditions is possible
- The viable seed obtained after separation can be sown in the nursery with minimum delay.

It is also possible to separate full but mechanically damaged seeds from full undamaged seeds. One method described by Lestander and Bergsten consists of placing the dry seeds in a drum partially filled with water. Centrifugal pressure is applied to the system by revolving the drum (5000 revolutions per minute has proved an effective speed) for a period sufficient to cause the damaged seeds to absorb enough water to make them sink, while the undamaged seeds absorb very little water and remain floating. In a seed lot of Pinus sylvestris known to have 26 per cent mechanically damaged seeds, it was found that 20 per cent of the seeds had sunk after 1 minute of drum rotation and 25 per cent after 5 minutes. About 98 per cent of the sinkers were damaged and only 2 per cent of the floaters. Germination in the sinkers was about 3 per cent and in the floaters 85 per cent (after 5 minutes' treatment and 21 days' germination test period). The same effect can be obtained by applying pressure to the liquid directly instead of by centrifuging, or by first applying a vacuum and then releasing it. The method is known as the PREVAC (Pressure-Vacuum) method.

This treatment is based on the fact that seeds with undamaged testas absorb water less readily than those with damaged testas, whereas the IDS treatment is based on the fact that a live imbibed seed releases moisture less readily on drying than a moistened dead seed. The PREVAC and IDS methods have been successfully used in combination to improve seed quality in Pinus caribaea and P. oocarpa.

In P. caribaea the combined treatments increased germination after 21 days from 75 per cent in the control to 87 per cent (and to 91 per cent after a second incubation period), in P. oocarpa from 93 per cent in the control to 99 per cent. Speed of germination after sowing was also improved from 4 per cent after 7 days to 35 per cent in P. caribaea, and from 6 per cent to 58 per cent in P. oocarpa. The schedules used were those devised for P. sylvestris and further improvement in results may be obtainable by adapting these to the tropical pines. In the initial experiment about half of the seeds separated as 'mechanically damaged' or as 'filled dead' actually germinated in P. oocarpa and about one third in P. caribaea; on the other hand a much higher proportion of these 'rejected but germinated' seeds showed signs of abnormal germination or reduced vigour than in the control. Figure illustrates the combined procedures in flow chart form and Figure the germinating seeds.

5

Seed Storage

INTRODUCTION

Storage may be defined as the preservation of viable seeds from the time of collection until they are required for sowing. When seed for afforestation can be sown immediately after collection, no storage is needed.

The best sowing date for a given species being raised in a nursery depends on:

- The anticipated date of planting, itself dependent on seasonal climate,
- The time needed in the nursery for planting stock of that species to reach the right size for out-planting.

Only rarely does best sowing date coincide with the best date for seed collection.

More often it is necessary to store the seed for varying periods which may be:

- Up to one year when both seed production and afforestation are regular annual events, but it is necessary to await the best season for sowing.
- 1–5 years or more when a species bears an abundant seed crop at intervals of several years and enough seed must be collected in a good year to cover annual afforestation needs in intermediate years of poor seed production.
- Long-term storage for purposes of conserving genetic resources. The period of storage will vary according

to the seed longevity of the species and the storage conditions, but will be measured in decades in species which are easy to store.

The storage facilities to be provided must be related to the amount of seeds and the period over which they are to be stored. It is a waste of money to create expensive facilities capable of maintaining viability for 10 years if the seeds will never stay longer than nine months between collection and sowing. It is equally wasteful to spend money on seed collection, extraction and cleaning if storage conditions are so inadequate that the seeds are 90 per cent dead before they reach the nursery.

For general accounts of seed storage of forest tree seeds, there are a number of useful references. They deal mainly or exclusively with temperate species. More intensive studies have been made of the storage of agricultural seeds and there is good reason to accept that the general principles established for agricultural crops apply also to forest trees. An excellent recent account of the subject as applied to agricultural seeds is contained in 'Principles and practices of seed storage' and there is also much useful information in the slightly older publications of Roberts and Harrington. Long-term storage for gene resource conservation is well covered by Cromarty *et al.*

NATURAL LONGEVITY OF TREE SEEDS

The period for which seed can remain viable without germinating is greatly affected by its quality at the time of collection, its treatment between collection and storage and the conditions in which it is stored. Nevertheless, seed longevity varies enormously from species to species even if they are given identical treatment and storage conditions.

Ewart divided seeds into three biological classes according to the time for which they are capable of retaining viability under 'good' storage conditions:

- *Microbiotic*: Seed life span not exceeding 3 years
- *Mesobiotic*: Seed life span from 3 to 15 years
- *Macrobiotic*: Seed life span from 15 to over 100 years.

Although Ewart's classes were useful in drawing attention to the differences in natural longevity of seeds of different species, his classification is too rigid to fit the variations between individuals, provenances and seed years in a single species, or the possible variations in storage conditions. It is not possible to define a standard set of 'good' storage conditions equally suitable to all species, because species vary in their requirements for optimum conditions. Yet storage life of a given species will vary greatly according to the conditions in which it is stored.

Today two major classes of seed are recognised:

1. Orthodox. Seeds which can be dried down to a low MC of around 5 per cent (wet basis) and successfully stored at low or sub-freezing temperatures for long periods.
2. Recalcitrant. Seeds which cannot survive drying below a relatively high moisture content (often in the range 20–50 per cent wet basis) and which cannot be successfully stored for long periods.

Within these two classes some further subdivision may be made, for example between orthodox seeds with or without hard coats and between recalcitrant seeds which can or cannot withstand low temperatures of below around 10°C. Within each of the main classes there are still considerable differences between species in the period for which viability is maintained under a given set of conditions. There may also be a distinction between truly recalcitrant species and species that are just difficult; the latter may turn out to behave in an orthodox manner if, for example, particular attention is paid to the methods of drying them.

HARD-COATED ORTHODOX SEEDS

Most, if not all, of the species which have been recorded as maintaining seed viability over a period of decades are hard-seeded. They include a number of tropical leguminous species. Examples of species of which at least some seeds maintained viability after lengthy periods of storage in herbaria, cited by Harrington from the work of Ewart and Becquerel are:

158 Years	Cassia Multijuga
149 Years	Albizzia Julibrissin
115 Years	Cassia Bicapsularis
99 Years	Leucaena Leucocephala

Ambient conditions in herbaria storage can be considered good (fairly low relative humidity and temperature) but well short of the combination of low initial MC, sealed storage and sub-freezing temperature now considered ideal for longterm storage of orthodox species.

Recent research has provided more precise information on conditions of storage, initial germination and final germination of some species, but over shorter periods. Examples are:

Species	**Conditions of Storage**	**Pre-storage germination %**	**Post-storage germination %**	**Period (years)**
Prosopis juliflora[1)]	Dry atmosphere of herbarium in S.W.	?	60	50
Acacia aneura[2)]	Closed containers at room temperature (20–25°C)	56	60	13
A. hemsleyi[2)]	" " "	96	96	13
A. holosericea[2)]	" " "	95	84	14
A. leptopetala[2)]	" " "	73	72	18
A. victoriae[2)]	" " "	80	60	18

As explained later in this chapter, modern thinking has defined low MC, low temperature and low oxygen pressure as the three most important constituents of the storage conditions which man should provide to maximize seed longevity in orthodox species. In the impermeable seedcoat nature has provided two of these constituents, a low MC and exclusion of oxygen. Full-sized but green leguminous seeds, sown immediately without drying, may germinate at once, indicating that the seedcoat has not yet developed an impermeable layer; no doubt the development of impermeability is synchronized in nature with the reduction of seed moisture by natural drying to the optimum content for longevity. Hard seeds are thus a potent factor in extending seed life in all conditions of storage but confer their most important benefits when storage facilities are limited and during the potentially dangerous period between collection and entry into long-term storage.

Not all leguminous seeds are equally long-lived, for example Koompassia malaccensis seeds have thinner seedcoats and deteriorate more rapidly in storage than species such as Parkia javanica, and they need no pretreatment to overcome seedcoat dormancy. In Sudan seeds of Dalbergia sissoo stored less well at room temperature than those of local Acacia, Albizzia and Tamarindus species, while in Australia seeds of Acacia harpophylla deteriorate rapidly unless stored in sealed containers at 2–4 °C.

ORTHODOX SEEDS WITHOUT HARD SEEDCOATS

Many species in important genera of forest trees fall into this group, *e.g.* Pinus, Picea, Eucalyptus. Experience in Australia is that mature seeds of all eucalypts can be kept viable for some years if stored with a low moisture content in sealed containers at 3°–5°C. The majority of species can be stored for 10 years at room temperature with relatively little loss of viability. Both E. deglupta and E. microtheca seeds deteriorate more rapidly if stored at room temperature, but storage life is improved if they are kept in air-tight containers at 3°–5°C and recent evidence suggests that storage at-18°C is even better.

In Thailand seeds of P. kesiya and P. merkusii retained good viability for four years if stored at below 8 per cent moisture content in sealed containers at 0°–5°C, while at least five years' good viability is possible withP. caribaea and P. oocarpa under similar conditions. Considerably longer periods have been recorded for some species of pine *e.g.* 30 years for Pinus resinosa in USA when stored in sealed containers at 1.1°–2.2°C. Tectona grandis is an orthodox tropical broadleaved species but, since it produces good seed crops in most years, there has been little stimulus to investigate optimum conditions for long-term storage.

According to evidence summarized by Bowen and Whitmore, most Agathis spp. are orthodox. For example, an appropriate treatment ofA. australis in one study (dried to 6 per cent MC, then stored in sealed containers at 5°C) preserved viability for 6 years (79 per cent germination compared with the initial 88 per cent), while storage at below freezing temperature maintained a germination of about 60 per cent for up to 12 years. The same seed stored at higher MC or temperatures (15–20 per cent MC. or 15°–20°C) had lost all germination power within 14 months. A australisseed is inherently longer lived than A. robusta which in turn is longer lived than A. macrophylla. Initial trials with the tropical A. macrophyllaindicated that good results could be obtained by drying fresh seeds from about 65 per cent to 20 per cent before despatch by air (period in transit 14 days) and by further drying in the recipient country for 5 days at 16°C and 14 per cent RH. final MC was 6 per cent and germination 75 per cent. However, later trials were inconsistent and less successful. With tropical species, it is likely that handling between collection and despatch and the largely uncontrollable conditions of air transit are more critical than in the easier temperate or subtropical species.

Orthodox species which rapidly lose viability unless they are given the optimum treatment include species in the mainly temperate generaPopulus, Salix and Ulmus. Many of these lose viability within a few weeks under natural conditions or if stored in ambient conditions of temperature and humidity, but can be stored for months or years if maintained at low temperature and low moisture content. Examples are ofUlmus americana stored successfully for 15 years at 3 per cent moisture content and-4°C, and Populus sieboldii stored for 6 years at-15°C over a desiccating agent in a sealed container. In Populus balsamifera and Salix glauca, reduction in germination after two years of sealed storage at-10°C was less than 6.5 per cent of initial germination; after three years there was very little change in Populus but up to 40 per cent reduction in Salix.

In the tropics Aucoumea klaineana is a good example of an orthodox species which is short-lived under ambient conditions. Germination of fresh seed is often over 90 per cent, but after 30 days' storage in room conditions there is a significant drop in germination and this falls to zero after 100 days. Storage at 0–5°C and 7–8 per cent MC in sealed containers with a chemical desiccator, Actigel, maintains over 50 per cent germination for at least 30 months. There is some indication that a further reduction of MC will conserve viability even better.

Thus one seed lot of initial germination 76 per cent in the laboratory and 79 per cent in sand, when stored in sealed containers with Actigel, had an MC of 4.6 per cent and a germination of 70 per cent in the laboratory and 79 per cent in sand after 30 months; the same seed lot stored in sealed containers without Actigel had an MC of 9.9–10.4 per cent and a germination of 54–63 per cent in the laboratory and 62–67 per cent in sand. Other species of this type include Entandrophragma angolensewhich has a seed life of 6 weeks in room conditions but up to 6 years in cold storage and Cedrela odorata which loses all germination capacity in 10 months at room temperature but suffers no loss in 14 months if stored at 5°C in a sealed jar.

Some species may need special treatment to prolong viability for more than a few months. Fagus sylvatica can be conserved overwinter by maintaining MC at 20–30 per cent and storing part-filled in sealed polythene bags at 0–5°C for 100 days. It is then suitable for sowing because such storage conditions constitute a suitable pretreatment to break dormancy. If longer storage is intended, MC should be reduced to 8–10 per cent by drying in a current of air at room temperature (15–20°C). The nuts are then placed in sealed containers and stored at-5° to-10°C and will keep for several years. Later research in France and Poland confirmed the above MC of 8–10 per cent and the advantages of sealed containers for long term storage. This technique has been successfully applied on a large scale (17 tons of beechnuts from 51 different sources) in France. Germination has been maintained over periods of 4 to 6 years.

Where storage conditions leave much to be desired, the longevity of orthodox seeds without hard coats can be expected to be much inferior to the hard-coated species. The nearer that conditions of storage approach the ideal for a given non-hardseeded species, the less the difference between its longevity and that of a hardseeded species. The best combination of MC and temperature will vary to some extent between species, for example the above-quoted 8–10 per cent MC for Fagus sylvatica is considerably higher than the 5–6 per cent considered ideal for many forest and agricultural seeds.

RECALCITRANT SEEDS

Recalcitrant seeds include a number of large seeds that cannot withstand appreciable drying without injury; it is of interest that the overwhelming majority of recalcitrant species listed by King and Roberts are woody. Temperate species such as Quercus andCastanea are commonly stored moist only for short periods over winter. Reduction of storage temperature to near freezing will prolong longevity. Bonner found that it was possible to store acorns of Quercus falcata for 30 months and still obtain over 90 per cent germination at the end of the period, provided that temperature was maintained at 3°C and MC between 33 per cent (initial) and 37 per cent (final). A lower MC or a higher temperature (8°C) both reduced germination. For Quercus robur MC should be maintained above 40 per cent. Recent research in Poland has demonstrated good results from storing this species at >40 per cent MC in air-dry peat or air-dry sawdust in milk cans at-1°C. It is important to allow free entry of oxygen and this is ensured by inserting several strips of cardboard at intervals between the lid and the edge of the can.

In these conditions germination after 3 winters was in the range of 38–75 per cent and after 5 winters was still about 12 per cent. Temperatures below-5°C killed all the acorns, while a temperature of +1°C encouraged excessive pregermination (60–75 per cent after 3 winters, with radicles up to 25 cm long, compared with 12 per cent and radicles <0.5 cm long at-1°C). There may be possibilities of storing seeds after emergence of radicles. Recent research in Poland has indicated that best results are obtained with the recalcitrant Acer saccharinum by maintaining MC at the same percentage (50–52 per cent) as when the seeds were freshly collected. For A. pseudoplatanus in the UK a minimum MC of 35 per cent is recommended, while in Poland an MC of 24–32 per cent and a temperature of-3°C have proved suitable to store samaras over three winters.

Most short-lived recalcitrant tropical species are constituents of the moist tropical forests, where conditions conducive to immediate germination (high humidity and high temperature) are prevalent throughout the year. Typical genera are Hevea, Swietenia, Terminalia andTriplochiton, as well as a number of Dipterocarp genera such as Dryabalanops, Dipterocarpus and Shorea and some species of Araucaria.Dryabalanops is injured if dried below 35 per cent moisture content (MC) but still survives only about three weeks at over 35 per cent MC. Triplochiton seed is naturally short-lived but can be stored for up to 22 months at a temperature of around 6° C and a moisture content of between 12 and 25 per cent. Azadirachta indica seeds also have a short period of viability, although the species occurs in dry, not moist, tropical forests and it is not clear whether it is a genuine recalcitrant or simply a short-lived orthodox species.

Orthodox and recalcitrant species sometimes occur within the same genus. In Acer and Ulmus, genera in which both orthodox and recalcitrant seed behaviour occur, the distinction in North American species is clearly between spring-and fallseeders. A. rubrum and A. saccharinumflower and seed in the spring. Their seeds are not dormant, and their storage behaviour is clearly recalcitrant. Other Acer species have fall-maturing seeds, which are dormant and orthodox in nature at maturity.

The same occurs in Ulmus. Seeds of U. crassifolia and U. serotinamature in the fall, and are orthodox in storage behaviour. Spring-seeding species of Ulmus are 'weakly' recalcitrant. InAraucaria, A. cunninghamii and other spp. in the Eutacta taxonomic group behave as orthodox. In Queensland seeds of A. cunninghamii of 5 provenances were air dried and stored at varying temperatures in sealed and unsealed containers. At the higher temperatures, +1.7°C and-3.9°C, germination started to drop after 17 months' storage and after 8 years was down to about half the initial germination rate in sealed containers and about one third in unsealed containers. At the lower temperatures of-9.4°C and-15°C, germination after 8 years' storage was little changed from the initial (41–44 per cent compared with initial 49 per cent), and there was virtually no difference between sealed and unsealed containers.

The rate of viability loss at the higher storage temperatures varied from provenance to provenance, but all stored better at the lower temperatures. Moisture content was not recorded but under local conditions air-dry seed is normally in the range of 16–23 per cent. Later trials with Papua New Guinea A. cunninghamii have shown that seeds can be dried from 21 per cent to 7 per cent MC without any effect on initial germination rate; effects on storage life are still under investigation. A. hunsteinii in the Intermedia group and A. angustifolia, A. araucana and A. bidwillii in the Colymbea group are apparently recalcitrant. Arentz found that high viability of A. hunsteinii could be maintained for at least 6 months by storage at 3.5°C and high MC; 37 per cent was significantly better than 32 per cent. Research reported by Tompsett confirmed that MC should be maintained above 32 per cent. Placing the seed in one polythene bag of 25 microns thickness inside a second bag is effective in maintaining viability. The double thickness of polythene maintains a high MC but allows for some exchange of oxygen which is necessary to preserve viability of A. hunsteinii. A. angustifolia also needs a high MC; seeds died if dried to less than 25–30 per cent.

For some temperate recalcitrant species, as indicated above, a relatively low temperature (just above or just below 0°C) has been found beneficial in extending the life of the seeds; low temperature to some extent compensates for the high MC which must be maintained to prevent the early loss of viability. In some tropical species, seeds are quickly killed if temperature is reduced too low, just as they are quickly killed if MC is reduced too low. Among woody species cited in King and Roberts are Theobroma cacao (killed below +10°C), Mangifera indica(damaged below +3° to +6°C) and, among the dipterocarps, Hopea helferi, Hopea odorata and Shorea ovalis (damaged below, respectively, +5°C, +10°C and +15°C).

This susceptibility to chilling damage at temperatures above 0°C compounds the difficulty of storing these recalcitrant species, which seldom maintain viability for more than a few weeks or at most months. This compares with a normal seeding periodicity of several years in most dipterocarps, so there is no possibility as yet of conserving seeds in a viable condition from one good seed year to the next.

Unlike orthodox species, in which viability is best preserved by maintaining a minimal respiration rate, it appears that active respiration is necessary to survival of seeds of most recalcitrants. Thus damage to recalcitrant seeds has been reported not only from inadequate MC and too low a temperature but also from lack of oxygen *e.g.* in Araucaria hunsteinii, Hevea brasiliensis and Quercus spp.

Whereas some temperate recalcitrant species have been stored successfully for several years, seed longevity in tropical recalcitrants can be measured in days or weeks. The amount of research on tropical species is still small, especially on forest species, and it is possible that seed longevity could be prolonged beyond a few weeks if the best combination of seed maturity, speed, conditions and degree of drying, and most suitable storage temperature could be determined for each species. King and Roberts suggest a research strategy.

FACTORS AFFECTING LONGEVITY IN STORAGE

SEED CONDITION

Even in ideal storage conditions seed will soon lose viability if it is defective from the start.

Factors to be considered are:

- *Seed maturity*: Fully ripened seeds retain viability longer than seeds collected when immature. Certain biochemical compounds, essential for preserving viability, may not be formed until the final stages of seed ripening. These include dormancy-inducing compounds in certain species, and dormancy is sometimes associated with seed longevity. In a few species *e.g.* Gingko biloba,Fraxinus excelsior, seed embryos are underdeveloped when the seed is shed. Maturation of these embryos is necessary before sowing but need not be done before storage. In Fraxinus excelsior drying of freshly collected samaras to 9–10 per cent MC, followed by storage in sealed containers at-3° C, gives satisfactory results provided that successive moist warm and moist cold treatments are applied after storage.

- *Parental and annual effects*: In seed harvest, quantity and quality often go together. The percentage of sound seeds in a high-yielding mother tree is usually higher than in one with a poor crop. Similarly, a given mother tree will have a higher percentage of sound seeds in a good crop year than in a poor one. Collection from high-cropping mother trees in a seed year is likely to yield seeds with the best longevity in storage. On the other hand, high-cropping 'wolf' trees should be avoided because of their potentially undesirable wood properties, even though they may produce long-storing seeds.
- *Freedom from mechanical damage*: Seeds damaged mechanically in extraction, cleaning, dewinging etc. rapidly lose viability. The danger is greatest for species which have thin or soft seedcoats. Excessive heat during extraction or drying also damages seed. Care should be taken to use the minimum times, lowest temperatures and minimum machine speeds necessary during the preparation of seed for storage. In some species, damage during dewinging may be reduced by partly restoring the moisture content between extraction from cones and dewinging, since moist seeds suffer less mechanical damage than dry ones.
- *Freedom from physiological deterioration*: Poor handling in the forest, during transit or during processing causes physiological deterioration of seeds even if mechanical and fungal damage are absent. Adequate ventilation of orthodox seeds is necessary to avoid rapid respiration and overheating, while recalcitrant seeds must be protected against excessive drying.
- *Freedom from fungi and insects*: For species stored at low temperature and low moisture content, the storage conditions themselves should prevent the

development of fungi and insects. It is necessary, however, to avoid collection of crops showing a high incidence of fungal or insect attack and to carry out all operations of collection, transport, processing etc. as quickly as possible to ensure seed is not already damaged before it goes into storage. Attack by fungi and insects is most rapid on the forest floor, so collection from the ground should be carried out as soon after fruit fall as possible. Fungicidal treatment cannot be generally recommended since it can be harmful to seeds; many fungicides are only effective when dissolved in water and are inappropriate for dry storage. Insects are usually killed if seeds are dried at temperatures above 40°–42° C. For seeds which cannot be dried, other measures may be needed. For example seeds of Quercus are fumigated with serafume or other chemicals or heated in warm water for control of weevils, while methyl bromide or carbon bisulphide are also commonly used to kill insects.

- *Initial viability*: Seed lots with high initial viability and germinative capacity have a higher longevity in storage than those with low initial viability. Germination tests, preceded if necessary by appropriate pretreatment to overcome dormancy, should be carried out on a sample of each seed lot before storage, in order to determine how long the seed is likely to retain viability in storage. Longevity of the viable seeds is correlated with the percentage which germinate in the initial test. As an example, samples of two seed lots of the same species, from which 80 per cent germination of fresh seeds is normally expected, might give results of 90 per cent and 50 per cent initial germination. Not only would storage of the second seed lot involve wasting space in storing dead seed, but even the 50 per cent of initially viable seeds are likely to lose their viability more quickly in storage than would the 90 per cent viable seeds in the first seed lot. Deterioration in initial viability may not be serious if the seeds are to be sown within a few weeks or months, but only good quality seed should be stored for long periods. In long-term storage of agricultural seeds for genetic conservation, it is recommended that no seeds should be accepted for storage which have an initial viability of less than 85 per cent of that considered typical for the species or variety in question. It may be noted that initial viability and germinative capacity are frequently the resultant of the factors described in previous paragraphs (seed maturity, mechanical damage, fungal or insect attack).

STORAGE CONDITIONS AND AGEING OF SEEDS

In common with all other living things, seeds are subject to ageing and, eventually, to death. In the case of orthodox seeds, the process of ageing and deterioration is so greatly affected by the conditions of storage that the 'age' of seeds, expressed solely in terms of the period elapsed since ripening and harvesting, is an inadequate measure of the degree to which they have 'aged' in the sense of losing viability and progressing towards the irreversible deterioration of death.

The term 'physiological age' is commonly used to describe the degree of deterioration of seeds measured by their reduced capacity for germination. Nomographs for the effects of temperature and MC on physiological ageing of seeds have been constructed for several agricultural crops. As an example, the nomograph for barley indicates that the same degree of deterioration (from initial 95 per cent to final 50 per cent germination) would occur in about 16 days in seeds stored at 25°C and 21 per cent MC, but in about 100 years in seeds stored at 8°C and 8 per cent MC. Both seed lots would have the identical physiological age, though stored for very different periods of time. Similar effects can be expected in orthodox seeds of forest trees.

A number of physiological changes in cell tissues may be associated with physiological ageing in seeds.

They include:

- Loss of food reserves caused by respiration, *e.g.* decrease in proteins and non-reducing sugars, accompanied by increase in reducing sugars and free fatty acids
- Accumulation of toxic or growth-inhibiting by-products of respiration
- Loss of activity of enzyme systems
- Loss of ability of dried proteid molecules to recombine to form active protoplasmic molecules on subsequent rehydration
- Deterioration of semi-permeable cell membranes
- Lipid peroxidation, leading to production of free radicals which react with, and damage, other components in the cell
- Alterations to DNA in cell nucleus, causing genetic mutations as well as physiological damage. It is still uncertain to what extent these various effects are the causes or only the symptoms of deterioration, but it has been suggested that the production of free radicals is the first effect of ageing and that damage to the several systems in the cells is the subsequent result of the release of free radicals.

Whatever the exact mechanism of seed deterioration, there is a consensus that, in orthodox seeds, loss of seed viability is largely governed by the rate of respiration. Any measures which reduce the rate of respiration without otherwise damaging the seed are likely to be effective in extending longevity during storage. These are the control of oxygen, the control of moisture content and the control of temperature. Inrecalcitrant seeds the safe minimum levels of oxygen, moisture content and temperature, and hence of respiration, are all considerably higher than those for orthodox seeds but, provided levels are maintained above the safe minima for each species, it appears that longevity can be extended by keeping them as close to the minima as possible in order to avoid an excessively high respiration rate.

STORAGE ATMOSPHERE

The most obvious method of reducing the rate of aerobic respiration is to exclude oxygen from the atmosphere surrounding the seeds. This can be done by replacing oxygen by other gases such as CO_2 or nitrogen, or by using a partial or complete vacuum. In an example with lettuce cited by Roberts, seeds were stored in sealed containers at 6 per cent MC and 18° C. After 3 years, seed stored in an atmosphere of pure oxygen had 8 per cent viability, those in air 57 per cent, those in nitrogen or argon or CO_2 78 per cent and those in a vacuum 77 per cent.

The value of excluding oxygen during storage of dry orthodox seeds has also been demonstrated in Pinus radiata. Best results were obtained with a storage atmosphere of nitrogen, followed by CO_2, while vacuum and air both gave poorer results. At the highest temperature used, 35°C, at which deterioration in viability was most rapid, the loss in final germination after 50 weeks' storage in sealed containers at 8 per cent MC was 8 per cent in nitrogen, 14 per cent in CO_2, 21 per cent in vacuum and 29 per cent in air. The same ranking was obtained by comparing the speed of germination and the vigour of germinated seedlings (measured as dry weight 49 days after sowing).

Although increases in seed longevity of this magnitude have been achieved experimentally, some of the methods are expensive to apply and the effects on seed life are less dramatic than the effects of differences in temperature and humidity. Exclusion of oxygen will prevent aerobic, but not anaerobic, respiration, whereas reduced MC and temperature will decrease the level of both. While systematic predictions have been made of seed longevity under a range of temperature and MC for several agricultural crops, similar quantitative predictions of the effect of oxygen levels on longevity are lacking.

One simple method which is recommended is to fill sealed containers as nearly full as possible. If there is only a small amount of air inside the container as compared with the volume occupied by the seeds, oxygen will be consumed and CO_2 produced. The resulting high CO_2/O_2 ratio is probably favourable for seed longevity in orthodox seeds.

Whereas the complete exclusion of oxygen from the storage atmosphere appears beneficial to most dry orthodox seeds, there is evidence that some oxygen is necessary for recalcitrant seeds. Seeds of Araucaria hunsteinii, which had an initial germination of 56 per cent, had all died within a month if stored in pure nitrogen, in two months if stored in 1 per cent oxygen, and in three months if stored in 5 per cent oxygen, while germination was still 18 per cent after four months' storage in 10 per cent oxygen. Storage in a polythene bag of 25 micron thickness, which was ventilated (21 per cent oxygen) periodically when opened for extraction of samples, gave results very similar to those in 10 per cent oxygen. King and Roberts record a general consensus that adequate ventilation (*i.e.* adequate oxygen), is necessary for the successful storage of recalcitrant seeds at relatively high MC, as well as for storage of imbibed seeds of orthodox species.

SEED MOISTURE CONTENT

The relationships of seed moisture content on a wet weight or fresh weight basis to seed MC on a dry weight basis, and of the equilibrium moisture content of seeds to the relative humidity of the surrounding atmosphere, are important in seed processing and are explained. They are equally important in seed storage. In the first case manipulation of RH can effectively change MC of seeds to the optimum for storage, in the second case MC can be maintained at or near that optimum by maintaining a suitable RH in the atmosphere around and between the seeds.

Effect of MC. In orthodox seeds, moisture content is probably the most important single factor in determining seed longevity. Reduction in MC causes a reduction in respiration and thus slows down ageing of the seed and prolongs viability. Harrington, cited by Barner, has related MC to various processes within and around the seed as follows:

Seed Moisture Content % (Wet Weight)	
Above 45 – 60 %	Germination begins
Above 18 – 20 %	The seed may heat (due to a rapid rate of respiration and energy release)
Above 12 – 14 %	Fungus Growth Can Occur
Below 8 – 9 %	Insect Activity Much Reduced
4 – 8 %	Sealed Storage is Safe.

Prevention of fungal activity is more easily achieved by controlling MC than by controlling temperature. If MC and RH are high enough, fungal activity is possible between-8°C and +80°C and it is easier to keep MC below 12–14 per cent (or RH to the equilibrium of around 65 per cent) than to maintain sub-zero temperatures.

Within the range of 4 to 14 per cent MC, Harrington has suggested a rule of thumb applicable to many agricultural species-the life of the seed is doubled for every 1 per cent decrease in MC, Schönborn found a relationship of a similar order when measuring the respiration rate, expressed in terms of CO_2 production, of Picea abies. At 20°C and 20 per cent MC the seed gave off 80 ml. CO_2 per hour per kg of seed; at 20°C and 5 per cent MC, the rate of CO_2 production was reduced to 0.11 ml/hr/kg, a reduction of nearly a thousand times for a difference of 15 percentage points in MC.

An MC of 4–8 per cent is considered safe for most orthodox species; 5 per cent ± 1 per cent is recommended for long-term storage for genetic conservation. Oily seeds will usually tolerate drying to a somewhat lower moisture content (calculated on the basis of total fresh weight) than will non-oily seeds. Drying below 4 per cent can lead to damage or more rapid loss of viability in some species, although certain species can be dried to a considerably lower MC. Betula papyrifera was successfully stored at 0.6 per cent MC without injury, while Schönborn succeeded in drying small samples of Picea abies, Pinus sylvestris, Pseudotsuga menziesii and Larix decidua down to 0 per cent MC without any observable drop in germination after 6 months, compared with germination at the normally applied 6–8 per cent MC.

Drying in this case was done, not by exposing the seeds to high temperatures but by leading a current of dry air through the seeds at 20° C. The same treatment killed Pinus strobus and Abies alba, and earlier attempts by Barton to store seeds of several species of Pinus and Picea at 0 per cent MC also failed. Below about 2 per cent MC desiccation injury becomes a strong possibility in many species. Drying to very low MC is also more costly than drying to the usual 4–8 per cent and is likely to be used only in exceptional cases. Methods of drying are described on pp. 95–107.

Some orthodox forest trees store best at appreciably higher MC. As mentioned on p. 134, 8–10 per cent is recommended for Fagus sylvatica. For seeds of Abies spp., an MC of 12–13 per cent is recommended for storage of one to three years, but for longer periods this should be reduced to 7–9 per cent. Species which benefit from storage at higher than average MC also need particular care in the timing and speed of drying.

Fluctuation in the moisture content of seed in storage due to open storage without humidity control or to frequent opening and resealing of sealed containers results in deterioration in the germinability of the seeds. In fact a steady MC slightly above the optimum is usually less harmful than one which fluctuates between the optimum and a higher moisture content.

Some cases have been reported in which the usual trend of decreasing seed longevity associated with increasing MC is reversed at or near the moisture content of fully imbibed seeds. If the species in question needs exposure to light in order to germinate, it is possible to store fully imbibed but ungerminated seeds for some time in the dark. Fraxinus americana was stored at 22° C at varying MCs with the following results:

MC %	Germination (%) After Storage Periods Indicated			
	1 Month	2 Months	3 Months	4 Months
6.0	98	92	96	94
9.5	94	88	76	4
18.6	81	22	0	0
Fully Imbibed (In Dark)	96	95	98	96

It has been postulated that imbibed seeds can repair damage to cell membranes, enzymes and DNA in the cell nucleus caused by free radicals in a way which is not possible for seeds at lower MC. Prolonged imbibed storage may, however, be difficult in practice, because of the need to maintain constant high moisture for imbibition and adequate oxygen without allowing the seeds to germinate or encouraging the multiplication of fungi and bacteria.

Moisture content is also important in recalcitrant seeds, but in this case the critical MC is the minimum to which it is allowable to dry the seeds rather than the maximum content for prolonged storage. For many of the large temperate hardwood seeds, moisture contents in the range of 25–79 per cent are appropriate. Storage should be carried out at close to the minimum safe MC, since the higher the MC the higher the respiration rate and the more rapid the loss of viability. Higher respiration rates release higher amounts of energy and there is a risk of overheating and death of the seed, unless great care is taken to provide adequate aeration.

High MC also increases fungal activity and the spread of rot. Wang quotes results from two seed lots of Acer saccharinum; germinability of one lot stored at 58 per cent MC and 1–2° C dropped from 94 per cent to 12 per cent after 6 months' storage, while that of the other, stored at 45 per cent MC at the same temperature, was still 78 per cent after 16 months. Loss of viability in this species may be sudden. Tylkowski found that seeds stored in sealed bottles at 50–52 per cent MC and-1° to-3°C had over 90 per cent germination after 18 months but this dropped to nearly zero after 24 months.

Less research has been done on tropical recalcitrant species, but there is some evidence *e.g.* in Triplochiton, that viability may be significantly prolonged if the minimum MC for the species can be determined and if particular care is taken over the period of drying down to that MC. Trials of Shorea platyclados in Malaysia indicated that a gradual reduction of MC to 20–27 per cent, followed by sealing in charcoal, sawdust or vermiculite at 15°–22° C allowed storage for at least one month, compared with the week or so of natural viability.

On the basis of experiments carried out on Shorea parvifolia and Dipterocarpus humeratus, Maury-Lechon *et al* recommended reduction of MC to between one quarter and one half of the initial MC in freshly collected fruits. Although tropical recalcitrant seeds cannot yet be stored for more than short periods, there is a growing body of useful research on the problem. King and Roberts contains a good summary of achievements and possible approaches.

STORAGE TEMPERATURE

Temperature, like moisture content, is negatively correlated with seed longevity; the lower the temperature the lower the rate of respiration and thus the longer the life-span of the seed in storage. Harrington suggested another rule of thumb for agricultural seeds-between 50°C and 0°C, every 5°C lowering of storage temperature doubles the life of the seed. For orthodox seeds, which can be dried to a low moisture content, still greater longevity can be assured by storage at sub-freezing temperatures. For long-term storage for genetic conservation of agricultural seeds, a temperature of-18°C has been recommended as the 'preferred' standard for most species and-10°C as an 'acceptable' standard for those species known to have an intrinsic high viability.

Much lower temperatures have been used with success on an experimental basis, *e.g.* in liquid helium at-269°C, but the high cost of maintaining such low temperatures for a long period would outweigh any (as yet unproven) advantages in increased longevity. Choice of storage temperature varies considerably according to species and the period for which the seed is to be stored.

The lower the temperature that has to be maintained in a cold store, the higher the cost, and provision of subfreezing temperatures may be unnecessary if seed is to be stored for only a year or two for afforestation projects. Holmes and Buszewicz noted that, in a number of experiments on conifers, the superiority of sub-freezing temperatures became evident only after prolonged storage over periods of about 5 years or more. Sub-freezing temperatures (-18°C) appear to prolong viability in tropical orthodox species such as Eucalyptus deglupta and Flindersia brayleyana.

Some seeds keep well at room temperature, *e.g.* many leguminous and rosaceous genera, Eucalyptus, Tilia and many other hard-seeded or stone fruits. Most species, however, only keep well for longer periods at lower temperatures. In 3–5 years' storage of most conifers and Alnusand Betula, the crucial temperature seems to lie at a maximum of +4°C. The temperature should therefore be kept at 1 to 4°C. For longer periods of storage, say 5–15 years, the temperature should be-4 to-10°C. For Abies, however, a temperature of-4°C is used for short storage periods and-10° to-20°C for longer periods.

Temperature and moisture factors are so interrelated that it is very difficult to separate them. Seeds at a relatively high moisture level can be stored for considerably longer periods at near freezing temperatures than at higher temperatures, while higher storage temperatures (30°C) are less harmful when the moisture content of the seed is low. In short, it can be said that the critical moisture content lies at a higher level when storage temperatures are low than when they are intermediate or high, *i.e.* to some extent, a low temperature can compensate for a high moisture content, and *vice versa*. It is, however, necessary to avoid any risk of freezing damage caused by ice formation in seeds of high MC. Roberts has suggested that 20 per cent MC may be the critical upper limit for storage at 0°C, 15 per cent for-20°C and 13 per cent for-196°C. If seeds are dried to 4–8 per cent MC as commonly recommended for orthodox species, there should be no danger of freezing damage, even at temperatures well below zero. As mentioned in Chapter 6, the equilibrium moisture content of many seeds at a given RH varies with temperature.

Barton and Crocker have shown that, at a range of RH from 35 per cent to 76 per cent, the amount of water contained by seeds increased progressively as temperature decreased from 30°C to 10°C. Species included Pinus as well as several agricultural crops. At low (35 per cent) RH moisture absorption by dry seeds was approximately the same at 5°C as at 10°C, but at higher (55 per cent and 76 per cent) RH the seeds absorbed less moisture at 5°C than at 10°C, thus reversing the trend above 10°C. Change of equilibrium moisture content with change of temperature can be of importance in open storage. In sealed containers the effect is minimal because the final EMC is dominated by the initial MC of the seeds and not the moisture of the enclosed air.

As with moisture content, repeated fluctuations in temperature lead to loss of viability. As far as possible, temperature should be maintained at a uniform level.

The effect of temperature on seed longevity of temperate recalcitrant species is similar to that of orthodox species-within certain limits the lower the temperature the longer the period of viability. Some tropical species are killed by temperatures above freezing *e.g.* some dipterocarps at <14°C, cacao at <10°C and mango at < 3–6°C. Seeds of Hopea helferi stored at 15°C with high moisture content in unsealed polythene bags retained 98 per cent germination after 37 days and 80 per cent after 60 days. Germination was much reduced if temperature was dropped to 10°C or raised to 25°–28°C. Shorea ovalis is another species which does not withstand low temperatures; it stores best at 21°C. Shorea talura, in contrast, stores well at 4°C and 40 per cent MC (wet weight basis); after six months germination was reduced from an initial 95 per cent to 69 per cent. Other species of dipterocarp have a much shorter seed life.

For most temperate recalcitrant species the lower the temperature down to 0°C the longer the safe storage period. Below-freezing temperatures, on the other hand, often kill recalcitrant seeds which need to be stored at a high moisture content. Some success has been achieved in storing Quercus seeds in the USA by maintaining them at 35–45 per cent moisture content and-1° to +3°C temperature. Temperature can be critical because less than-1°C will usually kill the seeds, while temperatures above 2° or 3°C cause excessive germination. In Europe more northerly species of Quercus can be stored at slightly lower temperature-1° to-3°C and 38–45 per cent MC.

LIGHT

Light, particularly ultra-violet light, is reported to be harmful to seed, but very few studies have been made. Use of opaque metal containers would be preferable to glass jars or bottles for species which are affected by light. But light appears to be much less important than either moisture content or temperature.

CHOICE OF STORAGE METHOD

A number of different storage methods are available, as described below. The main factors affecting choice are the seed characteristics of the species in question, the period for which it is to be stored and the cost. If more than one method is suitable to maintain viability for the required period, the simplest and cheapest will normally be chosen.

STORAGE AT AMBIENT TEMPERATURE AND HUMIDITY

Seeds can be stored in piles, single layers, sacks or open containers, under shelter against rain, well ventilated and protected against rodents. Best results are obtained in cool, dry climates. In these conditions several species of Pinus, Eucalyptus Pseudotsuga and Tectona will store satisfactorily for at least six months, while leguminous trees with impermeable seedcoats and naturally low MC, *e.g.* Acacia Prosopis, Robinia will retain viability for years.

DRY STORAGE WITH CONTROL OF MC BUT NOT OF TEMPERATURE

Orthodox seeds will retain viability longer, when dried to a low moisture content (4–8 per cent), as described, and then stored in a sealed container or in a room in which humidity is controlled, than when stored in equilibrium with ambient air humidity. Storage life is further prolonged if cool, but not controlled, temperature conditions can be provided, *e.g.* at high latitude or altitude and in a cellar or other room screened from direct sunlight.

Seed is sometimes stored in open containers in a room maintained at an RH of 15–20 per cent by dehumidifying machinery. In forestry it is more common to rely on predrying of the seed to the correct MC, followed by storage in full, sealed containers. Provided that the containers are not opened too frequently and that the sealing is effective, the method will maintain a low MC for many years. It is cheaper than using a humidity-controlled room, especially during periods when only a little seed is in store, and it is not subject to hazards of mechanical breakdown.

This method is suitable for a range of species including many Pinus and Eucalyptus species, for which it should maintain viability for one or more years.

DRY STORAGE WITH CONTROL OF BOTH MC AND TEMPERATURE

This storage treatment is the standard practice for many orthodox species which have periodicity of seeding but which are planted annually in large-scale afforestation projects. For many species a combination of 4–8 per cent MC and 0 to +5°C temperature will maintain viability for 5 years or more. Some cool-temperate genera benefit by storage at sub-freezing temperatures, *e.g.*-4°C or lower for Abies,-10°C forFagus,-18°C for Pinus strobus, Populus deltoides and others. Pinus merkusii is an example of a tropical pine which responds well to storage at low temperature and MC. 80 per cent germination was obtained after 3 years' storage at 2°C and 6–10 per cent MC of seeds of the Zambales (Philippines) provenance, while seeds stored in equilibrium with room temperature and humidity showed a significant loss of germination after 3–4 months. P. caribaeaand P. oocarpa behave similarly in this respect.

In addition to true seeds, this method is also suitable for certain types of fruits. For example in the Jari project of Brazil depulped, cleaned and dried stones of Gmelina arborea are successfully stored in sealed containers at 5°C and 6–10 per cent MC. The fresh stones have a germination of 90 per cent and after two years of storage germination is still 80 per cent.

DRY STORAGE FOR LONG-TERM GENE CONSERVATION

The preferred storage treatment for long-term conservation of gene resources of orthodox agricultural seeds is-18° C temperature and 5 per cent +-1 per cent MC. This is likely to be equally appropriate for orthodox seeds of forest trees requiring storage for genetic conservation. The quantity of seeds requiring this standard of storage is small in comparison with the quantities used each year for operational afforestation, and the cost per kg of seed is higher.

For many countries it would therefore be desirable that forest and agricultural crop genetic resources should share a common long-term storage facility. A good example is that of the Banco Latino Americano de Semillas Forestales at CATIE, Turrialba which has its own seed store (55 m^3 capacity at 5°C) for short or medium term storage, but also has access to the long-term storage facilities (at-20°C) of the Regional Genetic Resources Unit, which are also at Turrialba.

Loss of viability in storage, in addition to reducing the number of plants which can be produced by a given seed lot, may result in a shift in the genetic constitution of the seed being stored. This could be particularly important in forest trees which are predominantly outbreeding, variable populations. First, loss of viability may occur more rapidly in some genotypes than others; if losses are high, say 50 per cent of the total, the genotypes with short-lived seeds may be eliminated altogether. Yet they may have valuable traits for adaptation, growth or disease resistance as growing trees, and in any case they contribute to genetic variation in the species which it is the purpose of genetic conservation to preserve. Secondly, it is an accepted fact in agriculture that chromosome damage or change occurs and accumulates in the seed in storage, and that the risk of such heritable gene mutations depends not so much on the age of the seed as on changes in its viability.

A seed lot which has suffered a serious loss of viability is likely to have experienced some gene mutations among the survivors, but there is very little direct evidence that heritable mutations are induced under good storage conditions which lead to only small losses in viability.

The high standard of storage conditions recommended by the IBPGR and referred to above, if combined with regular testing of seed and regeneration as soon as germination falls to 85 per cent of the initial germination rate should minimize the risk of genetic change in storage. It is possible that still lower temperatures would increase longevity even more. Research on storage in liquid nitrogen has been pursued for some years and considerable progress has been made, but testing for several more years will be needed before the method can be recommended for general adoption in gene banks.

MOIST STORAGE WITHOUT CONTROL OF MC OR TEMPERATURE

Suitable for storage of recalcitrant seeds for a few months over winter. Seeds may be stored in heaps on the ground, in shallow pits in well-drained soils or in layers in well ventilated sheds, often covered or mixed with leaves, moist sand, peat or other porous materials. Seeds stored outdoors are kept moist by rain or snow, but those under shelter may need to be moistened periodically. The aim is to maintain moist and cool conditions, combined with good aeration to avoid overheating which may result from the relatively high rates of respiration associated with moist storage. This may be accomplished by regular turning of the heaps of seed or by inserting bundles of straw or twigs into them.

This method is suitable for short-term storage of large-seeded hardwood species in the temperate zone *e.g.* Quercus, Castanea, Aesculus. It is unlikely to be suitable for tropical recalcitrant species because ambient temperature is too high.

Outdoor stratification, a method of overcoming internal dormancy, is described. It is properly to be considered as a seed pretreatment, but it serves the incidental function of storing the seed for a few weeks or months and the method used is closely akin to those described.

MOIST COLD STORAGE WITH CONTROL OF TEMPERATURE

This method implies controlled low temperatures just above freezing or, less commonly, just below freezing. Moisture can be controlled within approximate limits by adding moist media *e.g.* sand, peat or a mixture of both to the seed, in the proportions of one part media to 1 part seed by volume, and remoistening periodically, or more accurately (but more rarely) by controlling the relative humidity in the cold store.

The latter type of control is often too expensive. Respiration rate is reduced and storage life prolonged by the low temperature, but seed should not be stored in sealed gas-proof containers which would limit oxygen supply. Closed polyethylene bags of 4–10 mil (100–250 microns) thickness will allow exchange of oxygen and CO_2 with air outside, while severely restricting exchange of moisture.

The method is suitable for the same temperate recalcitrant genera as listed in the previous section, and with temperatures of 0–5° C should extend viability up to 1½ to 2 years. Sub-freezing temperatures have given improved results in a few cases but frequently injure seeds with high MC and should be used only after research has demonstrated their applicability to the species in question.

Less is known about the application of this method to tropical species, but it merits much more investigation that it has so far received, for the dipterocarps and genera such as Araucaria, Agathis and Triplochiton. As mentioned earlier there is evidence that some species are killed at low but above-freezing temperatures and Gordon has proposed a division of recalcitrant seeds into those which can withstand temperatures below 10° C without loss of viability and those which cannot.

Tamari, summing up several years of research on dipterocarps in Malaysia, concluded that the best treatment for several species was:

- Dry at a temperature not above 35°C, to reduce MC to 35 per cent
- Seal with a fungicide inside polythene bags
- Store at 15°C, or for 3 weeks at 15°C followed by further storage at 10°C.

This treatment has been successful in extending longevity from a week or two up to two months in Hopea helferi, but this is still a long way from providing safe storage between seed years, reported to vary from 3–6 years apart in many dipterocarps. Storage at 3.5°C and MC over 32 per cent over periods of at least 6 months has been successful on the recalcitrant Araucaria hunsteinii.

In some recalcitrant species newly germinated seeds may retain viability better under moist cool storage conditions than ungerminated seeds. Gordon reported that some pregerminated seedlots of Quercus spp. showed no significant change in the number of living seedlings after one year's storage in 500 gauge (125 microns) polythene bags lightly sealed at 3°C, whereas a large proportion of the seeds which were viable but ungerminated when placed in the same bags died during the same period.

OTHER METHODS

Other storage methods have been used in the past, but are not yet of wide application.

They include:

- Storage of recalcitrant seeds in running (not stagnant) water.
- Storage under partial vacuum.
- Storage in gases other than air *e.g.* nitrogen or CO_2.
- Coating individual large seeds with paraffin or latex to prevent moisture exchange. This method may also be used to maintain moisture content during shipment.

STORAGE CONTAINERS

Some form of container is necessary for most seed storage, to facilitate access to, and handling of, individual seed lots while keeping them separate, to make the best possible use of storage space, to provide protection against animal and insect pests and, for some seeds, to prevent passage of moisture and gases between the enclosed and the outside atmosphere. Many types of container have been used for tree seeds.

They may be conveniently divided into:

- Materials freely permeable to moisture and gases
- Materials completely impermeable, when sealed, to moisture and gases
- Materials resistant, but not completely impermeable, to moisture.

MATERIALS FREELY PERMEABLE TO MOISTURE AND GASES

These include hessian or burlap sacks, cotton bags and containers of paper, cardboard and fibreboard. Hessian and cotton have the advantage that seed triers can be inserted through the cloth mesh to withdraw samples for testing without the need to open the mouth of the container. The resilience of the cloth will close the hole and avoid subsequent loss of seed, which is not possible with containers based on paper or paperboard Hessian and cotton are also robust materials which can be used more than once.

None of these materials is entirely proof against insect and rodent pests, and all are freely permeable to water vapour and gases. For orthodox seeds in uncontrolled conditions they are therefore suitable only for rather short storage periods; these can be extended in the case of hardcoated seeds or where ambient conditions are cool and dry. If seeds are stored in large containers after drying to the correct MC, the outer seeds themselves provide some barrier to the passage of moisture. Viability of the inner seeds may thus be preserved for a period even though there is some deterioration from increased MC in the outer layers. If a seed store has facilities for controlling both temperature and relative humidity, then permeable containers can be safely used for orthodox seeds for several years, provided that pests can be excluded.

For moist storage of recalcitrant seeds, open or freely permeable containers such as hessian sacks should be used in order to allow free exchange of air and so avoid the overheating which can occur if moist, rapidly respiring seeds are enclosed without adequate ventilation. Periodic spraying of the sacks may be necessary to maintain the high MC which is appropriate for this type of seeds.

MATERIALS COMPLETELY IMPERMEABLE WHEN SEALED, TO MOISTURE AND GASES

After drying of orthodox seeds to the correct MC, the MC may be maintained in storage by dehumidifying the whole storage space. Another very efficient way, commonly used in storing forest seeds, is to place the seed in sealed moistureproof containers. This avoids the need for expensive dehumidification equipment. For long-term storage the most effective method is a combination of moisture proof containers with controlled low temperatures provided by refrigeration.

An added advantage of most materials in this type is that they also exclude oxygen and so reduce still further the rate of respiration. Impermeable sealed containers are not suitable for storing recalcitrant seeds nor are they suitable for orthodox seeds at high MC, which deteriorate more rapidly in sealed than in open storage. Some seeds absorb moisture quickly, so it is important that they be sealed inside the container as soon as possible after drying is complete, preferably within the drying room itself.

Moisture proof containers include tin or aluminium cans and drums, glass jars of the Mason or Kilner types, plastic vials and laminated aluminium foil packages. Rigid and unbreakable metal cans provide maximum protection against mechanical damage to the seeds and are equally suitable for storage and subsequent shipment. Containers are only as moisture proof as their sealing. For rigid containers screw-top or clamp-down gasketed lids should be used, if periodic opening for seed extraction and subsequent resealing are anticipated; aluminium foil should be heat-sealed.

The effectiveness of sealing is particularly important in long-term storage. Three types of container are considered suitable for hermetically sealed long-term storage of agricultural seeds: glass jars or vials; metal cans; and laminated foil packets. They should be equally appropriate for orthodox forest seeds. But the report by IBPGR recommended sealed metal cans as the most reliable and convenient.

It noted that the seals on screw-cap jars are not always perfect and that further experience of the lasting qualities of laminated foil packets is needed before they can be recommended for general use in storage which will often last for several decades.

MATERIALS RESISTANT, BUT NOT COMPLETELY IMPERMEABLE, TO MOISTURE

They include polyethylene and other plastic films and aluminium foil. These materials are resistant to the passage of moisture but, over a long period of time, there will be a slow passage of water vapour tending to equilibrate the RH inside with that outside the container. Some of the figures quoted by Justice and Bass for transmittal of water vapour appear surprisingly high, *e.g.* 0.13 g per 100 square inches (645 cm^2) per 24 hours for low density polyethylene film 10 mil (250 microns) thick and about ten times this figure for low density film 1 mil (25 microns) thick.

However, the standard conditions for testing these materials are 0 per cent RH on one side and 90–100 per cent on the other. The RH gradient during storage is never so severe as this and hence the rate of passage of water vapour is much less rapid in practice. In one test using 6 mil (150 microns) high density polyethylene the rate of passage over two years from an outside RH of 95–100 per cent at 20°/30°C was four times that from an outside RH of 50 per cent at 10°C. The thicker the film, the greater the resistance to passage of water vapour and, for a given thickness, high density polyethylene is more resistant than low density.

Although polyethylene is not suitable for long-term storage of orthodox seeds for genetic conservation, it is very suitable for short-or medium-term storage and has given excellent results for up to 5 years' storage of Pinus caribaea and P. oocarpa seeds in Honduras, with no significant change in MC.

For Honduran conditions a thickness of at least 4–5 mil (100–125 microns) is recommended; thinner polythene can permit a significant passage of water vapour in time and is also subject to mechanical damage in handling. Harrington considered 3 mil (75 microns) high density or 5 mil (125 microns) regular suitable for temperate conditions and 7 mil (175 microns) high density or 10 mil (250 microns) regular as adequate for even severe tropical conditions. Proper sealing of bags is essential and can be done by a combination of heat and pressure. In the past hot irons were used, but sealing can now be done more efficiently and conveniently by commercial heat sealers, of which a number of different models is now on the market.

Different materials, each alone slowly permeable to water vapour, may become completely impermeable when laminated together. Various combinations of laminated polyethylene, aluminium foil and kraft paper proved completely impermeable to water vapour over a two year period, even when there was a high differential between the inside and outside RH.

USE OF DESICCANTS IN CONTAINERS

If orthodox seeds are dried to the correct MC and stored in sealed impermeable containers, the MC should remain constant for years. If, however, the seeds are stored in moisture resistant but not completely impermeable material such as polythene bags, or if it is necessary to open and reclose the containers periodically to extract seeds, there will be a slow build-up of moisture in time.

A convenient way to prevent this is to enclose some desiccant such as silica gel in the containers. The capacity of silica gel to adsorb moisture depends on the relative humidity of the ambient air, as shown in the following table:

Table 5.1 Moisture Content of Silica gel in Equilibrium With Various Relative Humidities

% RH	% H_2O Adsorbed Adsorbed	% RH	% H_2O
0	0.0	55	31.5
5	2.5	60	33.0
10	5.0	65	34.0
15	7.5	70	35.0
20	10.0	75	36.0
25	12.5	80	37.0
30	15.0	85	38.0
35	18.0	90	39.0
40	22.0	95	39.5
45	26.0	100	40.0
50	29.0		

A convenient method is to use silica gel treated with cobalt chloride, which changes colour from blue to pink about 45 per cent RH; the corresponding equilibrium MC for many orthodox species would be 7–9 per cent. Dried silica gel is enclosed with the seeds and, whenever the granules turn pink, the silica gel is removed and reactivated by drying in an oven at 175°C and cooling in a sealed container before reuse. A weight of silica gel equal to one tenth the weight of seeds is recommended. Care should be taken not to include too much silica gel which could lead to overdrying of the seeds. Even with silica gel of one tenth the weight of seeds, the MC of seeds enclosed at 6 per cent would be lowered to below 5 per cent during the initial phase of storage. More frequent reactivation of silica gel would preserve an equilibrium of RH and seed MC at lower levels than the 45 per cent and 7–9 per cent mentioned above but would forego the convenience of the colour indicator.

Another use for desiccants is where the MC of seeds is known to be higher than the optimum for sealed storage, for example because only air-drying is possible. As mentioned, the enclosure with the seed of approximately an equal weight of silica gel in sealed containers should reduce the MC of the seed to a suitable level and maintain it. As an example,

1 kg (oven-dry weight) of seed at initial 19% MC (dry weight basis) contains		190 g H_2O
1 kg (oven-dry weight) of seed at 6% MC (dry weight basis) contains		60 g H_2O
Therefore moisture to be removed	=	130 g H_2O
RH in equilibrium with 6% MC	=	25 % RH
At RH 25%, 1 kg silica gel adsorbs		125 g H_2O

Therefore a weight of silica gel equal to the weight of seed will reduce the initial 19 per cent MC to just over 6 per cent MC for storage.

CHOICE AND USE OF CONTAINER

The following factors, which should be considered when choosing the best storage container for a given use, are based on those listed by Stein *et al.*: When seed requires further drying in storage, do not use a tight-closing container because enclosing excess moisture is harmful to the seed. Use a tight-closing container if gain in seed moisture content can be damaging and relative humidity in the storage facility is high. Containers and seed can quickly gather unwanted condensation when brought out of cool or subfreezing storage. Warming to room temperature is recommended before opening a container brought out of such storage. 4 to 10 mil (100–250 microns) polyethylene bags will greatly restrict exchange of moisture, but still allow exchange of oxygen and carbon dioxide with air outside. Such exchange may be beneficial or harmful, depending on species.

A container that is easy to open and close is desirable when quantities of seed are likely to be added or removed repeatedly. In order to minimize temperature and relative humidity fluctuations, open only when necessary. Alternatively, store seed in small containers, so that the entire contents can be stored or emptied at one time. For orthodox seeds, fill containers completely to ensure minimum exchange of moisture between the seed and the entrapped air and, more importantly, to limit the amount of oxygen enclosed. When exchange of moisture through the container walls must be eliminated or restricted, the container must be made impermeable or of moisture resistant material. The longer the storage period and the higher the differential between external RH and RH within the container, the more impermeable the material must be.

When seeds are fragile and easily damaged, a rigid-walled container should be used. Moisture-proof plastic bags are often used as liners for rigid containers. Choose a container shape and stacking arrangement which facilitates uniform temperature and aeration throughout the storage facility. Some containers may be made of substances that are harmful to tree and shrub seeds. Unproven containers should be tested for toxicity.

Fig. 5.1 Airtight Containers Used for Storing seed, Division of Forest Research, CSIRO Canberra

Fig. 5.2 Interior View of Cold Storage Room at Humlebaek, Denmark

Fig. 5.3 Examples of Different Types of Container used for Storage or Shipment in Denmark

Static electricity can build up slowly on some materials such as PVC. This makes them difficult to clean between exhaustion of one seed batch and insertion of the next.

It should be stressed that no one container or packaging material can be the best for all sizes, conditions and objectives that occur in seed packaging. The relative merits of the various containers will have to be weighed against their disadvantages and costs before deciding the final choice.

DESIGN AND ENGINEERING OF SEED STORAGE FACILITIES

STORAGE CAPACITY

The weight of seeds to be kept in store can be estimated in the manner indicated and will depend on the annual planting area, the maximum number of years' seed supply to be stored at any one time because of seeding periodicity, and the number of seeds per kg, for each species. Weight of seed in kg can be converted to net volume in litres (or in g to cm^3) by a factor related to average specific gravity. An average factor of 2.0 is appropriate for many forest species and corresponds to an apparent specific gravity of 0.5 (true specific gravity would be slightly higher because of the air-spaces between the seeds).

For conversion from net volume to gross storage space, allowing for shelving, ventilation, air spaces within and between containers, access and fittings within the cold room, a factor of about X8 is commonly used; this is with fixed shelving. Use of mobile shelving may double the quantity of seed which may be stored in a given space; in this case a factor of about X4 is appropriate. Thus 500 kg of seed of S.G. 0.5 would need a gross storage space of 500 × 2 × 8 = 8000 litres or 8 m^3 if fixed shelving were used and 4 m^3 with mobile shelving. Where relatively few seed lots and large quantities of each lot are being stored, it is possible to use standard sizes of container, each filled to the brim, and for shelving space to be adapted to fit container size exactly. Under these conditions considerable savings in storage space can be effected. Thus in the Danish seed store at Humlebaek, which uses fixed shelving, a factor of only 3.12 has been calculated.

DESIGN AND EQUIPMENT

The design and machinery for refrigerated storage is a matter for refrigeration engineers. Some guidance as to the features which should be included in any quotation for installation may be obtained from the excerpts from the IBPGR report which appears the example of the facilities installed by the Regional Genetic Resources Project at Turrialba which appears. It should be noted that both these documents refer to long-term storage of agricultural seeds for purposes of genetic conservation.

It is essential that designs and equipment be adapted to local conditions and local resources. The best installation in the world is of little use if it cannot be maintained, so it is essential to investigate the local provision for servicing and spares before committing oneself to any particular item. The reliability of mains electricity services and the need for a voltage controller and standby generator are of primary importance. Ready availability of a spare compressor may also be necessary.

The correct siting of a seed store may reduce the need for much expensive equipment. For example a tropical country with variable climate and topography might solve many problems by moving its store from a hot humid coastal site to the dry rain-shadow side of a mountain at 2000 m. In such a case a well-ventilated room might provide perfectly suitable conditions for several years' storage for relatively 'easy' species such as pines and eucalypts and could be supplemented by one or more deep-freeze chests for small quantities of more 'difficult' species requiring sub-freezing temperature. The value of deep-freeze chests was stressed by the IBPGR and its comments are reproduced.

SEED SHIPMENT

The benefits of exemplary seed collection, processing and storage methods may be largely lost if care is not taken over shipment from seed store to nursery. It is seed viability at the time of sowing, rather than at the time of despatch from the seed store, which determines the number of healthy plants produced from a particular seed lot. It is therefore essential to provide shipment methods which will ensure the minimum loss of viability in the interval between storage and sowing. The selection of appropriate packing material will depend on the characteristics of the species, the quantity to be shipped, the length of time in transit, the mode of transport and the temperature and moisture conditions to which the shipment will be exposel.

High and fluctuating temperatures and adverse humidity are the chief causes of viability losses during shipment. These factors are identical with those that cause deterioration in freshly collected fruits between the collecting site and the processing depot, as described. However, seeds between storage and sowing should start with advantage of having had optimum conditions of temperature and moisture content during the storage period. In fact, maintenance of storage conditions during transit would be ideal, but is often not possible.

Provided that the initial moisture content of the seeds is correct, it can be easily maintained during transit by the use of sealed containers. In some cases the seeds can be despatched in the same containers in which they were stored. In others it may be advisable to transfer them from a large container in storage to a smaller container for despatch. Individual nurseries may require only a small quantity of a given seed lot. In addition, small and light packages are often less subject to mechanical damage in transit than large, heavy ones. Magini recommends separate packages of 1–20 kg but not larger. A variety of moisture-proof or moisture-resistant material is available, as described earlier in this chapter under storage containers.

Polyethylene of 4–8 mil (100–200 microns) has the advantage of restricting moisture passage while allowing exchange of oxygen and CO_2.

Sealed containers are highly suitable for orthodox species, of which the seeds must be kept dry during transit. The addition of a desiccant such as silica gel may be a useful additional insurance if there is any risk that the seeds may absorb moisture while being transferred from storage container to shipment container. Seeds of recalcitrant species, on the other hand, are best left unsealed, since the effect of some loss of moisture is less harmful than that of the overheating which can occur as a result of rapid respiration in sealed bags at ambient temperatures. They should be well-mixed with pulverized sphagnum moss, ground peat, coconut fibre or sawdust, that has been moistened and squeezed dry. A mixture of equal weights of dry packing and water will give adequate moisture content to these materials. In the case of international transit, however, an inert non-organic substance such as moist vermiculite is likely to be more acceptable to quarantine authorities.

Sealed moisture-proof containers should always be used for long journeys, *e.g.* form one country to another, of orthodox species of short longevity, provided that the initial MC is correct. But if orthodox seeds are being forwarded soon after collection and without having been dried to the appropriate MC for storage, it is preferable to ship in bags permeable to air rather than to seal with excessively high MC. A number of species with resistant seedcoats or pericarps, such as Tectona and many leguminous species, are able to withstand prolonged periods in ambient conditions; cotton or paper bags or hessian sacks are perfectly suitable for these species.

Large, moist seeds can be sealed individually with paraffin wax or latex. In the method described by Baldwin paraffin wax is heated to 71°–77° C and seeds or nuts dipped for a few seconds in a screen-type container, which should be shaken vigourously during the immersion. The waxed seeds should be packed in soft material so that the wax is not scraped off during transit. At the time of sowing the wax must be partly scraped off to permit the entry of water.

Protection against high or rapidly fluctuating temperatures is more difficult, but care should be taken to avoid placing the seeds close to local hotspots such as radiators and hot pipes. For very sensitive seeds, temperature effects can be mitigated by the use of insulating material in the packaging. Sub-zero temperatures do not usually affect dry seeds but may cause damage to recalcitrant seeds which must be kept moist. Premature germination is another risk which affects moist seeds. During storage, germination can be restricted by the use of low temperatures just above freezing, but the higher temperatures encountered during transit may induce germination in a substantial number of seeds. Seeds which are prone to germinate when held in moist packing may be treated with an inhibitor such as maleic hydrazide.

No matter what type of seeds is being despatched, it is necessary to take precautions against mechanical damage to seeds and against losses due to damage to the containers in transit. Double wrapping is often advisable, for example a sealed polythene bag should be placed inside a stout canvas bag. Stout drum cartons with sealed polythene or aluminium-foil containers inside provide an especially effective combination for seeds which need to be kept dry. If the inner bag is labelled, this is also an insurance against accidental defacement of the outer label. Clear labelling is essential and the consignee should be advised of despatch by means of an appropriate seed consignment note or seed issue form.

Stein et al. have provided a useful check list of helpful practices in seed shipment, reproduced hereunder:

- Double wrap the seed. Enclose the seed container in a sturdy, preferably rigid, outer container;
- Small or moderate size containers generally withstand shipment better than large containers;
- Fill containers completely to minimize air content and jostling of seeds during shipment;
- All packages should bear a good identifying label on the innermost covering and another one within the container;
- For long distances, shipment of sensitive seeds by air is desirable;

- Seed packages should permit ready opening and reclosing if destined for export to a country requiring fumigation. In addition a copy of the phytosanitary certificate should be readily available to quarantine authorities *e.g.* by sealing it in an envelope which is firmly attached to the outside of the package.

Seed storage facilities at nursery sites or district forest stations are inferior to those at the central seed store. Shipments should therefore be timed so that seeds can be sown with the minimum delay after receipt.

6

Seed Dormancy

Seed dormancy is defined as a state in which seeds are prevented from germinating even under environmental conditions normally favourable for germination. These conditions are a complex combination of water, light, temperature, gasses, mechanical restrictions, seed coats, and hormone structures.

Below are the different ratings:

- Very Dormant
- Dormant
- Moderately dormant

* Categories of semi dormant and intermediate dormancy

- Moderately non-dormant
- Non-Dormant (moapa 69 for instance)
- Very Non-Dormant (cuf 101)

As a practical matter for sprout producers, more dormant seed is generally easier to grow without having spoilage problems, especially in the summer. However, it generally has more hard seed, takes longer to sprout, and has a lower yield. It is also generally less expensive.

TYPES OF SEED DORMANCY AND THE ROLES OF ENVIRONMENTAL FACTORS

During seed maturation, the embryo enters a quiescent phase in response to desiccation. Seed germination can be defined as the resumption of growth of the embryo of the mature seed; it depends on the same environmental conditions as vegetative growth does. Water and oxygen must be available, the temperature must be suitable, and there must be no inhibitory substances present.

However, in many cases a viable (living) seed will not germinate even though all the necessary environmental conditions for growth are satisfied. This phenomenon is termed seed dormancy. Seed dormancy introduces a temporal delay in the germination process that provides additional time for seed dispersal over greater geographical distances. It also maximizes seedling survival by preventing germination under unfavourable conditions.

Two types of seed dormancy have been recognized, coat-imposed dormancy and embryo dormancy. Coat-imposed dormancy is dormancy imposed on the embryo by the seed coat and other enclosing tissues, such as endosperm, pericarp, or extrafloral organs. The embryos of such seeds will germinate readily in the presence of water and oxygen once the seed coat and other surrounding tissues are either removed or damaged.

There are five basic mechanisms of coat-imposed dormancy:

- *Prevention of water uptake.* Prevention of water uptake by the seed coat is a common cause of seed dormancy in families found in arid and semiarid regions, especially among legumes, such as clover (*Trifolium* spp.) and alfalfa (*Medicago* spp.). Waxy cuticles, suberized layers, and lignified sclereids all combine to restrict the penetration of water into the seed.
- *Mechanical constraint.* The first visible sign of germination is typically the radicle breaking through the seed coat. In some cases, however, the seed coat may be too rigid for the radicle to penetrate. Nuts with hard, lignified shells are examples of dormancy caused by mechanical constraint. Such shells must be broken by biotic or environmental forces for the seed to germinate. Even nonlignified tissues, such as the endosperm of lettuce seeds, can suppress expansion of the embryo. For the seeds to germinate, the

endosperm cell walls must be weakened by the production of cell wall–degrading enzymes.

- *Interference with gas exchange.* Some seed coats are considerably less permeable to oxygen than an equivalent thickness of water is— *e.g.*, less by a factor of about 10^4 in seeds of cocklebur (*Xanthium pennsylvanicum*). This lowered permeability to oxygen suggests that the seed coat inhibits germination by limiting the oxygen supply to the embryo. In support of this idea, investigators can break the dormancy of such seeds either by making a small hole in the coat with a pin (without weakening the coat mechanically), or by treating the coat with concentrated oxygen. However, other studies suggest that the oxygen consumption of the embryos from such seeds is considerably less than the amount of oxygen able to penetrate the seed coats under normal aerobic conditions. Thus the role of oxygen impermeability in seed coat dormancy remains unresolved.
- *Retention of inhibitors.* The seed coat may prevent the escape of inhibitors from the seed. For example, growth inhibitors readily diffuse out of isolated *Xanthium* embryos, but not from intact seeds.
- *Inhibitor production.* Seed coats and pericarps may contain relatively high concentrations of growth inhibitors that can suppress germination of the embryo. ABA is a common germination inhibitor present in these maternal tissues. In certain cases where repeated washing (leaching) removes dormancy, the effect is thought to be due to the loss of such inhibitory compounds.

The second type of seed dormancy is embryo dormancy, which refers to a dormancy that is inherent in the embryo and is not due to any influence of the seed coat or other surrounding tissues. In some cases, embryo dormancy can be relieved by amputation of the cotyledons. Species in which the cotyledons exert an inhibitory effect include European hazel (*Corylus avellana*) and European ash (*Fraxinus excelsior*). A fascinating demonstration of the cotyledon's ability to inhibit growth is found in species (*e.g.*, peach) in which the isolated dormant embryos germinate but grow extremely slowly to form a dwarf plant. If the cotyledons are removed at an early stage of development, however, the plant abruptly shifts to normal growth.

Embryo dormancy is thought to be due to the presence of inhibitors, especially ABA, as well as the absence of growth promoters, such as GA (gibberellic acid). The loss of embryo dormancy is often associated with a sharp drop in the ratio of ABA to GA.

SEED DORMANCY MAY BE PRIMARY OR SECONDARY

Different types of seed dormancy also can be distinguished on the basis of the timing of dormancy onset rather than the cause of the dormancy:

- Seeds that are released from the plant in a dormant state are said to exhibit primary dormancy.
- Seeds that are released from the plant in a nondormant state but which become dormant if the conditions for germination are unfavourable exhibit secondary dormancy. For example, seeds of *Avena sativa* (oat) can become dormant in the presence of temperatures higher than the maximum for germination, whereas seeds of *Phacelia dubia* (small-flower scorpionweed) become dormant at temperatures below the minimum for germination. The mechanisms of secondary dormancy are poorly understood.

ENVIRONMENTAL FACTORS CONTROL THE RELEASE FROM SEED DORMANCY

Various external factors release the seed from dormancy, and dormant seeds typically respond to more than one condition. Many seeds lose their dormancy when their moisture content is reduced to a certain level by drying. This method of breaking seed dormancy is called afterripening, and is usually performed in a special drying oven. On the other hand, if the seed becomes too dry (5 per cent water content or less), the effectiveness of afterripening is diminished. Another factor that can release seeds from dormancy is low temperature, or chilling.

Many seeds require a period of cold (0 to 10°C) while in a fully hydrated (imbibed) state in order to germinate. In temperate-zone species, this requirement is of obvious survival value, since such seeds will germinate not in the fall, but only in the following spring. Chilling seeds to break their dormancy is a time-honoured practice in horticulture and forestry and traditionally has been referred to as *stratification.* This term is derived from the old agricultural practice of allowing seeds with a chilling requirement to overwinter outdoors in layered mounds of moist soil. Today the seeds are simply stored in a refrigerator.

The third external factor that plays an important role in breaking seed dormancy is light. Many seeds have a light requirement for germination, which may involve only a brief exposure, as in the case of lettuce, an intermittent treatment (*e.g.*, succulents of the genus *Kalanchoe*), or even a specific photoperiod involving short or long days.

As was discussed, phytochrome is the main sensor for light-regulated seed germination. Interestingly, all light-requiring seeds exhibit seed coat dormancy, and removal of the outer tissues of the seed allows the embryo to germinate in the absence of light. The effect that light has on the embryo is thus to enable the radicle to penetrate the seed coat. This penetration often involves some enzymatic weakening of the enclosing tissues.

The Longevity of Seeds

How long can a seed remain dormant and still remain viable? Seed longevity is of practical importance because of ongoing efforts to preserve plant genetic resources for future agricultural crops by setting up seed gene banks. Spectacular claims of dormant seeds that remained viable for thousands of years have been made, but are considered highly controversial. Extreme examples of ancient seeds that have been reported to retain their viability include submerged lotus seeds found in a

3,000-year-old boat near Tokyo, barley seeds from the 3,000-year-old tomb of King Tutankhamen, and arctic lupine seeds associated with rodent burrows determined to be 14,000 years old. In most cases, however, a scientifically rigourous examination of the data has either disproved or raised serious doubts about the claimed antiquity of the seeds.

The most serious criticism is that the dates of the seeds have been inferred from the age of their immediate surroundings or associated artifacts rather than from direct measurements of the seeds themselves. This question raises the possibility that the seeds are much younger than the site at which they were found. In fact, microscopic examination of authenticated ancient cereal grains from various Middle Eastern sites has shown that cells and tissues of these seeds are no longer intact. Such seeds are clearly inviable.

Although the most sensational claims for seed longevity are almost certainly bogus, seeds of *Canna compacta* apparently can live for at least 600 years. Viable *Canna* seeds were obtained from inside a walnut in a tomb in Argentina. The *Canna* seeds had apparently been inserted into the immature seeds of a growing walnut fruit before the hard outer shell formed. Once the shell hardened and the nut dried out, the result was a rattle. Native people strung the rattles together to form a necklace. In this case, the seeds had to be at least as old as the walnut shell, and carbon dating of the shell indicated that it was about 600 years old.

Plant collections begun during the late eighteenth century in Europe—for example, at the British Museum in London and at the Museum of Natural History in Paris—have been reliable sources of seeds for viability determinations. *Cassia multijuga* (false sicklepod) seeds, collected, were still viable after being tested, W. J. Beal initiated the longest-running experiment on seed longevity by burying the seeds of 21 different species in unstoppered bottles in a sandy hilltop near the Michigan Agricultural College in East Lansing. After 100 years, only one species, *Verbascum blattaria* (moth mullein), remained viable.

Why are some seeds able to survive in a dormant state for hundreds of years, whereas others lose viability in less than 5 years? Almost nothing is known about the mechanisms that determine the longevity of seeds. If these mechanisms could be understood, we might someday be able to greatly increase the seed longevity of agriculturally important species and varieties, thereby enhancing our ability to preserve plant genetic resources for generations to come.

Genetic Mapping Of Dormancy: Quantitative Trait Locus (QTL) Scoring of Vegetative Dormancy Combined with a Candidate Gene Approach

Complex traits, *e.g.* dormancy, are affected by many different, often unlinked genes. Consequently, attempts to map them result in continuous, or quantitative, variation within a mapping population. Quantitative trait locus (QTL) mapping is used in these instances to map individual genes affecting the trait. In QTL mapping, inbred lines that differ in the trait of interest are crossed and an F_2 population is produced. The F_2 population has continuous variation for the trait of interest, and the goal of the analysis is to determine which chromosomal segments contain genes affecting the trait.

Using marker loci along each chromosome (loci that have different alleles between the parental inbred lines), the genotypes of entire chromosomal segments in each F_2 individual can be inferred as being homozygous for one or the other parental lines or heterozygous.

If the inheritance of a chromosomal segment is correlated with the trait of interest, then a gene affecting the trait is likely to be between the two marker loci. By analysing chromosomal segments along each of the chromosomes, the number and locations of genes affecting the quantitative trait can be determined.

Candidate genes are specific loci, identified by predicted biochemical function or homology to regulatory genes from other species, that are suspected of affecting the trait of interest. Molecular differences between the parental alleles at these loci can be used to determine whether they map to the same region as any of the QTLs, thereby supporting the hypothesis that a given gene contributes to regulation of the trait.

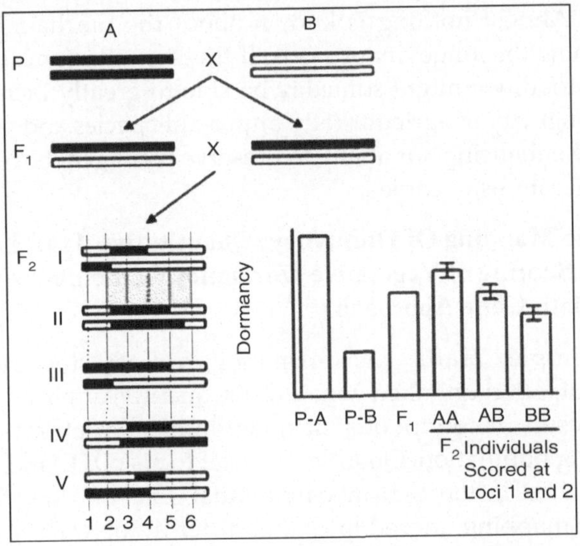

Fig. 6.1 A Two Parental (P) Inbred Lines, A & B, which Differ for a Trait of Interest (*e.g.* Dormancy) are Crossed to Produce Heterozygote F_1 Progeny which have an Intermediate Degree of Dormancy. Only one Chromosome Pair is Depicted for Simplicity. The F_1 Progeny are Crossed to Produce a Large Segregating F_2 Population (usually 100-500 Individuals are Analysed, here only Five Individuals, I-V, are Depicted). Because of Recombination During F_1 Meiosis, the F_2 Individuals have Varying Genetic Combinations of the Original Inbred Lines (Depicted by Shading of Chromosomes) and have Continuous Variation, from High to Low, in Degree of Dormancy. In Order to Estimate whether Segments of the Chromosome are Homozygous for one of the Parental-lines or Heterozygote, the F_2 Individuals are Scored for Marker Loci (1-6) along the Chromosome. For Example, Loci 1 & 2 are Identified as Homozygous for A-line Alleles in Individual III, as Heterozygous in Individuals I & V and as Homozygous for B-line Alleles in Individuals II & IV. The F_2 Individuals are also Scored for their Dormancy. After Scoring many F_2 Individuals a Correlation between the Genotypes at Locus 1 & 2 and Phenotype is Determined and therefore this Segment likely Contains at Least one Gene Affecting Dormancy (Bar Graph). The Analysis is Repeated for each Chromosomal Segment to Identify which ones are likely to Contain Genes Affecting Dormancy.

A Classification System for Seed Dormancy
The 'Whole-seed View'

Marianna G. Nikolaeva devised a dormancy classification system reflecting that dormancy is determined by both morphological and physiological properties of the seed. Based on this scheme, C. Baskin and J. Baskin have proposed a comprehensive classification system which includes five classes of seed dormancy.

The system is hierarchical with these five classes further divided into levels and types Baskin and Baskin:

- *Physiological dormancy (PD)*: PD (dormancy class A according to Baskin and Baskin, 2004) is the most abundant form and is found in seeds of gymnosperms and all major angiosperm clades. It is the most prevalent dormancy form in temperate seed banks and the most abundant dormancy class 'in the field'. PD is also the major form of dormancy in most seed model species 'in the lab', including *Arabidopsis thaliana, Helianthus annuus, Lactuca sativa, Lycopersicon esculentum, Nicotiana* spp., *Avena fatua,* and several cereals. The molecular mechanisms of PD are the focus of the Tansley review by Finch-Savage and Leubner-Metzger. PD has three levels: deep, intermediate and non-deep.
- *PD deep:* Embryos excised from PD-deep seeds either don't grow or will produce abnormal seedlings. GA treatment does not break their dormancy. Ca. 3-4 months of cold (subtype a) or warm (subtype b) stratification are required before germination can take place. Examples: *Acer platanoides* (PD deep subtype a); *Leptecophylla tameiameiae* (PD deep subtype b).
- *PD intermediate:* Embryos excised from PD-intermediate seeds produce normal seedlings. GA promotes germination in some (but not all) species. Seeds require 2-3 months of cold stratification. Dry storage (after-ripening) can shorten the cold stratification period. Example: *Acer pseudoplatanus* (PD intermediate).

- *PD non-deep:* The great majority of seeds have non-deep PD. Embryos excised from these seeds produce normal seedlings. GA treatment can break this dormancy and depending on species dormancy can also be broken by scarification, after-ripening in dry storage, and cold (0-10°C) or warm (>15°C) stratification. Based on patterns of change in physiological responses to temperature five types of non-deep PD can be distinguished. Most seeds belong to type 1 or 2, in which the temperature range at which seed germination can occur increases gradually during the progression of non-deep dormancy release from low to higher (type 1, *e.g. Arabidopsis thaliana*) or from high to lower temperature (type 2, *e.g. Helianthus annuus*). In addition, the sensitivity of the seeds to light and GA increases as non-deep PD is progressively released. The molecular mechanisms of Arabidopsis seed dormancy cycling have been investigated by transcriptome analyses.

Five Types of Non-deep Physiological Seed Dormancy (PD) According to Baskin.

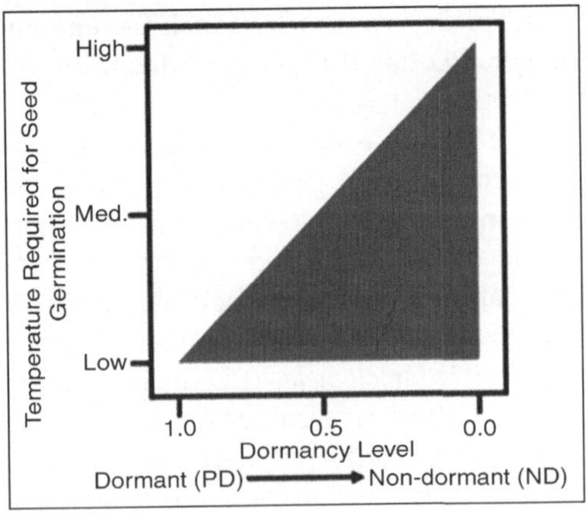

Fig. 6.2 PD Non-deep Type 1

Temperature range for germination increases during dormancy release as a continuum from low to high. Example: *Arabidopsis thaliana*

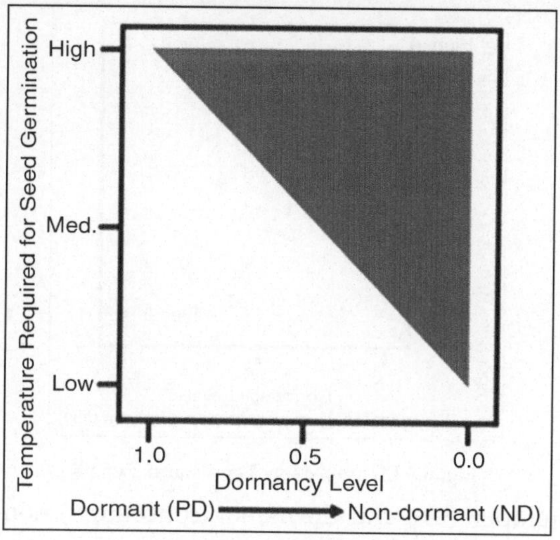

Fig. 6.3 PD Non-deep Type 2

Temperature range for germination increases during dormancy release as a continuum from high to low. Example: *Helianthus annuus*

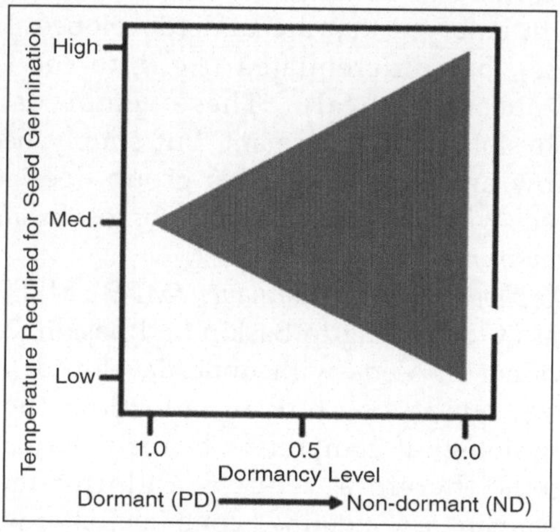

Fig. 6.4 PD Non-deep Type 3

Temperature range for germination increases during dormancy release as a continuum from medium to high and low. Example: *Aster ptarmacoides*

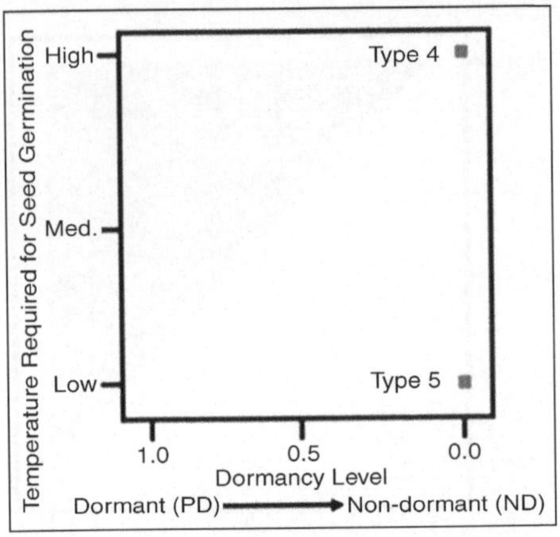

Fig. 6.5 PD non-deep Type 4 and Type 5

No temperature and dormancy continuum, non-dormant seeds germinate only at:—high temperature (Type 4). Example: *Callicarpa americana*- low temperature (Type 5). Example: *Gentianella quinquefolia*

- *Morphological dormancy (MD)*: MD (dormancy class B according to Baskin and Baskin,) is evident in seeds with embryos that are underdeveloped (in terms of size), but differentiated (*e.g.* into cotyledons and hypocotyl-radical). These embryos are not (physiologically) dormant, but simply need time to grow and germinate. This group does not include seeds with undifferentiated embryos. Example: *Apium graveolens* (Apiaceae).
- *Morphophysiological dormancy (MPD)*: MPD (dormancy class C according to Baskin and Baskin, 2004) is also evident in seeds with underdeveloped (in terms of size) embryos, but in addition they have a physiological component to their dormancy. These seeds therefore require a dormancy-breaking treatment, *e.g.* a defined combination of warm and/or cold stratification which in some cases can be replaced by GA application. In MPD-seeds embryo growth/ emergence requires a considerably longer period of time than in MD-seeds. Seeds with undifferentiated

embryos like the Orchidaceae also have a morphological and a physiological component of dormancy, but they are not considered in this classification scheme. Examples for MPD: *Trollius* (Ranunculaceae), *Fraxinus excelsior* (Oleaceae). There are eight known levels of MPD, based on the protocol for seed dormancy break and germination.

Type of MPD = Morphophysiological Dormancy	**W = warm Stratification; C = cold Stratification Temperature Requirement**		**GA Requirement for Dormancy Release Treatment**	**Example**
	To Break Dormancy	**At Time of Embryo Growth**		
Non-deep simple MPD	W or C	W	yes	*Anemone coronaria*
Intermediate simple MPD	W + C	W	yes	*Aralia mandshuria*
Deep simple MPD	W + C	W	(yes)	*Fraxinus excelsior*
Deep simple epicotyl MPD	W + C	W	(yes)	*Hydrophyllum macrophyllum*
Deep simple double MPD	C + W + C	W	?	*Smilacina racemosa*
Non-deep complex MPD	C	C	yes	*Erythronium albidum*
Intermediate complex MPD	C	C	yes	*Trollius* spp.
Deep complex MPD	C	C	no	*Delphinium tricorne*

- *Physical dormancy (PY)*: PY (dormancy class D according to Baskin and Baskin, 2004) is caused by one or more water-impermeable layers of palisade cells in the seed or fruit coat. In seeds PY-seeds, prevention of water uptake develops during maturation drying and the covering layer(s) control water movement (often associated with hardseededness). Seeds will remain dormant until some factor(s) render the covering layer(s) permeable to water. In nature, these factors include high temperatures, widely fluctuating temperatures, fire, drying, freezing/thawing and passage through the digestive tracts of animals. In seed technology, mechanical or chemical scarification can break PY dormancy. Once PY is broken, *i.e.* the seed or fruit coat becomes permeable to water, the seeds can germinate over a wide range of ambient conditions. Unlike PD-seeds, which may re-enter (secondary) dormancy after primary dormancy is broken, once the coat of PY-seeds becomes permeable it generally cannot revert to complete impermeability. Thus, the timing of dormancy break in nature is a more critical event in the life cycle of plants with PY, than it is in those with PD. The mechanism for PY-break must therefore be fine-tuned to the environment.

Specialized Structures for Water-impermeability

PY is associated with the main mechanical covering layer(s) of the seed and/or fruit coat. In most hardseeded species a palisade of radially elongated cells prevents water uptake. This palisade layer(s) prevent water uptake by their physical arrangement as a tissue and the chemical coatings/impregnates of the cells (heavy ligninfication, suberin-cutin matrix, waxes). In several cases specialized structures are associated with the control of water-impermeablility.

The figure on the right shows the testa (seed coat) structure of a typical legume seed (Fabaceae). Water-impermeability of PY-dormant legume seeds is due to a palisade layer of Malphighian cells in the exotesta. The the lens (strophiole, not shown) is the spezialized structure localized in the hilum region that controls water-impermeability.

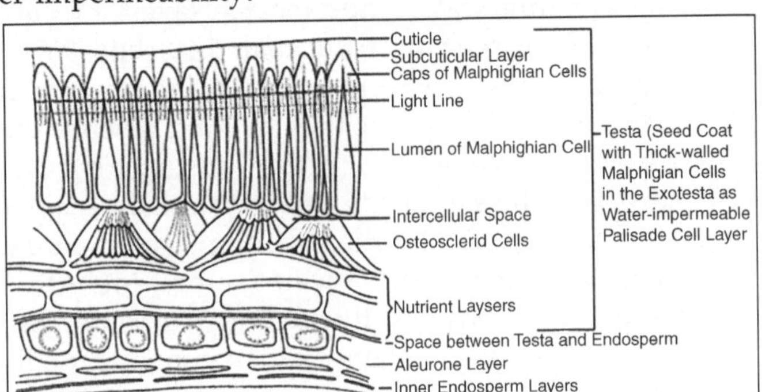

In PY-dormant Fabaceae species (Rosids) the lens (strophiole) is the spezialized structure localized in the hilum region that controls water-impermeability. The hardseededness and water-impermeability of many legume seeds is due to a palisade epidermal layer of thick-walled Malpighian cells in the outer testa (exotesta).

PY-dormancy of legume seeds is released if the lens is disrupted and a 'water-gap' allows water uptake. In most legume seeds stress, *e.g.* by heating, causes disruption (pulling apart) of the relatively thin-walled cells of the lens. In some legume species 'pop-up lenses' are evident. There is strong evidence that the lens is the weak point in the palisade layer of PY-dormant Fabaceae seeds. It is however not the only place of water entry: The lens functions as an environmental 'signal detector', it may act as regulator of the rate of water entry into the seed, thereby affecting seed and seedling vigour. Examples for PY-dormant Fabaceae seeds with lens are *Melilotus* and *Trigonella* species.

In PY-dormant Ancardiaceae species (Rosids), *e.g. Rhus* spp., the endocarp consists of three water-impermeable palisade layers (macrosclereids, osteosclereis, brachysclereids) and the outer crystalliferous layer. The carpellary micropyle is a discontinuity in the macroslereid layer and the specilized structure that controls water-impermeability. No discontinuity occurs in the osteosclereid and brachysclereid layers, and these layers block water entrance to the carpellary micopyle in dormant seeds. Dormancy release by heating causes formation of a blister near the carpellary micropyle via uplifting of the osteosclereid and brachysclereid layers. During blister formation, a slit is formed in these layers, therby creating an opening for water entrance.

Different types of chalazal plugs/caps are the spezialized structures that control water-impermeability of other seeds, *e.g.* in PY-dormant species of the Malvales clade (Rosids) families Bixaceae, Cistaceae, and Malvaceae. A suberized 'stopper' formed from the nucellus is the spezialized structure that controls water-impermeability of the Geraniaceae (Rosids).

An imbibition lid is the spezialized structure that controls water-impermeability of the Cannaceae (Monocots), the only Monocot family with PY species:

- *Combinational dormancy (PY+PD)*: Combinational dormancy, PY+PD (dormancy class E according to Baskin and Baskin), is evident in seeds with water-impermeable coats (PY) combined with physiological embryo dormancy (PD non-deep). Within the Ancardiaceae the genus *Rhus* includes species with PY+PD- dormancy (*e.g. Rhus aromatica*) and species with only PY-dormancy (*e.g. Rhus glabra*). Embryos of freshly harvested mature PY+PD-dormant seeds of winter annuals, *e.g. Geranium* spp. (Geraniaceae, Rosids) and *Trifolium* spp. (Fabaceae, Rosids), have some conditional dormancy (PD non-deep). This PD is released during after-ripening storage, even of the seed coat remains water impermeable (PY). Embryos of PY+PD-dormant *Ceanothus* spp. (Rhamnaceae, Rosids) are more deeply dormant (but still PD non-deep). In this case PY is released first and the subsequent water uptake during imbibition is followed by the release of the embryo dormancy (PD non-deep) during a few weeks of cold stratification. Thus, release from PY and PD of PY+PD-dormant seeds seems to be by independend events and the timely order can be species-specific.

Evolution of Seed Structure and Seed Dormancy

A general scheme of the evolutionary connection between seed structure and dormancy class is shown below.

MD and MPD are present in B-type seeds, but can also be typical of some specialized species. MD is thought to be the ancestral dormancy type among seed plants and is the most primitive dormancy class. The dispersal of seeds with an underdeveloped embryo that need time to grow might have evolved as an ancient strategy to disperse germination over time. MD and MPD are not only typical for primitive angiosperms, but also for primitive gymnosperms like the Zamiaceae,

Ginkgoaceae, Podocarpaceae and Taxaceae. Evolution of larger embryo size in MD seeds resulted in non-dormant (ND) seeds. Concurrently, the gain of physiological dormancy mechanism(s) led from seeds with MD to seeds with MPD, which upon gain in embryo size led to PD seeds.

PD is the most phylogenetically widespread dormancy class. This class of dormancy is distributed over the entire phylogenetic tree from gymnosperms and the basal angiosperms to the higher core eudicot Rosid clade. As ND is also distributed over the entire phylogenetic tree it has been proposed that gain and loss of PD occurred at several times and at several levels of seed evolution. The most phylogenetically restricted and derived dormancy classes are PY and PY+PD.

The occurrence of an impermeable seed or fruit coat combined with a ND embryo (PY) or a PD embryo (PY+PD) is probably the adaptation to specialised life strategies or habitats. PY and PY+PD are the only dormancy classes not found in gymnosperms, and PY is only evident in one Monocot family (Cannaceae). A conceptual model for the evolution of PY and PY+PD within the Ancardiaceae has been proposed. Within this family the genus *Rhus* includes species with PY+PD- dormancy (*e.g. Rhus aromatica*) and species with only PY-dormancy (*e.g. Rhus glabra*).

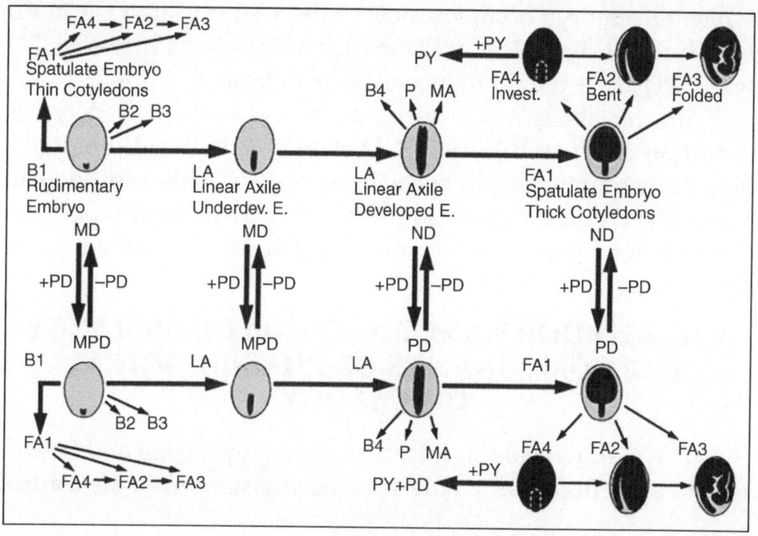

Anatomical evidence for PY of extinct *Rhus* spp. suggests that PY had evolved in the Ancardiaceae by 43 Ma in the Middle Eocene. The model begins in pre-Eocene times with an ancestral species that has large, non-dormant (ND), recalcitrant seeds. By the middle Eocene, a derived species with relatively small, orthodox seeds and a water-impermeable covering layer had evolved, *i.e.* a PY-dormant seed evolved. By the Oligocene, PD had been added to the seed dormancy mechanism, *i.e.* a PY-dormant seed evolved.

Climatic drying (Eocene), followed by climatic cooling (Eocene-Oligocene transition), are proposed as primary selective agents in the development of PY. An evolutionary connection between PY and recalcitrance is suggested by the relatively high concentration of these two states in the Rosid clade. Phylogenetic data and fossil evidence seem to support the PY → PY+PD evolutionary sequence in Ancardiaceae, which also may have occured in Fabaceae.

Summary of General Trends in Angiosperm Seed Evolution with Respect to Seed Type and Dormancy Class

Seeds with small embryo and abundant endosperm (B1 seed type) are primitive and evolution shows a general trend (indicated by arrows) towards mature seeds with little or no endosperm in which the embryo occupies most of the seed (through LA to FA seed types). Gain or loss of PD to each of these seed types (B1, LA and FA1) alters the dormancy class as indicated.

Similar changes can also occur in the other seed types. Addition of PY to FA4-type ND or PD seeds is indicated as a side branch occurring in specialized species. This addition can be reversed and PY can also be added to other seed types (not shown). Seed types and dormancy classes are described in the figure above.

EMBRYO DORMANCY AND COAT DORMANCY THE COMPONENTS OF PHYSIOLOGICAL DORMANCY

The hierarchical classification system by Baskin and Baskin accurately reflects the 'whole-seed' ecologists view of the control of germination by dormancy. At the molecular level very little is known about MD, MPD, PY, PY+PD and deep PD. Recent work by Cadman et el. has provided insight into molecular mechanisms of non-deep PD. Together with earlier physiological work (Finch-Savage and Leubner-Metzger) it is clear that the intrinsic molecular mechanisms determining dormancy can have an embryo and/or a coat component. The terms embryo and coat dormancy are used to distinguish between these two mechanisms, but it should be emphasized that they are not used as part of a classification system for 'whole-seeds' sensu Baskin and Baskin.

Embryo dormancy and coat dormancy are components of PD; their sum and interaction determines the degree of 'whole-seed' PD. Embryo dormancy is characterized by a block that inhibits extension growth and therefore excised embryos do not grow. Coat dormancy, is characterized by a block that is conferred by the covering layers.

Non-dormant embryos excised from coat-dormant seeds will therefore extend and grow. 'Coat' is used in a loose sense and can be any embryo covering structure, *e.g.* testa, endosperm and/or pericarp and terms like testa dormancy and endosperm dormancy can be used to specify these.

For example, mechanical resistance from combined testa and endosperm dormancy, which is greater than the embryo growth potential opposing it, appears to be the cause of non-deep PD in seed model systems like *A. thaliana* and Solanaceae species. When embryo and coat dormancy are considered as components of non-deep PD the influence of ABA and GA on dormancy and the control of germination can be summarised as follows:

EMBRYO DORMANCY

Embryo dormancy (embryo component of non-deep PD): A dormant embryo is characterized by a high ABA/GA ratio, high ABA sensitivity and low GA sensitivity. Embryo dormancy release involves remodelling of hormone biosynthesis and degradation towards a low ABA/GA ratio, a decrease in ABA sensitivity and an increase in GA sensitivity. Thus ABA dominates the embryo dormancy programme, and GA the embryo germination programme. A non-dormant embryo is characterized by increased growth potential, the ability for cell extension growth and the ability to induce the release of coat dormancy.

COAT DORMANCY

Coat dormancy (coat component of non-deep PD): The combination of an embryo with low growth potential and mechanical constraint from the seed covering layers can result in dormancy. GA can release this coat dormancy by increasing the embryo growth potential and/or by reducing the mechanical constraint.

There are two forms which are distinguished based on whether the covering layer consists of dead (e.g. outer testa) or living (e.g. endosperm) tissue:

- *Testa dormancy*: ABA during seed development determines the subsequent GA requirement for germination since ABA influences the testa characteristics (*e.g.* thickness) and GA the embryo growth potential.
- *Endosperm dormancy*: Endosperm weakening can be either part of the coat dormancy release or part of the germination programme. Since the endosperm is in most cases living tissue it can actively participate in regulating embryo constraint by influencing both the ABA/GA ratio and sensitivity to these hormones. GA acts by increasing the embryo growth potential and by promoting endosperm weakening which is achieved though ABA-independent and ABA-inhibited mechanisms.

Induction, Maintenance and Release of Physiological Dormancy by Plant Hormones and Environmental Signals

There is considerable evidence that abscisic acid (ABA) is an important positive regulator of both the induction of dormancy and the maintenance of the dormant state in imbibed seeds following shedding:

- ABA-deficiency during seed development is associated with absence of primary dormancy in the mature seed, whereas over-expression of ABA biosynthesis genes can increase seed ABA content and enhance seed dormancy or delay germination.

- ABA produced by the seed itself during seed development can impose a lasting dormancy, whereas, maternal ABA or ABA application during seed development both fail to induce a lasting seed dormancy, but has other functions.
- In *Arabidopsis thaliana*, the members of the AtNCED gene family encode enzymes catalyzing the key regulatory step in ABA biosynthesis. ABA synthesis in the embryo and the endosperm both seem to contribute to the induction of seed dormancy.
- High ABA contents are present in the imbibed seeds of the strongly dormant *A. thaliana* ecotype Cape Verde Island (Cvi) and decrease as dormancy is lost. A recent transcriptome analysis with this ecotype strongly supports the view that increased ABA biosynthesis is associated with the dormant state.
- *De novo* ABA biosynthesis during imbibition of dormant, but not non-dormant, seeds has been demonstrated in the *A. thaliana* ecotype Cvi, as well as in other species including *Nicotiana plumbaginifolia, Helianthus annuus,* and *Hordeum vulgare*. This de novo ABA biosynthesis has been interpreted as a mechanism for dormancy maintenance.
- Work with the strongly dormant *A. thaliana* ecotype Cvi shows that dormancy may depend on an intrinsic balance of gibberellin (GA)- and ABA-biosynthesis and catabolism, which will determine the dominance of either of the hormones. While PD release of Cvi seeds occurs effectively by after-ripening, stratification or inhibition of ABA biosynthesis, the addition of GA appears less effective. GA treatment of dormant Cvi seeds caused a transient increase in ABA levels, suggesting that in dormant seeds a feedback mechanism exists that maintains a high ABA/GA ratio. Thus, the net result of the dormant state is characterized by

increased ABA biosynthesis and GA degradation. It appears to be the ABA/GA ratio, and not the absolute hormone contents, that controls germination.

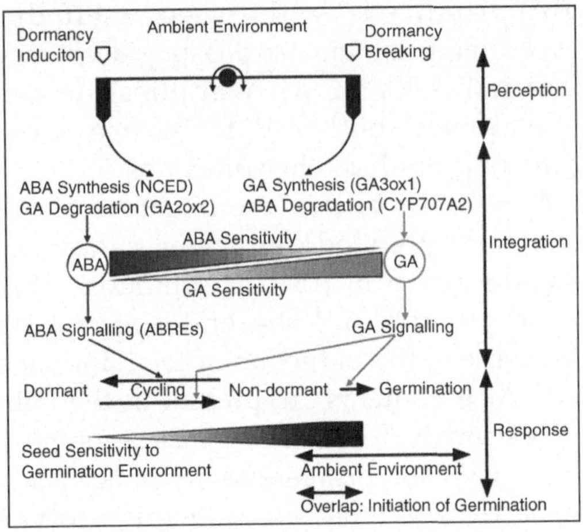

Model for the Regulation of Dormancy and Germination by ABA and GA in Response to the Environment

According to this model ambient environmental factors (*e.g.* temperature) affect the ABA/GA balance and the sensitivity to these hormones. ABA synthesis and signalling (GA catabolism) dominates the dormant state, whereas, GA synthesis and signalling (ABA catabolism) dominates the transition to germination. The complex interplay between hormone synthesis, degradation and sensitivities in response to ambient environmental conditions can result in dormancy cycling. Change in the depth of dormancy alters the requirements for germination (sensitivity to the germination environment); when these overlap with changing ambient conditions, germination will proceed to completion.

VARIATION OF THE SEED DORMANCY TRAIT IN ARABIDOPSIS AND NICOTIANA

ARABIDOPSIS THALIANA

Non-dormant seeds of *Arabidopsis thaliana* (*Arabidopsis*, Brassicaceae) germinate in the presence of water, oxygen, light and a suitable temperature, but dormant *Arabidopsis* seeds do not germinate at these favourable ambient conditions. *Arabidopsis* is native to Europe and central Asia. Flowering time and seed dormancy are key traits that determine the timing and lenght of the *Arabidopsis* natural life cycle. For both traits extensive natural variation is present among the different *Arabidopsis* accessions, which determine the variation observed in life cycles and the climatic adaptations.

In Europe, Arabidopsis flowers most abundantly in spring and early summer, and mature seeds are dispersed from May to July. These seeds exhibit a certain degree of conditional dormancy (PD non-deep), most of them germinate in the fall and survive winter as rosettes and therefore are winter annuals. Under greenhouse conditions these Northern European winter annual accessions flower late, but are very responsive to vernalization (cold treatment), which under natural conditions synchronizes flowering in springtime. In general, most accessions collected from nature in Northern Europe are late flowering are typical winter annuals; Southern populations are of both types, summer and winter annuals.

Seed dormancy is a quantitative trait, determined by several genes with an additional strong impact of the environment. The analysis of natural alleclic variation at seed dormancy (PD nondeep) loci of *Arabidopsis thaliana* was performed by exploiting these differences of accessions in the degree of dormancy. The laboratory strains Columbia (Col) and Landsberg *erecta* (L*er*) have low dormancy, whereas the Cape Verde Island (Cvi) and C24 accessions have deep dormancy. Recombinant inbred lines (RILs)/ near isogenic lines (NILs) between Cvi and L*er* were used in a quantitative trait loci (QTL) approach and identified several loci, named '*Delay Of Germination 1* to *12*' (*DOG1* to *DOG12*), that determine *Arabidopsis* seed dormancy. *DOG1*, for which the Cvi allele increased the level of seed dormancy, explains 12 per cent of the variance observed in seed dormancy in these RIL population.

The *DOG1* gene has been cloned and is a member of a small gene family of unknown molecular function. The functional allelic variation present in Arabidopsis is caused by polymorphisms in the cis-regulatory region of the *DOG1* gene resulting in considerable expression differences between *DOG1* allels of the accessions analysed. Alternative splicing leading to DOG1 proteins that differ in the C-terminal domain also appears to be important for dormancy.

Seed dormancy and germination of *Arabidopsis* are controlled by phytohormones and an interaction between the growth potential of the radicle and the mechanical resistance of the seed covering layers.

Two-step seed germination of Arabidopsis is visible as:

1. Testa rupture and
2. Endosperm rupture.

Only the endosperm rupture step is inhibited by ABA, but ABA during seed maturation is involved in determining the degree of Arabidopsis seed dormancy. Germination of dormant Arabidopsis seeds is blocked prior to testa rupture, and GA is required for its induction. Seed dormancy of mutants affected in ABA and GA levels and sensitivity is altered: ABA-deficiency (*aba1* mutant) and ABA-overproduction (*cyp707a* mutants) lead to non-dormancy and increased dormancy, respectively. The ABA-insensitive mutant *abi3* is non-dormant. GA-deficiency (*ga1* mutant) leads to increased dormancy. Mutations in DELLA-type repressors mediating of GA-responses in seeds lead either to enhanced (gain-of-function) or to reduced (loss-of-function) dormancy.

Control of germination by the endosperm - *Arabidopsis* seed dormancy is primarily determined by the endosperm: Arabidopsis endosperm layer is sufficient and necessary for seed dormancy. Embryos from dormant seeds had a lesser growth potential than those from nondormant seeds. However, the endosperm layer was found to be the primary determinant of seed dormancy.

Arabidopsis endosperm (aleurone) cells responded to nitric oxide (NO), GA, and ABA, with NO being upstream of GA in a signaling pathway that leads to vacuolation (GA-induced, ABA-inhibited) of protein storage vacuoles. Dormancy release and the GA signal lead to Arabidopsis endosperm rupture which involves these microscopic changes that are typical for endosperm weakening.

Control of germination by the seed coat—*Arabidopsis* testa mutants: Completion of germination in seeds with PD-type coat dormancy requires that either the embryo growth potential increases to overcome the mechanical constraint, and/or the mechanical constraint associated with the seed covering layer(s) is reduced.

Two forms of mechanical constraints and release mechanisms can be distinguished:

1. Living seed covering layers where a regulated tissue weakening occurs prior to germination and the tissue itself can produce enzymes for this process, *e.g.* of endosperm or inner testa;
2. Mostly dead seed covering layers where predetermined breaking points facilitate tissue rips prior to germination, *e.g.* outer testa (this section) or pericarp. The testa is maternal tissue and the reduced seed dormancy phenotype is inherited maternally.

A series of *Arabidopsis* testa mutants show reduced dormancy that is caused by alterations of the testa characteristics. Examples are *tt* (*transparent testa*), *ttg* (*transparent testa glabra*), and *ats* (*aberrant testa shape*). The testa mutants highlight the importance of the testa structure as a constraint to radicle emergence. The GA requirement for *Arabidopsis* seed germination is determined by testa characteristics, embryonic growth potential and by embryonic ABA.

Arabidopsis seed dormancy genes: These genes are represented by *Arabidopsis* mutants affected in seed dormancy and include hormone-related genes, and other genes that affect dormancy via the testa characteristics (testa mutants; see paragraph above) or by different mechanisms, *e.g. fus3* (*fusca3*), *lec1* and *lec2* (*leafy cotyledons*), *dag1* and *dag2* (*DOF affecting germination*, DOF-type transcription factors), *rdo1* to *rdo4* (*reduced dormancy*), *cts* (*comatose*), and *DOG1* (*delay of germination*).

NICOTIANA SPP. – TOBACCO

Nicotiana spp. seed dormancy and ABA: The onset of dormancy in *Nicotiana tabacum* is correlated with a peak in ABA content at approximately 15-20 days after pollination (DAP), and a rapid decline in ABA content follows during further seed maturation. Tobacco seeds harvested after DAP 25 are dark-brown, the embryos are mature and have white cotyledons, the products of maturation-specific genes have accumulated, dormancy has been established, desiccation tolerance has been acquired, and the moisture content is low.

Seed dormancy is not established in transgenic tobacco expressing an anti-ABA antibody that causes deficiency in free ABA, resulting in precocious germination, embryos with green cotyledons, reduced accumulation of storage proteins, and desiccation intolerance. *Nicotiana* species differ in the degree of seed dormancy (PD non-deep): *N. tabacum* and *N. sylvestris* have a low level of dormancy, while *N. plumbaginifolia* has a somewhat higher degree of dormancy. The high degree of seed dormancy of the post-fire annual tobacco, *Nicotiana attenuata,* can be induced by ABA and terpenes and smoke-exposure, light and GA are required for dormancy release.

The wilty mutants *aba1* and *aba2* of *Nicotiana plumbaginifolia* have reduced ABA contents and exhibit precocious germination and reduced primary dormancy). ABA-deficiency of the *aba2* mutant is due to a mutation in the *ABA2* gene, encoding zeaxanthin epoxidase, a key step in ABA biosynthesis. Antisense- and sense-ABA2 transformation of *N. plumbaginifolia* resulted in decreased and increased ABA biosynthesis and seed dormancy, respectively. Experiments suggested that, as in Arabidopsis and tomato, also in *Nicotiana* species only ABA produced by the seed itself, but not maternal ABA, is necessary to impose a lasting dormancy.

Tobacco dormancy can be released during after-ripening, *i.e.* a period of dry storage of freshly harvested, mature seeds. A further decline in ABA content, decreased sensitivity to ABA and increased sensitivity to GA are involved in the after-ripening-mediated transition from the dormant to the non-dormant state of many species.

The work of Grappin *et al.* demonstrated this for *N. plumbaginifolia* and showed in addition *de novo* ABA biosynthesis in imbibed fresh (dormant), but not after-ripened (non-dormant) seeds. Promotion of ABA-delayed seed germination of *N.*

plumbaginifolia by light or GA involves stimulation of ABA degradation and inhibition of ABA synthesis Tobacco photodormancy: Light is required for at least two aspects of tobacco seed germination.

First, in photodormant tobacco seeds germination in darkness is blocked at a step before testa rupture and neither neither testa nor endosperm rupture occur even after several weeks of dark-imbibition. Brief treatment of imbibed photodormant seeds with red light activates the phytochrome signal transduction pathway resulting in the release of photodormancy and the promotion of germination. Genetic and physiological experiments suggest that tobacco photodormancy is mainly under maternal control. Gibberellin (GA) can substitute for the red-light trigger needed to release photodormancy and to induce testa rupture and subsequent endosperm rupture of tobacco seeds imbibed in the dark. Red light has been shown to up-regulate the biosynthesis of bioactive GA in germinating seeds of lettuce and Arabidopsis.

Fresh tobacco seeds are photodormant and after-ripening contributes to the release of photodormancy. This effect varies greatly for different seed batches as reported for several tobacco cultivars. The GA requirements for photodormancy release of fresh and completely photodormant after-ripened seed batches are equal. Non-photodormant tobacco seeds have lost the GA requirement for dark-germination, which could be due to increased GA sensitivity and/or increased endogenous GA levels. Light is also required for a second aspect of tobacco seed germination, it promotes the speed of endosperm rupture of non-photodormant tobacco seeds.

GA is also not only involved in inducing dark-germination of photodormant tobacco seeds, it also promotes ABA-delayed endosperm rupture of dark-imbibed non-photodormant seeds, and osmoticum-delayed testa and endosperm rupture of light-imbibed seeds. Finally, endogenous ethylene and brassinosteroids also promote the germination of non-photodormant tobacco seeds and counteract the inhibitory effects of ABA on endosperm rupture, but ethylene and brassinosteroids do not release tobacco photodormancy.

7

Quiescence

Quiescence is a state of suspended growth of the embryo, or a resting condition of the seed. It involves factors in the seed itself which put it into a resting state (such as dessication). Quiescent embryos will resume growth at any time upon exposure to favourable conditions (water, oxygen and warmth).

Dormancy is a state that requires a special event or 'trigger' before the embryo can resume growth, such as fire, scarification or cold treatment. Until such an event occurs, the seed is prevented from germinating.

Fast Plants seed is quiescent but not dormant. It does not require a special event to resume development and growth. Many wild brassicas have dormant seed, whose dormancy can be broken by treatment with gibberellin an other plant growth hormones..

PLANTS EXHIBIT MITOTIC SENESCENCE POSTMITOTIC SENESCENCE AND CELL QUIESCENCE

Plants exhibit both types of senescence (below Figure). An example of mitotic senescence in plants is the arrest of apical meristem; the meristem consists of nondiffer-entiated, germline-like cells that can divide finite times to produce cells that will be then differentiated to form new organs such as leaves and flowers. The arrest of apical meristem is also called proliferative senescence in plant literature. This is similar to replicative senescence in yeast and animal cells in culture, as discussed above. Another example of mitotic senescence is the arrest of mitotic cell division at early stages of fruit development. Fruit size is a function of cell number, cell size and intercellular space, and cell number is the major factor. Cell number is determined at the very early stage of fruit development and remains unchanged thereafter.

Postmitotic senescence occurs in some plant organs, such as leaves and floral petals. Once formed, cells in these organs rarely undergo cell division; their growth is mainly contributed by cell expansion; thus, their senescence, unlike mitotic senescence, is not due to an inability to divide. This type of senescence involving predominantly somatic tissues is very similar to that

Shoot apical meristem
Early fruit development
Early leaf development
Mitotic/proliferative senescence
Early fruit development
Early leaf development
Mitotic/proliferative senescence

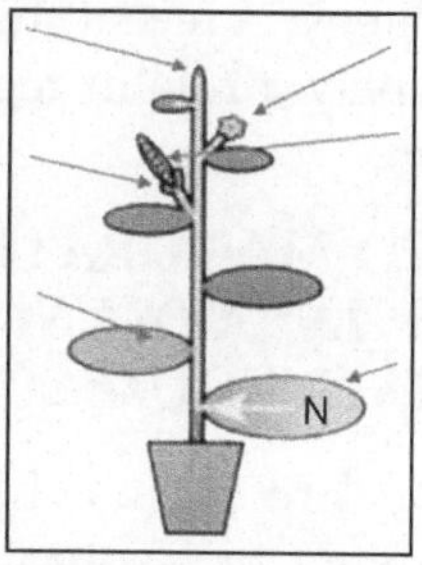

Floral senescence (sepal and petal)
Carpel senescence (fruit)
Leaf senescence
Postmitotic senescence

Figure Mitotic and postmitotic senescence in plants. Mitotic senescence occurs in SAM, in fruits and leaves that are at very early stages of development. In contrast, postmitotic senescence occurs in leaves, flowers and fruits that are at late stages of development (thus leaf senescence, flower senescence and fruit senescence, respectively).

Floral senescence (sepal and petal)

Carpel senescence (fruit)

Leaf senescence

Postmitotic senescence

Figure Mitotic and postmitotic senescence in plants. Mitotic senescence occurs in SAM, in fruits and leaves that are at very early stages of development. In contrast, postmitotic senescence occurs in leaves, flowers and fruits that are at late stages of development (thus leaf senescence, flower senescence and fruit senescence, respectively). Of such animal model systems as Drosophila and Caenorhabditis elegans whose adult bodies, with exception of germline, are postmitotic.

Cell quiescence also occurs in plants. Cells of apical meristems will stop dividing under unfavourable conditions. For example, the apical meristems of many trees will stop proliferative process when they perceive the short-day photoperiod signal; short day often means that the winter season is coming. These meristem cells retain their division capability during winters and will resume division activity when spring is coming. Therefore, the short-day-induced cell quiescence is an evolutionary fitness strategy. A recent study shows that ethylene and abscisic acid may play a role in regulating the temporary 'arrest' of tree meristem.

SEED MATURATION

DEVELOPING AN INTRUSIVE PHASE TO ACCOMPLISH A QUIESCENT STATE

Plants, as sessile life forms, have evolved diverse mechanisms to circumvent unfavourable growth conditions, among them interruption of the life cycle is one of the most successful strategies.

Spermaphyta, or seed plants, are characterised by the formation of the seed, a structure originated from the fertilised ovule, that includes the embryo and other maternally derived tissues. Embryogenesis within the seed allows the entry into a quiescent state that represents an evolutionary advantage since it facilitates dispersal and resuming of growth under optimal environmental conditions.

Seed formation is an intricate process that can be roughly divided into proper embryogenesis (cell division and morphogenesis), followed by a maturation phase, characterised by storage compound accumulation, acquisition of desiccation tolerance, growth arrest and the entry into a dormancy period of variable length that is broken upon germination. In essence, seed maturation involves all structures comprised within the seed, but predominantly the embryo and the endosperm originated by a double fertilisation event.

Maturation leads to a developmental end-point in the endosperm, whereas the embryo retains the regenerating capacity after germination. Despite these differences, both embryo and endosperm share many features concerning the physiological changes and underlying molecular mechanisms associated with maturation.

In this review, we will re-examine minor aspects of seed maturation as a physiological process opposed to germination and will focus on recent findings related to central transcriptional regulators that participate in gene expression programmes associated with embryo and endosperm maturation. In the past, the study of seed specific gene expression has led to the idea of different regulatory mechanisms in monocot- and dicotiledoneous species. However, a closer watch uncovers a limited perception, probably sustained on a knowledge biased from the different prevailing tissues in the seed of the two phylogenetic groups. Current data, clearly points to the participation of similar and sometimes the same factors in both organs.

Moreover, new roles, out of the seed, have been discovered for regulators considered to be seed-specific and new functions within the seed assigned to previously known regulators unrelated to this organ. Altogether, these findings are enabling to perceive seed maturation as an 'intrusive phase' in the developing embryo, similar to other phases introduced in the course of evolution at different times and in different taxa to produce growth arrest in a reversible manner. In addition, extensive studies of regulatory networks are facilitating the identification of master regulators, responsible for the 'seed fate', which directly participate in transcriptional control during maturation or modulate the activities of other factors acting under their influence.

PHYSIOLOGY OF SEED MATURATION

The maturation phase is started once the embryo and endosperm have completed the morphogenesis and patterning stages. This phase is characterised by a growth arrest, followed by the synthesis and accumulation of reserves, whose degradation upon germination will provide nutrients to the growing seedling before the photosynthetic capacity is fully acquired. Early and mid phases of maturation are dominated by the action of ABA, initially synthesised in the maternal tissues and later on, although to a lower extent, in the embryo and endosperm.

Transcription of major seed storage protein genes occurs mainly during this period. Subsequently, ABA levels decline and late maturation follows characterised by the synthesis of LEA (Late Embryogenesis Abundant) proteins, associated to the dehydration process and acquisition of desiccation tolerance. During this stage, accumulation of storage metabolites prevails in the form of carbohydrates (endosperm) or lipids (embryo), a quiescent state is accomplished and dormancy, the inability to grow under otherwise favourable conditions, can be established. Maturation is not an obligatory process and if embryos are removed from the seed and the ABA effects eliminated, they can proceed through the germination phase and develop into normal seedlings.

In certain plants, like mangroves, embryogenesis proceeds directly to the seedling state. Similarly, so-called viviparous mutants in other plants display an analogous behaviour. In addition to ABA, other hormones are important in seed development, like auxins, cytokinins and gibberellins (GAs). In particular, the synthesis and requirement of active GAs during the maturation phase have been demonstrated in elegant experiments in maize embryos. It is now widely accepted that maturation is not determined by ABA alone but instead by the ABA/GA balance. Exciting results on metabolites as signals, as well as metabolism and accumulation of nutrients during seed development have been extensively covered in recent publications and are outside the scope of this review.

MUTATIONS AFFECTING SEED DEVELOPMENT

Seed mutants have been an important source of information about the maturation phase both in monocot and dicot species. In cereals, due to the importance of the endosperm (the first world crop), seed mutants have been mostly seek on the basis of modifications in this organ. While this has resulted in the identification of important mutations affecting maturation outputs, many embryo mutants remain overlooked. In dicot species, *e.g. Arabidopsis,* a great number of seed developmental mutants display altered phenotypes on maturation features, but many of them are not specific to this phase.

Instead, they are altered in basal activities required for normal embryo development with subsequent effects into the maturation phase. In addition, certain mutants impaired in seed maturation show abnormal embryonic behaviour. Although this situation has initially made difficult to establish the boundaries between embryo development and maturation proper, it has enabled the identification of master genes that determine a state of competence under which maturation gene expression programmes occur.

GENE EXPRESSION PROGRAMMES ASSOCIATED WITH SEED MATURATION

As previously described, physiological and metabolic conditions prevailing in the seed during the maturation phase lead to the accumulation of storage compounds and other products conferring desiccation tolerance. Accordingly, gene expression programmes are primarily related to these processes. From early studies, it was known that most abundantly expressed genes in the seeds correspond to seed storage proteins, oleosins, LEA proteins and enzymes implicated in carbohydrate and lipid biosynthesis. Consequently, many of these genes have for a long time served as molecular markers, specific to this phase.

With the introduction of new high-throughput technologies, seed maturation has been investigated on a genome-scale basis. Transcriptome analysis has been performed in developing seeds of monocot and dicot species and allowed to identify new seed-specific genes, to redefine patterns of gene expression and to recognize new groups of co-regulated genes. The forthcoming years will probably see a great advance in the transcriptome analysis of seed mutants and the consequent deciphering of regulatory networks underlying seed maturation. An important fact to point is that many of the final outputs of the maturation-induced gene expression programmes are common in monocot and dicot species, no matter if they occur in the embryo or in the endosperm.

One such a case is a group of seed storage proteins *(SSP)* genes, encoding specific dicot albumins and monocot prolamins, which can be evolutionary traced to a common ancestor. Gene promoter *cis* -acting motives and interacting transcription factors have been shown to be functionally exchangeable between both systems, indicating a remarkable conservation in the machinery responsible for the maturation gene expression programmes. In the following sections we will summarise the current knowledge of important regulatory sequences and interacting transcription factors present in these promoters, in the framework of known key regulators of seed development and seedspecific expression.

MATURATION REGULATORY ELEMENTS IN DICOT SPECIES

Regulatory *cis* -acting elements required for specific expression of *SSP* genes have been determined in numerous dicot species and can be illustrated on the 2S albumin/ napin gene promoters. Besides high sequence conservation, functional relevance of these elements has been demonstrated by site-specific mutagenesis and gain of function experiments. The best-characterised motives include the RY element, the ACGT box and the AACA motif, representing putative targets for B3, bZIP and MYB transcription factors, respectively. Alternative strategies, like the analysis of mutants with altered features in the seed, have also led to the identification of genetic loci affecting the maturation programme. In *Arabidopsis* four loci: *LEC1, LEC2, FUS3* and *ABI3* are fundamental in the control of different aspects of seed development.

LEC1 is a homologue of the CAAT binding factor HAP3 subunit and LEC2, FUS3 and ABI3 belong to the B3 family of transcription factors. In terms of phenotypic alterations FUS3, LEC1 and LEC2 belong to the Leafy Cotolyden (LEC) type and loss of function in any of them result in the display of leaf primordia features (*e.g.* trychome formation) in the cotyledons, precocious growth of root and apical meristem, alterations in anthocyanin and storage product accumulation and reduction in the establishment of desiccation tolerance and dormancy. Functions of these genes are not completely redundant, acting in an overlapping manner.

Although structurally related to FUS3 and LEC3, ABI3 is not considered of the LEC type and loss of its function results in a failure to degrade chlorophyll, altered storage product accumulation, loss of desiccation tolerance and dormancy and ABA insensitivity upon germination.

Mutations in any of these four regulators impaired the maturation programme and shift embryo development towards germination. Recently, exciting results have been obtained concerning their mode of action. The McCourt's group has described the ability to fully complement a *fus3-3* loss-of-function mutant by expressing the FUS3 protein in the protodermal tissue of the embryo. Anthocyanin and trichome production in the *fus3* mutant requires the product of the TTG1 gene and the authors show that FUS3 is a negative regulator of TTG1 mRNA in the protodermal tissue.

In addition, restoration of SSP accumulation was shown in the same complemented mutant and a similar effect displayed in the *fus3-3/ ttg1* double mutant. However, the *ttg1* mutation could not rescue other *fus3* -impaired functions, like desiccation tolerance and dormancy, indicating that FUS3 action occurs only partially through the TTG1 product. Up-regulation of FUS3 by auxins in the embryo was also demonstrated and the positive and negative regulation of ABA and GA synthesis by FUS3, acting as a nexus of hormone action during embryogenesis.

Moreover, accumulation of SSPs in parenchyma cells of adult leaves miss-expressing FUS3 in the epidermis suggests a cell-nonautonomous mechanism in its mode of action.

Other investigations have disclosed a positive regulation of LEC1 over FUS3 and ABI3 and their activation of SSP genes in a hierachical manner. Complex genetic and molecular interactions have been uncovered among these factors and deserve further examination.

In addition to the general 'seed-competence' state generated by these factors, it has been demonstrated that they can particularly act through direct interactions with regulatory elements present in the promoters of output genes of the maturation phase. Functional assays for LEC2, FUS3 and ABI3 have corroborated such mechanisms on the RY element of different SSP gene promoters. Nevertheless, the action of these factors is a necessary but not sufficient requisite for the expression of the target genes, since mutations affecting other critical elements or their interacting factors, result in a poor (or absent) expression.

In this respect, the ACGT boxes as putative binding elements of bZIP proteins are reported targets of AtbZIP10 and 25 in SSP promoters and of ABI5 in *Em* promoters, in both cases in concerted interaction with ABI3. Contribution of other elements, like AACA boxes, is known to be critical as well, although the interacting factors have not been identified yet. It is worth mentioning the high level of conservation, both in sequence and functionality, detected among different gene promoters in monocot and dicot species that encourages for the isolation of similar factors to those previously characterised in the alternative group.

Maturation Regulatory Elements in Monocot Species

Seed maturation has been extensively studied in cereal species, due to the importance of the endosperm as the major food and feed tissue in agriculture. The cereal endosperm is structured into different cellular domains comprising the aleurone, the starchy endosperm, embryo surrounding tissues and transfer cells. The starchy endosperm is the principal storage tissue, where carbohydrates and SSP are accumulated during the maturation phase. Among the numerous known mutants affecting endosperm traits, many are altered in the pigmentation of the outer aleurone layer or the deposition of reserves in the starchy endosperm.

Cereal SSP genes are among the first plant genes characterised and functionally studied. The bipartite endosperm box and the AACA motif are important regulatory elements, repeatedly found in the promoters of SSP genes. These *cis* -elements are bound by TFs of the bZIP, DOF and R2R3MYB classes including BPBF and SAD Dof proteins, OPAQUE2-like bZIP proteins BLZ2 and BLZ1 and R2R3MYB factor GAMYB. Full activation is achieved by the synergistic effect of different TF combinations, suggesting that they are part of a regulatory complex.

In support, protein-protein interactions have been detected among them. Although conserved RY elements are also present in the promoters of these genes, direct regulation by a B3-type transcription factor has not been reported so far. Nevertheless, it is worth mentioning that the VP1 gene (the monocot orthologue of ABI3) is weakly expressed in the starchy endosperm, while highly expressed in the aleurone and embryo during the maturation phase, where it participates in the activation of LEA genes in an ABA dependent manner.

It is also remarkable that key factors participating in maturation programmes in the cereal endosperm, like GAMYB, BPBF or SAD, are also essential regulators in the post-germination phase. Consistent with a mode of action based on exchangeable regulatory complexes under the influence of external TFs, this represents an example of how regulators can be recruited to perform different tasks depending on the context.

In the seed framework, GAMYB, BPBF and SAD different actions are mediated by VP1 modulation. Maturation phase changes induced in the embryo of monocot seeds have been studied to a lesser extent, but strong similarities to the situation in the dicot embryo exists, like the well-known participation of VP1 in the regulation of *LEA* and globulin *SSP* genes and the conserved interactions with bZIP orthologous to ABI5 factors.

Modules, Overlaps and Hierarchies in the Structure of Seed Maturation Programmes

Maturation within the seed is a multipart process that affects both the embryo and the endosperm, leading through sequential steps into quiescence. As a whole, it can be divided into overlapping programmes of gene expression to accomplish different tasks, like synthesis of storage compounds, acquisition of desiccation tolerance or the establishment of dormancy. For a process with such a modular structure it is not surprising to discover that individual tasks might be implemented in different parts of the plant with functions unrelated to the seed.

For instance, many of the genes related to desiccation tolerance can be induced in other organs under certain stress conditions. Furthermore, mutant analyses have allowed the identification of individual regulators that operate over a wide range of modules (or gene expression programmes) and that are therefore considered 'master regulators' of the process (*e.g. LEC* genes). Individual switching on of these genes results in the definition of a 'seedcompetent' state that affects a precise set of tasks of the maturation phase, which are globally controlled by these factors in an overlapping, rather than a hierarchical manner. On top, at a different level of regulation, it has been shown in *Arabidopsis* that the master *LEC* genes are repressed outside the embryo by the CHD3-chromatin-remodeling factor *PICKLE.*

Driving the Maturation Programme out of the Seed

Taking into account the described organisation of the maturation programme, it is conceivable to execute independent parts by manipulating selected regulators. In fact, different reports have shown that miss-expression of particular regulators can turn on precise expression programmes of seed maturation out of the seed. An interesting finding was the discovery of an ABI3-factor, initially thought to be a seed specific regulator, as an important player in the induction of dormancy in buds. Like specific programmes of seed maturation, this process is associated to the growth inhibitory action of ABA, in which ABI3 is known to be implicated. Again, this supports the idea of maturation being ancillary or intrusive to embryo development and points towards possible mechanisms that could make it rise, with subsequent evolutionary advantages.

Remaining Questions

In recent years, important contributions have been made in different aspects of seed maturation, like studies on metabolism of storage compounds, identification of key regulatory elements or transcriptome analyses of the process at a whole-genome scale. The identification of key regulatory transcription factors involved in the process allows addressing important and still opened questions. It remains unclear to what extent these key regulators are conserved in the different phylogenetic groups, for instance there is no evidence yet for a role of LEC genes in seed maturation of monocot species.

Although conservation in the regulatory network that controls SSP is remarkable, extensive studies must be performed to provide information on other regulatory networks operating under the maturation programme to allow further comparisons. In particular, information concerning expression programmes in the dicot endosperm, or associated with the establishment of dormancy is still very limited. Another key and recurrent issue in seed biology are the differences between embryo and endosperm, linked to the still controversial origin of the later. Involvement of key regulators of maturation programmes is significantly similar in the embryo and endosperm aleurone. A deeper knowledge of maturation in both systems and the influence of maternal and dosage effects can shed new light into this question.

ESCAPE FROM WATER OR REMAIN QUIESCENT? LOTUS TENUIS CHANGES ITS STRATEGY DEPENDING ON DEPTH OF SUBMERGENCE

Flooding of the soil drastically reduces the availability of soil oxygen, and this can damage the growth and survival of the roots on which plants depend. When water is sufficiently deep to cover part or all of the shoot, the stress is intensified as shoots become directly affected by shortages of carbon dioxide and oxygen imposed by slow gas diffusion through water. The severity of the stress thus depends on water depth. Accordingly, two contrasting strategies may be required to deal with partial or complete submergence.

In rice, maize and Paspalum dilatatum submergence of the shoot base can promote elongation (escape strategy) while complete submergence can also strongly induce this in rice seedlings, Rumex palustris and other species. In response to partial submergence, tolerant plants increasingly allocate carbon and nutrients towards shoot growth, permitting faster elongation in order to 'escape' from the water. In contrast, some plants are able to tolerate long periods of complete submergence; they maintain their basic metabolism by respiring reserve carbohydrates until water drawdown. This second strategy is called quiescence.

To date, the ability to adopt the quiescence strategy has been described for certain specific different cultivars of rice, for one overwintering ecotype of Ranunculus repens and for Rumex crispus. However, the possibility that individual plants of one species or ecotype can adopt either strategy depending on water depth has not been examined before. We now address this question in the legume Lotus tenuis. In addition to elongation and quiescence effects, submergence of some or all the plant can trigger changes in root porosity and in the carbohydrate metabolism of reserve organs (*e.g.* crowns and tap roots) to maintain root respiration and facilitate shoot elongation in the absence of adequate rates of photosynthesis.

In legume species, previous reports on this topic mostly focused on flood-sensitive Medicago sativa (alfalfa). The usual observation was severely damaged plants and an accumulation of water-soluble carbohydrates (WSCs) in crowns [from 2–6 per cent to 11–16 per cent dry weight (d. wt.)] due to the lack of growth and sugar demand under waterlogged conditions and with little change in starch levels. However, there have been no comparable studies for a flood-tolerant legume such as L. tenuis, which is able to maintain carbon fixation and plant growth during long-term flooding. If plants become completely submerged this can lead to a dramatic decline of the carbon balance and energy status of the plants and to plant death. However, some plants are able to sustain their basic metabolism by consuming reserve carbohydrates.

In some wetland species, this is supplemented by underwater photosynthesis. Starch reserves can be mobilized during submergence and can readily provide soluble sugars for plant respiration in anaerobic tissues. However, this capacity – which reflects the plant's ability to survive with little or no oxygen or photosynthesis – differs greatly among plant species. For instance, the consumption of starch reserves in tubers of Scirpus maritimus allows the plant to survive complete submergence for nearly 3 months, while rhizomes of Juncus effusus survive only 4 d under anaerobic conditions. In accordance, our study also evaluated the potential use of carbohydrates in crowns of L. tenuis plants subjected to submergence. Consequently, we included in the present study the role of crown carbohydrates (WSCs and starch) in responses of L. tenuis to partial or complete submergence over 30 d.

These were combined with analyses of shoot elongation, tissue porosity, morphological traits, shoot number, plant biomass and the utilization of crown carbohydrates. We show that increasing flooding depth induces alternative strategies by otherwise identical plants that are centred on faster shoot elongation under partial shoot submergence conditions and on quiescence under complete submergence linked to utilization of crown reserve carbohydrates. MATERIALS AND METHODS Plant material.

The genus Lotus is native to the Mediterranean basin and widely distributed throughout the world, with several species adapted to stressful soil conditions poorly tolerated by other forage legumes such as M. sativa (alfalfa), Trifolium pratense (red clover) or Trifolium repens (white clover). In this regard, L. tenuis Waldst. and Kit. ex Willd. (syn. Lotus glaber Mill.) is a notable perennial with a long growing season. It possesses awelldeveloped crown (2 cm of the transition zone between shoots and roots that functions as a storage reserve tissue able to support shoot growth) and a taproot with extensive lateral root branching. Leaves are pentafoliate and the species is an important forage crop for flood-prone soils and is naturalized in several plant communities of the Flooding Pampa grasslands of Argentina.

Experimental details Seeds of L. tenuis ('Pampa INTA') were germinated in an incubator (25°C) in polystyrene boxes containing cotton and absorbent white paper saturated with water. After 2 d, germinated seeds were transplanted to 4 L plastic pots (three seedlings per pot) filled with sand and topsoil (1: 1) from a lowland grassland of the Flooding Pampa (3 _ 33 per cent organic carbon; for further details) and transferred to a glasshouse at the Faculty of Agronomy at the University of Buenos Aires. Seedlings were subsequently thinned to one plant per pot and grown for 6 months at 22+6 8C and a photosynthetic photon flux density (PPFD) of 1400+40 mmol m22 s21.

Flooding treatments Four treatments were applied for 30 d to 6-month-old plants following a fully randomized design with eight replicates:

- *Control*: Watered daily to field capacity;
- *Waterlogging*: Saturated soil flooded to 2–5 mm above the soil;
- *Partial submergence*: Water level maintained 6 cm above the soil surface; and
- *Complete submergence*: Plants submerged in water 8–10 cm deep to ensure no leaves emerged above water level during the experiment.

Soil oxygen availability was determined by measuring oxygen diffusion rates (ODRs) at a depth of 5 cm with platinum microelectrodes. Flood water was replaced weekly and root zone temperature checks showed these were similar for all treatments (P ¼ 0.88). Tissue porosity Shoot and root porosity was measured at the end of the flooding period by pycnometry. The porosity in aerial (shoot) and submerged tissues (roots) allowed comparison of the capacity for internal aeration from shoot to root among L. tenuis plants under the different treatments. Shoot number and length Shoots per plant were counted and measured at the beginning and end of the experiment. Shoot length was expressed as the average of the five longest shoots per plant. Both variables provide information on the strategy developed by the plants in response to submergence. Biomass responses and leaf greenness Plants were harvested for biomass and chlorophyll at the beginning and end of the experiment using randomly chosen individuals (n ¼ 8).

Plants was separated into leaves, stems, shoots, crown and roots for dry mass determinations after drying for 72 h at 80 8C. In addition, the ratio of leaf to total shoot biomass and of crown to total biomass was calculated for each plant. Leaf chlorophyll was measured in fully expanded young leaves using a portable chlorophyll meter (Model SPAD-502, Minolta, Ramsey, NJ, USA) at the end of the experiment. Carbohydrate analyses For WSCs and starch, samples of crown tissue weighing approx. 0.1 g (d. wt.) were milled and heated to 80 8C in 25 mL of 80 per cent ethanol for 1 h.

The supernatant was filtered twice, diluted with 25 mL of distilled water and heated to 60 8C for 1 h. All supernatants were made up to 100 mL with 80 per cent ethanol and aliquots mixed with anthrone reagent [200 mg of anthrone in 75 per cent (v/v) H_2SO_4], left to stand for 30 min, shaken and heated for 10 min in an 80 8C water bath (Yemm and Willis, 1954). Absorbance was recorded at 620 nm, and total soluble carbohydrate concentration was calculated based on a glucose calibration curve. To determine starch, the remaining residues were oven-dried at 37 8C for 24 h, suspended in 10 mL of distilled water and heated in a boiling water bath for 4 h.

The resulting homogenate was incubated with 0.7 mL of a solution containing 18 U mL21 of amyloglucosidase in an acetate buffer at pH 4.5 and 37 8C overnight. The amounts of glucose released were analysed by the anthrone method as described above. WSCs and starch content (mg per plant crown) were calculated as the product of WSCs or starch concentration (mg g21) and crown biomass (g) at the beginning and end of the experiment.

The difference between these two values represented the change in WSCs or starch content during the course of the 30 d experiment. Statistical analyses All variables were analysed using one-way analysis of variance (ANOVA) with Tukey's honestly significant difference tests. These were done a posteriori to identify differences among treatments (P, 0.05). Normality and the homogeneity of variances were previously verified. The variables involving proportions were arcsine p x transformed before analyses.

In addition, orthogonal contrasts were performed to compare data between day 0 and day 30. Statistical analyses were performed using the STATISTICA package for Windows (StatSoft, Tulsa, OK, USA). All results are presented as nontransformed means+s.e. RESULTS Flooding effects on soil aeration The ODR under control conditions remained between 74.3 and 78.3 _ 1028 g cm22 min21, indicating well-oxygenated soil conditions. In the waterlogged soil, the ODR decreased slowly over 6 d to values reported as non-limiting for root growth (25.5+3.2 _ 1028 g cm22 min21; see Stolzy and Letey, 1964). By day 10, ODRs in waterlogged soil decreased further to 1.5+0.7 _ 1028 g cm22 min21, and similar values were recorded up to the end of the 30 d long experiment.

The ODR under partial and complete submergence conditions decreased rapidly from 77.3+3.7 to 6.9+1.1 _ 1028 g cm22 min21 during the first 3 d, and remained near zero until the end of the experiment, indicating anaerobic soil. Plant tissue porosity Root porosity was lower under control conditions (12.8 per cent) and higher in treatments involving excess water (P, 0.05, Table). Values ranged from 21.6 to 32. 5 per cent for plants growing under waterlogged or in partial or completely submerged conditions (Table). In contrast, constitutive shoot porosity in well-drained plants was always higher than root porosity (*e.g.* 24.6 per cent vs. 12.8 per cent) and did not increase under soil waterlogging or under complete submergence.

An increase in shoot porosity was seen only in partially submerged plants (P, 0.01). Shoot number and length The number of shoots of L. tenuis increased during the course of the experiment except in completely submerged plants (Fig.). The magnitude of the increase was lower in partial submergence conditions than under control and waterlogging conditions. Thus, the shoot number of partially submerged plants was 22.1 per cent less than in control and waterlogged plants.

Instead, partially submerged plants prioritized elongation of the emerging shoots since the five longest shoots of the plant were 30 per cent longer than under control or waterlogging conditions (P, 0.01; Fig.). In contrast, completely submerged plants did not increase the number or length of their shoots (P. 0.7) but, importantly, all plants survived the 30 d complete submergence treatment. The lack of change in these variables is evidence of the quiescence syndrome of L. tenuis plants when wholly submerged in water. Plant biomass responses and flooding depth Increasing flooding depth had a negative effect on growth in biomass.

At the end of the experiment, total plant biomass of partially submerged plants was 30.3 per cent below that of control plants and 64.4 per cent less than in waterlogged plants (P, 0.05). Under complete submergence, biomass accumulation during the experiment was negative (P ¼ 0.072; cf. day 0 vs. day 30 in Fig.). Final shoot biomass was progressively lowered by increased flooding depth: waterlogged, partially submerged and completely submerged plants finishing with a shoot biomass of 21.7, 33.5 and 64.3 per cent, respectively, below that of well-drained plants (P, 0.05 for all cases; Fig.). Different parts of the shoot were affected differently. Leaf biomass was depressed more than stem biomass as flooding depth increased.

Accordingly, the leaf-to-shoot biomass ratio was smaller in partially submerged and completely submerged plants than in control and waterlogged plants (P, 0.05; Table). Completely submerged plants had a lower leaf-to-shoot biomass ratio and much lower chlorophyll leaf content (Table). Crown biomass at final harvest was less under partial submergence and complete submergence than in other treatments (33.3 and 81.3 per cent lower mass, respectively; P, 0.05 in all Cases). However, important differences were noted: in partially submerged plants, crown biomass was little different from the initial mass 30 d previously, while it was much lower than the starting mass in completely submerged plants.

The reduction in the crown biomass of completely submerged plants was disproportionately larger than the reduction in total biomass, as indicated in the lower crown-to-

total-biomass ratio (Table). Root growth was also differentially affected by the treatments: it ceased in both partially submerged and completely submerged plants (P. 0.25; cf. day 0 vs. day 30 in Fig.), but continued similarly under control and waterlogged conditions (Fig.).

Thus, partially submerged and completely submerged plants registered a root biomass that was 42.8 and 63.0 per cent lower, respectively, than that of control and waterlogged plants by the end of the experiment. WSCs and starch in plant crowns WSCs and starch accumulated in plant crowns during the course of the experiment under control, waterlogging and partial submergence conditions. The magnitude of the accumulation differed among treatments for WSCs but not for starch content. Crown WSCs were similar in concentration in well-drained controls, waterlogged and partially submerged plants but substantially depressed by complete submergence.

Total accumulation per crown over 30 d (DWSCs) was, however, reduced by both waterlogging and partial submergence, while a large loss in total WSCs per crown was seen in completely submerged plants over time. Similar but less marked effects were also seen for starch. Importantly, complete submergence was the only treatment that provoked reductions in WSC and starch concentration.

8

Plant Disease Resistance

Plant disease resistance is crucial to the reliable production of food, and it provides significant reductions in agricultural use of fuel, land, water and other inputs. There are numerous examples of devastating plant disease impacts, as well as recurrent severe plant disease issues. However, disease control measures are reasonably successful for most crops. Across large regions and many crop species, it is estimated that diseases typically reduce plant yields by 10 per cent every year in more developed settings, but yield loss to diseases often exceeds 20 per cent in less developed settings.

Plant disease resistance derives both from pre-formed defences and from infection-induced responses mediated by the plant immune system. Relative to a disease-susceptible plant, disease resistance is often defined as reduction of pathogen growth on or in the plant, while the term disease tolerance describes plants that exhibit less disease damage despite similar levels of pathogen growth. Disease outcome is determined by the three-way interaction of the pathogen, the plant, and the environmental conditions (an interaction known as the disease triangle). Defence-activating compounds can move cell-to-cell and systemically through the plant vascular system, but plants do not have circulating immune cells so most cell types in plants retain the capacity to express a broad suite of anti-microbial defences.

Although obvious *qualitative* differences in disease resistance can be observed when some plants are compared (allowing classification as 'resistant' or 'susceptible' after infection by the same pathogen strain at similar pathogen inoculum levels in similar environments), a gradation of *quantitative* differences in disease resistance is more typically observed between plant lines or genotypes. Plants are almost always resistant to certain pathogens but susceptible to other pathogens; resistance is usually pathogen species-specific or pathogen strain-specific. Note that plant defence against herbivory (plant resistance to insect pests) exhibits some mechanistic similarities to, but also differences from, plant disease resistance (plant resistance to microscopic organisms).

Common Mechanisms of Plant Disease Resistance Pre-formed structures and compounds that contribute to resistance Plant cuticle/surface Plant cell walls Antimicrobial chemicals (for example: glucosides, saponins) Antimicrobial proteins Enzyme inhibitors Detoxifying enzymes that break down pathogen-derived toxins Receptors that perceive pathogen presence and activate inducible plant defences Inducible plant defences that are generated after infection Cell wall reinforcement (callose, lignin, suberin, cell wall proteins) Antimicrobial chemicals (including reactive oxygen species such as hydrogen peroxide, or peroxynitrite, or more complex phytoalexins such as genistein or camalexin) Antimicrobial proteins such as defensins, thionins, or PR-1 Antimicrobial enzymes such as chitinases, beta-glucanases, or peroxidases Hypersensitive response - a rapid host cell death response associated with defence mediated by 'Resistance genes.'

Plant Immune Systems and Plant Defence Signal Transduction Plant immune systems show some mechanistic similarities and apparent common origin with the immune systems of insects and mammals, but also exhibit many plant-specific characteristics. As in most cellular responses to the environment, defences are activated when receptor proteins directly or indirectly detect pathogen presence and trigger ion channel gating, oxidative burst, cellular redox changes, protein kinase cascades, and/or other responses that either directly activate cellular changes (such as cell wall reinforcement), or activate changes in gene expression that then elevate plant defence responses. Plants, like animals, have a basal immune system that includes a small number of pattern recognition receptors that are specific for broadly conserved microbe-associated molecular patterns (MAMPs, also called pathogen-associated molecular patterns or PAMPs). Examples of these microbial compounds that elicit plant basal defence include bacterial flagellin or lipopolysaccharides, or fungal chitin.

The defences induced by MAMP perception are sufficient to repel most potentially pathogenic microorganisms. However, pathogens express effector proteins that are adapted to allow them to infect certain plant species; these effectors often enhance pathogen virulence by suppressing basal host defences. Importantly, plants have evolved R genes (resistance genes) whose products allow recognition of specific pathogen effectors, either through direct binding of the effector or by recognition of the alteration that the effector has caused to a host protein. R gene products control a broad set of disease resistance responses whose induction is often sufficiently rapid and strong to stop adapted pathogens from further growth or spread. Plant genomes each contain a few hundred apparent R genes, and the R genes studied to date usually confer specificity for particular strains of a pathogen species.

As first noted by Harold Flor in the mid-20th century in his formulation of the gene-for-gene relationship, the plant R gene and the pathogen 'avirulence gene' (effector gene) must have matched specificity for that R gene to confer resistance. The presence of an R gene can place significant selective pressure on the pathogen to alter or delete the corresponding avirulence/effector gene. Some R genes show evidence of high stability over millions of years while other R genes, especially those that occur in small clusters of similar genes, can evolve new pathogen specificities over much shorter time periods.

The use of receptors carrying leucine-rich repeat (LRR) pathogen recognition specificity domains is common to plant, insect, jawless vertebrate and mammal immune systems, as is the presence of Toll/Interleukin receptor (TIR) domains in many of these receptors, and the expression of defensins, thionins, oxidative burst and other defence responses. Some of the key endogenous chemical mediators of plant defence signal transduction include salicylic acid, jasmonic acid or jasmonate, ethylene, reactive oxygen species, and nitric oxide. Numerous genes and/or proteins have been identified that mediate plant defence signal transduction. Cytoskeleton and vesicle trafficking dynamics help to target plant defence responses asymmetrically within plant cells, towards the point of pathogen attack. Plant immune systems can also respond to an initial infection in one part of the plant by physiologically elevating the capacity for a successful defence response in other parts of the plant.

These responses include systemic acquired resistance, largely mediated by salicylic acid-dependent pathways, and induced systemic resistance, largely mediated by jasmonic acid-dependent pathways. Against viruses, plants often induce pathogen-specific gene silencing mechanisms mediated by RNA interference. These are primitive forms of adaptive immunity. In a small number of cases, plant genes have been identified that are broadly effective against an entire pathogen species (against a microbial species that is pathogenic on other genotypes of that host species). Examples include barley MLO against powdery mildew, wheat Lr34 against leaf rust, and wheat Yr36 against stripe rust.

An array of mechanisms for this type of resistance may exist depending on the particular gene and plant-pathogen combination. Other reasons for effective plant immunity can include a relatively complete lack of coadaptation (the pathogen and/or plant lack multiple mechanisms needed for colonization and growth within that host species), or a particularly effective suite of pre-formed defences (see above). Plant Breeding for Disease Resistance Plant breeders focus a significant part of their effort on selection and development of disease-resistant plant lines.

Plant diseases can also be partially controlled by use of pesticides, and by cultivation practices such as crop rotation, tillage, planting density, purchase of disease-free seeds and cleaning of equipment, but plant varieties with inherent (genetically determined) disease resistance are generally the first choice for disease control. Breeding for disease resistance has been underway since plants were first domesticated, but it requires continual effort. This is because pathogen populations are often under natural selection for increased virulence, new pathogens can be introduced to an area, cultivation methods can favour increased disease incidence over time, changes in cultivation practice can favour new diseases, and plant breeding for other traits can disrupt the disease resistance that was present in older plant varieties. A plant line with acceptable disease resistance against one pathogen may still lack resistance against other pathogens.

PLANT BREEDING FOR DISEASE RESISTANCE TYPICALLY INCLUDES

Identification of resistant breeding sources (plants that may be less desirable in other ways, but which carry a useful disease resistance trait). Ancient plant varieties and wild relatives are very important to preserve because they are the most common sources of enhanced plant disease resistance. Crossing of a desirable but disease-susceptible plant variety to another variety that is a source of resistance, to generate plant populations that mix and segregate for the traits of the parents. Growth of the breeding populations in a disease-conducive setting. This may require artificial inoculation of pathogen onto the plant population. Careful attention must be paid to the types of pathogen isolates that are present, as there can be significant variation the effectiveness of resistance against different isolates of the same pathogen species. Selection of disease-resistant individuals. Breeders are trying to sustain or improve numerous other plant traits related to plant yield and quality, including other disease resistance traits, while they are breeding for improved resistance to any particular pathogen.

Each of the above steps can be difficult to successfully accomplish, and many highly refined methods in plant breeding and plant pathology are used to increase the effectiveness and reduce the cost of resistance breeding. Resistance is termed *durable* if it continues to be effective over multiple years of widespread use, but some resistance 'breaks down' as pathogen populations evolve to overcome or escape the resistance.

Resistance that is specific to certain races or strains of a pathogen species is often controlled by single R genes and can be less durable; *broad-spectrum resistance* against an entire pathogen species is often quantitative and only incompletely effective, but more durable, and is often controlled by many genes that segregate in breeding populations. However, there are numerous exceptions to the above generalized trends, which were given the names vertical resistance and horizontal resistance, respectively, by J.E. Vanderplank. Crops such as potato, apple, banana and sugarcane are often propagated by vegetative reproduction to preserve highly desirable plant varieties, because for these species, outcrossing seriously disrupts the preferred plant varieties. See also asexual propagation. Vegetatively propagated crops may be among the best targets for resistance improvement by the biotechnology method of plant transformation to add individual genes that improve disease resistance without causing large genetic disruption of the preferred plant varieties.

Host Range There are thousands of species of plant pathogenic microorganisms (Plant Pathology), but only a small minority of these pathogens have the capacity to infect a broad range of plant species. Most pathogens instead exhibit a high degree of host-specificity. Non-host plant species are often said to express *non-host resistance*. The term *host resistance* is used when a pathogen species can be pathogenic on the host species but certain strains of that plant species resist certain strains of the pathogen species. There can be overlap in the causes of host resistance and non-host resistance. Pathogen host range can change quite suddenly if, for example, the capacity to synthesize a host-specific toxin or effector is gained by gene shuffling/ mutation, or by horizontal gene transfer from a related or relatively unrelated organism. Epidemics and Population Biology Plants in native populations are often characterized by substantial genotype diversity and dispersed populations (growth in a mixture with many other plant species).

They also have undergone millions of years of plant-pathogen coevolution. Hence as long as novel pathogens are not introduced from other parts of the globe, natural plant populations generally exhibit only a low incidence of severe disease epidemics. In agricultural systems, humans often cultivate single plant species at high density, with numerous fields of that species in a region, and with significantly reduced genetic diversity both within fields and between fields. In addition, rapid travel of people and cargo across large distances increases the risk of introducing pathogens against which the plant has not been selected for resistance.

These factors make modern agriculture particularly prone to disease epidemics. Common solutions to this problem include constant breeding for disease resistance, use of pesticides to suppress recurrent potential epidemics, use of border inspections and plant import restrictions, maintenance of significant genetic diversity within the crop gene pool, and constant surveillance for disease problems to facilitate early initiation of appropriate responses. Some pathogen species are known to have a much greater capacity to overcome plant disease resistance than others, often because of their ability to evolve rapidly and to disperse broadly. Disease resistance in fruit and vegetables There are a number of lines of defence against pests (that is, those animals that cause damage to the plants we grow) and diseases in the organic garden, principal among these being the practice of good husbandry, creating healthy soil and ensuring high standards of garden hygiene. But no matter how diverse and healthy the garden eco-system may be, there will always be a degree of disease and pest presence.

In many ways, some level of pathogen population in the garden can be not only acceptable but desirable as they are indicative of a generally healthful and diverse environment, and add to the overall robustness of the system as an immunity to such detrimental influences will build up, particularly in a balanced polycultural regime. Indeed, most of the plants we grow will tend to be selected because they are trouble free, and those that are more susceptible to attack will have fallen by the wayside over time. However, most farmers find it unacceptable that the food crops they grow are damaged by pests.

For these crops there has been considerable research and selective breeding carried out in order to find cultivars that are resistant or immune to pest and disease damage. Breeding for plant disease resistance generally has involved finding suitable genetic material amongst existing stocks or in the wild, which is then incorporated into commercial varieties. Example: The apple In the case of apples, in which research is being carried out in order to develop resistance to diseases such as apple scab (*Venturia inaequalis*), powdery mildew (*Podosphaera leucotricha*), orchard fireblight (*Erwinia amylovora*), woolly apple aphid (*Eriosoma lanigerum*) and collar rot (*Phytophthora cactorum*), the main sources of resistant material used in breeding programmes such as those being run by East Malling Research Station in England or Hortresearch in New Zealand are major gene resistances derived from crab-apples.

The Vf gene for black spot resistance is derived from the ornamental crab-apple species *Malus floribunda*. Most black spot resistant cultivars developed around the world carry this gene, but there are some selections that carry the Vr (from M. pumila) or Vm (from M. micromalus) gene. Major gene resistances to powdery mildew are derived from M. robusta (Pl1) and M. zumi (Pl2), and the apple cultivar *Northern Spy* has a long-standing reputation for its major gene resistance to woolly apple aphid. Since early this century this resistance has been used to develop woolly aphid resistant rootstocks such as MM.106 and M.793. Much later it was shown that the cultivar was also very resistant to collar rot and a useful breeding parent for this resistance. Resistance and immunity Some plants can tolerate the presence of large numbers of insects without being severely affected.

This is not very satisfactory however as insects will still cause damage, and in fact further breeding and population expansion of the pest species is supported. Other varieties are less attractive to pests, but this can be difficult to sustain or demonstrate.

The most valuable form of resistance is where the pest cannot survive as well on one variety as on another. In some cases this can actually make the plants immune to attack, as is the case with the lettuces *Avoncrisp* and *Avondefiance* which were bred at the Institute of Horticultural Research, Wellesbourne during the 1960s, which are fully resistant to lettuce root aphid

(*Pemphigus bursarius*). Trade-off of breeding for resistance Sometimes however there can be a *trade-off*, for those varieties which have increased immunity or resistance may be lacking in other qualities such as flavour, yield or quality. Celery resistant to the Fusarium fungus (*Fusarium oxysporum spp.*) may not succumb to this disease, but may also be unacceptably short, ribby and low yielding.

Further, a cultivar that is resistant to one disease may be more susceptible to another that is equally important. A lettuce cultivar that is resistant to mosaic virus may be sensitive to corky root disease, whilst another that resists corky root may be vulnerable to downy mildew (*Brim lactic*).

Another drawback to resistance is that depending on the host pathogen system, resistance is sometimes not long lasting as new pathogen strains quickly develop, and further research and breeding is constantly needed. Availability of resistant varieties Resistant varieties are not available for all crops. For several of the most damaging plant diseases, such as Potato blight (*Phytophthora infestans*) and white rot (*Sclerotic cepivorum*) of the Allium family, no acceptable resistant cultivars are yet available.

In addition, commercial seed companies and plant breeders rarely invest resources into developing resistant cultivars for more minor or speciality crops, which often tend to be those of greater interest to the organic grower. In general it is probably fair to say that resistance will not fully guarantee total crop protection, but choosing resistant varieties should rather be considered as a part of an overall Integrated pest management strategy, especially against virus diseases. In particular they can be especially useful where the threat from specific pests and diseases is high. The table below illustrates a number of pest and disease resistant vegetable crop varieties, although should not be considered comprehensive.

Table 8.1 Pest and Disease Resistant Crops

Crop	Variety	Comments
French Bean	Aigullion	Resistant to bean mosaic virus and anthracnose
	Hildora	Tolerant of bean mosaic virus

(*Contd...*)

	Maxi Nektar Queen Farba Hilda	Tolerant of bean mosaic virus Resistant to bean mosaic virus Resistant to bean mosaic virus Resistant to bean mosaic virus
Broad Bean	Futura	Tolerant of chocolate spot
Brussels sprouts	Cavalier Braveheart F1	Resistant to light leaf spot Resistant to powdery mildew and light leaf spot
Cabbage	Stonehead F1	Resistant to mildew
Calabrese	Emperor F1 Sampson F1	Highly tolerant of black rot and downy mildew Highly resistant to black rot and downy mildew
Carrot	Fly Away F1 Newmarket	Bred for resistance to carrot fly Good resistance to splitting
Cucumber	Bush Champion F1 Marketmore Burpless Tasty Green F1 Slice King F1 Cumlaude F1 Media F1	Resistant to cucumber mosaic virus Resistant to cucumber mosaic virus Resistant to mildew and tolerant of heat Resistant to downy and powdery mildew, gummosis and angular leaf spot Tolerant of powdery mildew Tolerant of powdery mildew
Leek	Swiss Giant, Zermatt Alvitta Conora	Moderate rust resistance Rust Tolerant Good resistance to rust
Lettuce	Alexandria Lisbusa	Highly resistant to downy mildew and bolting Resistant to downy mildew, tolerant of mosaic virus, root aphid and tipburn

(*Contd...*)

	Sylvestra	Resistant to downy mildew and aphids
	Little Gem	Resistant to root aphid
	Barcelona	Resistant to aphids and mildew
	Iglo	Resistant to downey mildew
	Revolution	Resistant to mildew and bolting
	Smile	Resistant to aphids, mildew, tipburn and bolting
Parsnip	Avonreister	Very good resistance to canker
	Gladiator F1	High resistance to canker
	Tender and True	Good canker resistance
Pea	Ambassador	Resistant to powdery mildew, entation virus and fusarium wilt
	Cavalier	Good resistance to powdery mildew.
	Greenshaft	Resistant to downy mildew and fusarium wilt
	Rondo	Resistant to fusarium wilt
Potato (first early)	Colleen	Good resistance to blight and scab
	Premiere	Resistant to blight and spraing
	Pentland Javelin	Good all round disease resistance, including golden eelworm and scab
	Swift	Resistant to golden eelworm and tolerant to blackleg
Potato (second early)	Cosmos	Resistant to blight and common scab
	Osprey	Very resistant to scab and eelworm
Potato (maincrop)	Harmony	Very resistant to scab and partially resistant to white and golden eelworm
	Milva	Blight resistant
	Remarka	Good all around disease resistance
	Admiral	Good resistance to blight and scab
	Cara	Blight resistant
	Valor	Good overall disease resistance

(Contd...)

	blight resistance	combined with high eelworm and
Pepper	Bell Boy F1 Mandy F1	Mosaic virus resistant Highly resistant to mosaic virus
Sweetcorn	Golden sweet F1	Highly resistant to smut
Tomato	Alicante Libra F1 Shirley F1	Good resistance to greenback and mildew Resistant to fusarium crown and root rot Resistant to fusarium, cladosporium and TMV

Bibliography

Albina F Musil: *Identification of Crop and Weed Seeds*, Delhi, Scientific Publication, 2003.

Alexander C. Martin and William D. Barkley: *Seed Identification Manual*, Delhi, Scientific Publication, 2010.

Amarjit S Basra: *Handbook of Seed Science and Technology*, Delhi, Scientific Publication, 2007.

Avinash Ramdeo: *A Handbook of Seed Industry : Prospects and its Costing*, Delhi, Scientific Publication, 2011.

Bewley, J. Derek, and Michael Black: *Seeds Physiology of Development and Germination. The Language of Science*, New York: Plenum Press, 1994.

Brajesh Tiwari: *Seed Production of Field Crops*, New York, Oxford Book Company, 2010.

Baskin C. C. and J. M. Baskin: *Seeds: Ecology, Biogeography, and Evolution of Dormancy and Germination*, Delhi, Academic Press, 1998.

Corner EJH: *The Natural History of Palms*. Berkeley, CA: University of California Press, 1966.

Cronquist, Arthur: *An Integrated System of Classification of Flowering Plants*. New York: Columbia University Press, 1981.

D. Kumar: *Crop Response to Abiotic Stresses: International Review and Annotated Bibliography*, Delhi, Scientific Publication, 1997.

D.K. Jha: *Laboratory Manual on Seed Pathology*, Delhi, Vikas Publication, 1995.

Dhirendra Khare and Mohan S. Bhale: *Seed Technology*, , Delhi, Scientific Pub, 2000.

E.V. Divakara Sastry and Kayam Singh Shekhawat: *Production and Protection of Seed Spices*, , Delhi, Aavishkar Publication, 2011.

Edwar Clodd: Animism : *The Seed of Religion*, , Delhi, Cosmo Publication, 2007.

G Nagaraj: Oilseeds : *Properties, Processing, Products and Procedures*, Delhi, New India Publication, 2009.

G.S. Saharan, Naresh Mehta and M.S. Sangwan: *Diseases of Oilseed Crops*, Delhi, Indus Publication, 2005.

Gautam Ghosh: *Agro's Dictionary of Seed Science and Technology*, Delhi, Agrobios Publication, 2007.

Gurnam Singh: *Seed Pathology*, Delhi, Gene Tech Books, 2008.

Gurnam Singh: *Seed Science and Technology*, Delhi, Gene Tech Books, 2008.

Gurnam Singh: *Seed Testing*, Delhi, Gene Tech Books, 2008.

H. Panda: *Fruits, Vegetables, Corn and Oilseeds Processing Handbook*, Delhi, Asia Pacific Business Press, 2010.

Hari Har Ram and Rakesh Yadava: *Genetic Resources and Seed Enterprises: Management and Policies*, Delhi, New India Publishing Agency, 2007.

J. Renugadevi, P. Srimathi, R.R. Renganayaki and V. Manonmani: *A Handbook of Seed Testing*, Delhi, Agrobios, 2011.

Jagdish Prasad: *Marketing of Farm Inputs Seed, Fertilizer and Irrigation*, Delhi, Mittal, 2005.

Jones, Samuel B., and Arlene E. Luchsinger: *Plant Systematics. McGraw-Hill Series in Organismic Biology*. New York: McGraw-Hill, 1979.

Index